A DISSERTATION

ON THE

FREEDOM OF NAVIGATION

AND

MARITIME COMMERCE,

AND SUCH

RIGHTS OF STATES, RELATIVE THERETO,

AS ARE FOUNDED

ON THE LAW OF NATIONS:

ADAPTED MORE PARTICULARLY

TO THE UNITED STATES;

AND INTERSPERSED WITH

MORAL AND POLITICAL REFLECTIONS,

AND HISTORICAL FACTS.

WITH

AN APPENDIX,

CONTAINING SUNDRY STATE PAPERS.

BY WILLIAM BARTON, M. A.

MEMBER OF THE AMERICAN PHILOSOPHICAL SOCIETY,
PHILADELPHIA, AND OF THE ROYAL ECONOMICAL SOCIETY, VALENCIA, SPAIN.

THE LAWBOOK EXCHANGE, LTD.
Clark, New Jersey
2005

ISBN 1-58477-509-2

The quality of this reprint is equivalent to the quality of the original work.

Printed in the United States of America on acid-free paper

THE LAWBOOK EXCHANGE, LTD.
33 Terminal Avenue
Clark, New Jersey 07066-1321

Please see our website for a selection of our other publications and fine facsimile reprints of classic works of legal history:
www.lawbookexchange.com

Library of Congress Cataloging-in-Publication Data

Barton, William, 1754-1817.
A dissertation on the freedom of navigation and maritime commerce, and such rights of states, relative thereto, as are founded on the Law of Nations : adapted more particularly to the United States and interspersed with moral and political reflections, and historical facts / by William Barton.
p. cm.
Originally published: Philadelphia: J. Conrad, 1802.
ISBN 1-58477-509-2 (alk. paper)
1. Freedom of the seas. 2. War, Maritime (Intemational law) I. Title.

KZA1348.B37 2005
343.09'66—dc22

2004054849

A DISSERTATION

ON THE

FREEDOM OF NAVIGATION

AND

MARITIME COMMERCE,

AND SUCH

RIGHTS OF STATES, RELATIVE THERETO,

AS ARE FOUNDED

ON THE LAW OF NATIONS:

ADAPTED MORE PARTICULARLY

TO THE UNITED STATES;

AND INTERSPERSED WITH

MORAL AND POLITICAL REFLECTIONS,

AND HISTORICAL FACTS.

WITH

AN APPENDIX,

CONTAINING SUNDRY STATE PAPERS.

BY WILLIAM BARTON, M. A.

MEMBER OF THE AMERICAN PHILOSOPHICAL SOCIETY, PHILADELPHIA, AND OF THE ROYAL ECONOMICAL SOCIETY, VALENCIA, SPAIN.

PUBLISHED BY

JOHN CONRAD, & CO. NO. 30, CHESNUT-STREET, PHILADELPHIA; M. & J. CONRAD, & CO. NO. 144, MARKET-STREET, BALTIMORE; AND RAPIN, CONRAD, & CO. WASHINGTON CITY.

H. MAXWELL, PRINTER.

1802.

TO THOMAS JEFFERSON, L.L.D.

PRESIDENT

OF THE UNITED STATES OF AMERICA;

EMINENTLY DISTINGUISHED

BY HIS TALENTS AND VIRTUES,

AND

RENDERED STILL MORE ILLUSTRIOUS

BY

THE APPROVING VOICE OF HIS COUNTRY;

THE FOLLOWING DISSERTATION

IS INSCRIBED,

WITH SENTIMENTS OF

THE HIGHEST RESPECT

AND THE GREATEST

PERSONAL CONSIDERATION,

BY

THE AUTHOR.

LANCASTER, IN PENNSYLVANIA;
NOVEMBER, 1801.

PREFACE.

THE welfare of the United States is intimately connected with the subject of the following dissertation. As a great commercial, as well as agricultural nation, their interests are involved in the just and secure establishment of those rights, upon which the exercise and protection of their foreign trade depend.

As long, however, as arbitrary and unreasonable interpretations of the Law of Nations, shall be permitted to direct the conduct of several and independent states, with respect to their foreign trade; so long will those injurious infractions of their respective maritime rights, which have furnished so many pretexts for naval wars, be continued: and so long also will the irritation, that is naturally provoked by such acts of injustice, supply a constant source of both public and private evil. Hence the obvious necessity of establishing an explicit code of Maritime Law, founded on principlies which shall conform to that invariable standard of natural equity, that constitutes the only true basis of the LAW OF NATIONS: and the period of a general peace in Europe, is the most eligible season for the accomplishment of so desirable a purpose.

The principles of this Law are immutable in their nature. When we find, therefore, jurists and civilians greatly differing from, and contradicting each other, in their several constructions of the Law of Nations; and thereby subjecting many of the most important rights of independent states, to litigation, and to the control of others; it is a plain indication that some of their interpretations must be erroneous. Such, unquestionably is the fact.

The cause of those fallacious theories, with which many writers have sophisticated their respective systems of general jurisprudence, may be more generally traced, it is presumed, to national prejudices and the bias of particular interests, than to defect of judgment. But whatever may be the source of such errors, the evils are the same: and, in order to remedy these, it becomes necessary to remove the cause; by substituting, in the place of an artificial code of Maritime Law, one, that shall be conformable to the principles of natural justice and the rights of independent nations.

Influenced by these considerations, the writer has ventured to investigate some of the leading principles, upon which, alone, he conceives the Law of Nations can be rested, as its true foundation. In doing this, he has endeavoured to point out the fallacy of relying on the mere speculative opinions of jurists, however learned and ingenious: and he has also made an essay towards ascertaining those legitimate principles of Natural Law, with their true interpretation, which apply to some of the most essential maritime rights of commercial states.

The various controversies that frequently arise between nations, concerning these rights, evince the uncertainty in which the rulers of states are involved, with regard to their just construction. Notwithstanding all that had been written by Grotius, on the Rights of War and Peace, we find Pufendorf declaring his opinion, long afterwards, that the question of Free Navigation remained unsettled:....In a letter addressed to M. Groning, by this celebrated writer on Universal Law, (respecting a design which the former had announced, of writing a treatise on Free Navigation,) he makes these observations.... "It is a curious subject; and what no person as yet, that I know of, has particularly handled."...."The question is certainly, one of those which have not yet been settled, upon any clear and undeniable principles, so as to afford a general rule to mankind."....When it is recollected, that this letter was written in 1692,....twenty-three years after its writer published his treatise on the Law of Nature and Nations, and nearly seventy years after the publication of Grotius's book on War and Peace; let it be asked, whether the words, quoted from the letter, do not clearly imply a non-acquiescence of M. Pufendorf, in Grotius's doctrines (at least in some of them,) concerning Free Navigation, and, consequently, of all those who had adopted similar opinions?....It must be observed that M. Pufendorf has not, himself, treated at all on the subject of Neutrality.

Subsequent writers have left the subject in the same obscurity; and, indeed, some of them have contrived to involve it in additional perplexity. From this it can never be relieved, without recurring to first principles. The writer of these sheets claims no other merit, on the present occasion, than that of having endeavoured to draw the attention of his countrymen to a more ample discussion of the subject, than either his leisure or abilities will permit him to do. He has contributed his mite, with an earnest desire to promote the cause of justice and of truth: and it will afford him real pleasure to find the same object pursued, with a similar disposition, by those who may be more competent to decide on its merits.

The witer's situation, in an inland town, deprived him of access to some books, as well as other sources of information, which might have enabled him to render this little tract less defective. This circumstance, he trusts, will be admitted by a candid and generous public, as at least a partial apology for such errors and omissions, as may appear in the work:....And, with respect to imperfections of any kind, which shall be found in it, he craves the same liberal indulgence from the generosity of his fellow-citizens.

It will probably be thought by some, that the writer's strictures on the conduct of Great Britain, with respect to Neutral nations, and particularly towards this country, are edged with too much asperity. He regrets, extremely, that the nature of the subject, and a due regard to truth, imposed on him a necessity of placing certain principles and measures of the British government in such point of view, as does not exhibit the rulers of that nation in the most favorable light. It would have afforded him great satisfaction, if the policy of their administrations which have successively held the reins of government in that country, for many years past, had been (in regard to their exterior relations) more compatible with the dignity of a great and enlightened nation, and less derogatory from the rights of other states:....Yet he thinks it due to justice and candor, to acknowledge, that the acquiescence in the principles of the Armed Neutrality....offered by Mr. Fox, while Secretary of State for Great-Britain (by his letters to M. Simolin, in 1782,) evinced a just and liberal policy,....worthy of that eminent statesman, and honourable to his country. To some individuals in England, of distinguished worth and character, the writer of this is personally under obligations, which will always command his grateful respect and esteem. In fact, he is so far from feeling any illiberal sentiment towards the people of the British empire,....a great proportion of whom he believes to be truly estimable,...that it would yield him very sincere pleasure to behold them participating in real happiness, along with the great community of nations; under a government as free, as the radical defects of a monarchical system will admit; and administered by wise, just and liberal men.

It may be proper to notice, in this place, that, in the present undertaking, the writer has neither consulted, nor been counselled by any person, in public or private station:....Whatever merit or demerit the work may possess, is, therefore, wholly imputable to himself.

PRELIMINARY OBSERVATIONS;

CONTAINING

AN INVESTIGATION OF THE TRUE PRINCIPLES

OF THE

LAW OF NATIONS.

IN taking a preliminary view of the important subject before us, we readily perceive that it branches itself into several principal divisions. The facts and observations, which compose the present treatise are therefore arranged under separate heads, in conformity to such division as appears most obvious, in order to give them the greater perspicuity. These are, in substance, as follow:

I. Containing an examination of the Law of Nations, in relation to the Principle, that FREE SHIPS MAKE FREE GOODS, as understood and acted upon, by most of the principal maritime powers of Europe, prior to the formation of the Treaty of Armed Neutrality, in 1780.

II. Shewing that the position of FREE SHIPS MAKING FREE GOODS was recognized and fully established, as a fundamental principle in what is sometimes styled the MODERN Law of Nations; for the regulation of that important maritime right, claimed by neutrals; conformably to the doctrine laid down in the treaty of Armed Neutrality.

III. Treating of Neutrality, and the Rights of Neutrals, as deduced from the nature of war.

IV. Designating what articles ought to be considered as Contraband of war, and defining the right of Search; according to the true construction of the Law of Nations, now generally received.

V. Containing miscellaneous observations and reflections, arising out of the main subject; together with the general result.

Such is the outline of our plan: and, to elucidate the several points treated of, under their respective heads, in this distribution of the subject, copious notes are subjoined; together with an appendix, containing some of the principal documents, referred to in the text.

The principles, on which the several propositions now under discussion are founded, are unequivocally admitted to appertain to the Law of Nations, by those who controvert the truth of the propositions, or the principles themselves: By that Law, therefore, the litigated points must be decided.

It is evident, that to be enabled to decide justly, on this subject, it is necessary to understand, with precision, what the Law of Nations really is: and as a true definition of this law thus becomes a primary and indispensible requisite, we shall endeavour to obtain a correct conception of its meaning and extent. In adducing the opinions of sundry eminent writers, on this occasion, the number and length of the quotations will, it is expected be justified by the importance of the subject, and by the desire we experience to give to our own arguments all the additional weight they can derive, from the sanction of distinguished names in the science of morals and universal jurisprudence.

" Every man (says M. Barbeyrac) who will be happy, must needs, in order to make himself so, regulate his conduct after some certain manner; and God, as author and parent of all the human race, does prescribe to all men, without exception, the duties, which tend to procure them that happiness, that they passionately seek after*."

"Whatever is inconsistent with the general peace and welfare, or good of mankind, is inconsistent with the Law of human nature, wrong, and intolerable†."

"The Law of Nations is the Law of Nature applied to social life, the affairs of societies and of independent political bodies‡."

"Since the Law of Nature comprehends all the Laws promulgated to mankind by right reason; and men may be considered either as particulars, singly, or as they are united in certain political bodies or societies; we call that Law by which the actions of particulars ought to be governed, the Law of Nature; and we call that the Law of Nations, which determines what is just and unjust in society, or between societies. And therefore the precepts, the Laws of both, are the same: Nay, the Law of Nations is the Law of Nature itself, respect-

* Historical and Critical Account of the Science of Morality, prefixed to Pufendorf's treatise on the Law of Nature and Nations.

† Wollaston's Religion of Nature delineated, sect. 1. 3. 9.

‡ Heineccius's methodical System of Universal Law, book ii. sect. 1. It is *this* work only, of Heineccius, which we refer to, under his name.

ing or applied to social life, and the affairs of societies and independent states. Hence we may infer, that the Law of Nature doth not differ from the Law of Nations, neither in respect of its foundation and just principles, nor of its rules; but solely with regard to its objects*."

Every Republic, State, or political society of men, aggregated under one common civil government, is considered as one moral person; in contradistinction to the physical persons individually considered, who collectively constitute those societies. "Now (says Heineccius), if every society be, as it were, one person, it must, by consequence, be subject to the same Law as individuals, or physical persons: and therefore all the duties which the Law of Nature prescribes to particular persons, ought likewise to be religiously observed by all societies, greater or lesser†."

The Law of Nations is called by Koehler‡, *Jus naturale Societatum*,... the natural Law of Societies.

Professor Hutcheson (in his Elements of the Law of Nature, chap. ii.) maintaining the well known principle, admitted in society, that no

* Heinec. book i. sect. 21, 22. † Ibid. book ii. sect. 20.
‡ Spec. Jur. Gent.

private right can hold good against the general interest of all, goes on to say; "For, a regard to the most extensive advantage of the whole system ought to control and limit all the rights of individuals, or of particular societies."—"Whatever (says he) appears necessary for preserving an amicable society among men, must necessarily be enjoined by the Law of Nature: and, in whatever circumstances the maintaining of peace in society requires, that certain actions, possessions, or claims, should be left free and undisturbed to any one, he is justly deemed to have a right so to act, possess, or claim from others."....But the "Right" here spoken of, must nevertheless be understood, as one conformable to the maxim of Natural Law, that no Right can be founded on an injury*: for, as Vattel† truly observes, "the first general law, which the very end of the society of nations discovers, is, that each nation ought to contribute all in its power to the happiness and perfection of others."

Agreeable to the spirit of this quotation from Vattel, is the following observation of

* See Rutherforth's Institutes of Natural Law, book i. chap. ii. sect. 6.

† See his Preliminaries, sect. 13.

the celebrated Pufendorf: " It is (says he) a fundamental Law of Nature, that every man ought, as far as in him lies, to promote and preserve a peaceful sociableness, (such a disposition of one man towards all others, as shall suppose him united to them by benevolence, by peace, by charity,) with others; agreeable to the main end and disposition of the human race in general*."

" By the Law of Nations (says professor Rutherforth) we mean such rules, as nations or civil societies are obliged to observe, in their intercourse with one another†." Now, it has been stated, that " the Law of Nations is the Law of Nature itself, applied to social life, and the affairs of societies and independent states;" and that the precepts, consequently the obligations, of both, are the same, and derived from the same source. Hence, in order to ascertain their origin, it is necessary to have recourse to the faculties of the human mind. " Thus far (observes Pufendorf‡,) most are agreed, that the Law of Nature is to be drawn from man's Reason; flowing from

* Law of Nature and Nations, book ii. chap. iii. sect. 15.

† Instit. of Nat. Law, book i. chap. i. sect. 13.

‡ Book ii. chap. iii. sect. 13.

the true current of that faculty, when unperverted: on which account, the holy scriptures declare it to be *written in the hearts of men;* Rom. ii. 15. This we judge to be a most manifest truth, that although the sacred writings do throw in a more enlarged light, to direct us in the clearest view of Nature's Law; yet the same law may, without any extraordinary assistance, be found out and solidly demonstrated by the bare force of Reason; such as God first implanted, and still preserves, in mankind." Wollaston* reasons in like manner, on this point, when he says, "It is true, that whatever will bear to be tried by right Reason, is right; and that which is condemned by it, wrong....To be governed by Reason is the General Law, imposed by the Author of Nature upon them, whose uppermost faculty is Reason: as the dictates of it, in particular cases, are the particular Laws, to which they are subject...Man's uppermost faculty is Reason: from hence it follows, that the great law imposed upon him is, to be governed by Reason."

Vattel† expressly acknowledges, that "the necessary and the voluntary Law of Nations

* Rel. of Nat. del. sect. 1. 3. 9.

† In his preface.

are both established by Nature; but each in a different manner: the first as a sacred law, which Nations and Sovereigns ought to respect in all their actions; the second, as a rule which the welfare and common safety obliges them to admit, in their transactions with each other. The necessary law proceeds immediately from Nature; and that common mother of men recommends the observance of the voluntary Law of Nations, in consideration of the state in which nations are found with respect to each other, and for the advantage of their affairs. This double law, founded on certain and invariable principles, is capable of demonstration."

Grotius has attempted to establish the doctrine, that there exists a separate and distinct species of the Law of Nations, founded on tacit consent, or acquiescence; which he denominates the Arbitrary Law of Nations. But, says Barbeyrac*, " Mr. Pufendorf often justly refutes Grotius: and, to be convinced that Grotius had, as to several matters, even false, or at least very confused ideas, there needs no more than to examine one single notion of his, which runs through his whole system; I

* See his Hist. and Crit. account of the science of morality.

mean, that pretended distinction of his, between the Law of Nature, and a certain arbitrary Law of Nations, which he conceives to be founded on the tacit consent of the people.*"

This erroneous notion of Grotius, respecting the existence of an arbitrary Law of Nations, founded on tacit consent, is adopted by Vattel†; but in terms so qualified, as to exempt it, in some measure, from the imputation of error, to which Grotius's definition is justly obnoxious: yet the doctrine is fundamentally false: "There is (says this writer) another kind of the Law of Nations, which authors call arbitrary, because it proceeds from the will or consent of nations. States may acquire rights, and contract obligations by express engagements, by pacts and treaties: there results from these a conventional Law of Nations, pe-

* In Parrhasiana (Tom. i. p. 346.) is this observation respecting Grotius: "If he was not thoroughly acquainted with the art of thinking justly, the philosophy of his time being still very obscure, he has supplied, in a great measure, that defect, by the force of his good sense. If, without the help of art, he has shewn so much delicacy of taste and true discernment; what could he not have done, had he been entire master of that art of reasoning justly, and of rightly methodizing his thoughts, which has since prevailed."

† In his preface.

culiar to the contracting powers. Nations may also (continues Vattel) bind themselves by tacit consent: upon this is founded, whatever manners have introduced among different people, and which form the customs of nations, or the Law of Nations founded on custom. It is evident that this Law can impose an obligation only on those nations, who have adopted those customs by long use. Both derive all their force from the Law of Nature, which prescribes to nations the observance of their engagements, whether express or tacit. The same Law of Nature ought to regulate the conduct of states, in relation to the treaties they conclude, and to the customs they adopt."

The fallacy of the doctrine contained in this last extract, and which Vattel has borrowed from Grotius, is readily detected. For it is evident, that no custom of any people or nation, however sanctioned by long use or prescription, can ever, either by tacit acquiescence or express engagements, be made to impose a legitimate obligation of conformity thereto; if such custom be repugnant to moral rectitude, or to the unalienable rights of mankind, derived from Nature. When we speak of the moral obligation we are under, to fulfil our engagements, whether tacit or express; it follows as the necessary result, that the engagements must be such, as enjoin nothing, as a duty, which is in any wise morally wrong, or contrary to the paramount injunctions of the Law of Nature. Vattel appears to have been sensible of the unsoundness of the doctrine, which Grotius has endeavoured to establish, of his alleged distinction between the Law of Nature and his arbitrary Law of Nations. This may be collected, from the modified sense in which he has adopted that pretended distinction, as it is justly styled by Barbeyrac: for, when treating of the customary law of nations....which he considers as being founded by tacit consent, on some custom generally established, either between all the polished nations of the world, or only between those of a certain part, as of Europe, for example,....he observes, "That this law is binding only on those nations, which have adopted it:....But, that even between them, the custom is of no force, if it contain any thing unjust or illegal;" and in this case (continues Vattel*) "every nation is under an

* Preliminaries, sect. 26....See also book ii. sect. 161.

obligation to abandon it,....nothing being able to oblige or permit a nation to violate a Natural Law."

This notion of Grotius, that a law founded on the consent of nations, imposes an obligation, resulting from the mere circumstance of such consent, is manifestly opposed to the very principle, from which natural or moral obligations derive their validity. Hence Heineccius* has said...." None, I think, will rashly go into the opinion of those learned men, who hold the consent of all nations, or of all the more civilized nations, to be the principle of Natural Law. For it is not true, that what all nations agree in, is also conformable to the Divine will" And Dr. Turnbull, commenting on the text of Heineccius in this particular, remarks, that "we find a wonderful consent, almost of all nations, in many things which none will assert to be of the Law of Nature or Nations; as in Polytheism, Idolatry, Sacrifices, Robbery committed in a foreign territory, &c." But Grotius acknowledges (as the learned Dr. Kennet remarks) that, in establishing the foundation of the Laws of Nature and Nations, he made use of the testimonies of historians,

* Book i. chap. iii. sect. 71.

orators, and even poets; as well as those of philosophers*." "He chose (according to

* The very mention of philosophers, in connection with our subject, (although quoted from an English divine), may probably afford a new occasion for that senseless rant about "modern philosophers"...."French philosophers," &c....with which some men, who ought to have shewn more respect to truth and candor, have debased themselves. A total perversion of the meaning of the term, Philosophy, furnishes to such men, whose object is to propagate, by sophistry and deception, principles destructive of free government,....a copious theme of the most illiberal abuse of all those, who endeavour to investigate political, moral or religious truth. The author of a valuable little book, entitled the Spirit of Despotism, (published in London in 1795,) shews, that the fashionable invectives against philosophy and reason, are a proof of the spirit of despotism. We think the following observations, extracted from that work, are so well founded, and apply so pointedly in this instance, as to merit attention.

"Philosophy, so far from deserving contempt, is the glory of human nature. Man approaches, by contemplation, to what we conceive of celestial purity and excellence. Without the aid of philosophy, the mass of mankind, all over the terraqueous globe, would have sunk in slavery and superstition, the natural consequences of gross ignorance. Men at the very bottom of society, have been enabled, by the natural talents they possessed, seconded by favorable opportunities, to reach the highest improvements in philosophy; and have thus lifted up a torch in the valley, which has exposed the weakness and deformity of the castle on the mountain, from which the oppressors sallied, in the night of darkness, and spread desolation with impunity. Despots, the meanest, the basest, the most brutal and ignorant of the human race, would have trampled on the rights and the happiness of men, unresisted, if Philoso-

Dr. Kennett†) rather to insist on authorities taken from the historians, civilians, and cano-

phy had not opened the eyes of the sufferers, and taught them to despise those giants of power, as they appeared through the mists of ignorance, who ruled a vassal world with a mace of iron. Liberty is the daughter of Philosophy; and they who detest the offspring, do all that they can to vilify and discountenance the mother.

"But let us calmly consider, what is the object of this philosophy, so formidable in the eyes of those who are bigotted to ancient abuses,....who hate every improvement, and who wish to subject the many to the control of an arbitrary few. Philosophy is ever employed in finding out whatever is good and whatever true. She darts her eagle-eye over all the busy world, detects error and mischief, and points out modes of improvement. In the multiform state of human affairs, ever obnoxious to decay and abuse, it is her's to meditate on the means of melioration. She wishes to abolish nothing, but what is a nuisance. To build, to repair, to strengthen, and to polish; these are the works which she delights to plan; and, in concerting the best methods of directing their accomplishment, she consumes the midnight oil. How can she disturb human affairs, since she dwells in contemplation, and descends not to action?....Neither does she impel others to action, by the arts of delusive eloquence. She applies to reason alone; and if reason is not convinced, all that she has done, is swept away, like the web of Arachne.

"But it is modern philosophy, and French philosophy, which gives such umbrage to the lovers of old errors, and the favorers of absolute power; just as if philosophy were mutable, by time or place. Philosophy, by which I mean the investigation of the good and true, on all subjects, is the same,....like the sun, whether it shines in China or Peru. Truth and good are eternal and immutable; and therefore philosophy, which is solely

nists; than on philosophical deductions from the nature of man and the reasons of things." Is it, then, a matter of surprize, that, relying on such authorities, Grotius's conceptions of many subjects were "false" and "very confused?"

attached to these, is still one and the same, whether ancient or modern,....in England or in France.

"It is sophistry, and not philosophy, which is justly reprobated; and there has, at all times, been more sophistry displayed by the sycophant defenders of despotism, than by the friends to liberty. England has ever abounded with sophists, when the high prerogative notions, toryism, and jacobitism, and the servile principles which flow from them, have required the support of eloquence; either written or oral. Besides our modern Filmers, we have had an army of ten thousand mercenary speakers and writers, whose names are as little remembered as their venal productions. Such men, contending against the light of nature, and common sense, have been obliged to seek succour of sophistry. Theirs is the philosophy, falsely so called, which deserves reprobation."...."As we value a free press, or wish to preserve a due esteem for genius and science, let us ever be on our guard, when we hear great men possessing neither genius nor science, rail against philosophy. Let us remember, that it was a Roman tyrant, in the decline of all human excellence, (when Providence permitted such monsters to shew the world the deformity of despotism) who wished to extinguish the light of learning, by abolishing the finest productions of genius. There are men, in recent times, who display all the propensities of a Caligula:....Be it the people's care, that they never possess his power."

† See his Preface to Pufendorf's Law of Nature and Nations.

Wolfius* observes, that "nations (i. e. sovereign states, in their independent, political capacity,) acknowledge, among themselves, no other law, than that which nature herself has established." "Nations, it is true (continues this author,) can only be considered as so many particular persons, living together in the state of nature; and, for that reason, we ought to apply to them all the duties and rights, which Nature prescribes to, and lays upon mankind; as they are born naturally free, and are only bound to each other by the single knot Nature herself has tied. The law which arises from this application, and the obligation resulting from it, proceed from that immutable law founded on the nature of man; and, in this manner, the Law of Nations certainly belongs to the Law of Nature: it is therefore called the Natural Law of nations, with respect to its origin, and the necessary law, in relation to its obligatory force. This law is common to all nations; and that which does not respect it, in its actions, violates a law common to all people."

From a collected view of the testimonies here adduced, it is evident, that the Law of

* Preface to his *Jus Gentium.*

Nations, in the general import of the term, or what is strictly styled the Natural Law of Nations, is founded on, and incorporated with, the Law of Nature; and, that there is no other difference between them, than what is necessarily produced by their application to objects and purposes, in some respects differing as to their extent. In fact, every modification or branch of the Law of Nations....whether of the necessary and internal Laws of Nature and of Conscience, as they are called by some, or the external and voluntary Law of Nations, so styled,....must rest on the same immutable foundation, the great original precepts of Nature herself, from whence their obligation is entirely derived. The observation of Pufendorf* is, therefore, perfectly correct, when he asserts, that there is no other voluntary or positive Law of Nations, than that which Hobbes† divides into the Natural Law of men and the Natural Law of states, properly in-

* See book ii. chap. iii. sect. 23.

† *De Cive*, chap. xiv. sect. 4, 5.—Vattel acknowledges that the author discovers great abilities in this work, "notwithstanding his paradoxes and detestable maxims." He has certainly well defined the Law of Nations, when he stiles it the Law of Nature applied to states or nations.

vested with a true and legal force, and obligatory, as the ordinance of a superior power.

To possess, legitimately, any obligatory force, every stipulation in the ordinances or positive laws of nations, must be founded on such rights, as are deducible from the immutable principles of natural justice: and, in this sense, Pufendorf is justified by reason, when he denies, as he and the best writers on the same subject do, that there is any positive Law of Nations, proceeding from a superior:.... that is to say, there is not any, considering such positive law as a rule (for directing the conduct of nations towards each other,) invested with that essential property of a law.... an obligatory force,....and resting solely on human authority, abstracted from natural right. For, in national pacts and treaties, rules of conduct might, by possibility, be prescribed, purporting to derive their authority from the consent of the contracting parties; which rules might, nevertheless, have a direct tendency, in their operation, to disfranchise one or both of the parties of some unalienable natural right; and, consequently, one essential to their well-being. Thus, a rule of that description, so prescribed, would operate a radical injury; and therefore it could not, though under the denomination of Law, possess that characteristic property of genuine law....a rightful obligatory force; being repugnant to the paramount obligations of natural justice. Injury and injustice, on the one part, and real benefits and right, on the other, can never, by any possibility or any terms, naturally comport with each other. Accordingly, Wollaston* has well observed, that "whatever is inconsistent with the general peace and welfare, or good of mankind, is consistent with the Laws of Human Nature,....wrong, intolerable." Every thing, therefore, that tends to disturb the public peace of nations, and either to prostrate or diminish their general welfare, is an infringement of their natural rights; and, as such, is manifestly unlawful: And it is from the principles here laid down, that the maxim of the Law of Nature and Nations is derived....That no right can be founded on an injury. The maxim, adopted into the code of our municipal laws....that *Consensus tollit errorem*,....is wholly inapplicable to the Law of Nature and Nations, as must evidently appear; with the exception of those things, enjoined

* Rel. of Nat. delin. sect. 6.

by the voluntary and positive Law of Nations, that are either indifferent in themselves, and not immoral or unlawful in their nature: Because, as it has been shewn, the dictates of Natural Law are paramount, in their obligation, to the positive injunctions of any human precept, which either contravene the immutable principles of natural justice, or violate the unalienable rights of man, derived from Nature herself.

The author of the Persian Letters makes the following remark, which is, unfortunately, too well founded in truth, with respect to the perversion of right to which it alludes...."As the Law of Nature and Nations is commonly doctored, one would imagine there were two sorts of justice; one, to regulate the affairs of private persons; the other, to compose the differences that arise between people and people: as if the Law of Nations were not itself a civil law, not indeed of a particular country, but of the world. The magistrate ought to do justice between citizen and citizen; every nation ought to do the same, between themselves and another nation. This second distribution of justice requires no maxims but what are used in the first."....But the design of our present pursuit is not, to inquire what have been the actual violations of the indefeasible Rights of Nations; but, to investigate the nature of those rights, and the validity of the obligations which their correlative duties impose: unless, indeed, in such instances, as it becomes necessary to adduce, in order to illustrate or explain our main subject.

Such, then, being the objects of this dissertation, it is conceived, that a fair induction from what has been already premised, satisfactorily establishes the two following important propositions; as the foundation, upon which the superstructure of the Rights of Nations, with respect to each other, must be raised:....the truths contained in these propositions being derived from the unerring dictates of natural equity and right reason; and their conformity to the principles, thus dictated, supported by the testimony of many celebrated authors.

1st. That the Law of Nations, properly so called,....though apparently compounded of two distinct systems of law....or consisting of two several species of rules of action, operating on different objects upon different principles,...is, in reality, one grand system; deriving the duties it enjoins from the immutable and unerring source of natural justice; and, consequently, attaching to them universal obligation. And that the obligations thus imposed by this great Natural Law....respecting the duties it enjoins to be performed towards those who possess the correlative rights,....are homogeneous in their quality, and uniform in their operation; excepting so far a sa different modification of the objects to which they apply, necessarily varies the mode of their application, according to the limits of the objects, respectively: but, nevertheless, in such quality and degree, as not to change the essential properties of the obligation itself or of its relative right.

2d. That (as a corollary from the preceding proposition) neither any indispensible duty of morals,....consequently, none enjoined by a religion of Divine origin; nor any unalienable natural right; can lawfully have the obligation that enjoins the one, invalidated; or the benefits accruing from the other, annulled;....either by express pacts or treaties*, or by voluntary

* "There are things just and permitted by the necessary Law of Nations, which states may agree to establish between each other; and which they consecrate and strengthen by man-

or implied customs or consent; though under the fictitious sanction of such pretended obligations, as contravene the precepts of Nature's Law.

ners and customs. There are also those that are indifferent, which different states may agree to establish at pleasure by treaties, or introduce such custom or such practice as they shall think proper. But all treaties and all the customs contrary to what the necessary Law of Nations prescribes, or that are such as it forbids, are unlawful." Vattel, Prelim. sect. 9.

A DISSERTATION

ON THE

FREEDOM OF NAVIGATION

AND

MARITIME COMMERCE.

SECTION I.

SHEWING THAT FREE SHIPS MAKE FREE GOODS; ACCORDING TO THE LAW OF NATIONS, AS UNDERSTOOD AND GENERALLY ACTED UPON, PRIOR TO THE YEAR 1780.

HAVING stated, in the introduction, what the Law of Nations really is, as we proposed; we shall now proceed to examine the truth of the proposition, that, by the Law of Nations, the goods of an enemy cannot be taken, on board the ship of a friend.

In the investigation of this subject, we have proposed to pursue the inquiry under two heads;....

1st. Relating to the sanction (as far as it could be thus sanctioned) which the doctrine, contained in the proposition before us, derived from the Law of Nations, as it was understood and acted upon, prior to the year 1780.

2d. Relating to the express recognition of the principle asserted in the same proposition, and the practice thereon; in pursuance of the treaty of Armed Neutrality, in 1780, and of the subsequent adoption of the principles of that Treaty, by almost all of the great maritime states,....manifested by their public official acts.

In this view of the subject, the year 1780 forms a new æra, with respect to the legitimate regulation of the maritime rights and interests of nations, in their mutual intercourse; and, therefore, from that epoch we properly date the commencement of what is usually styled the modern Law of Nations.

We shall then, in the first place, test the controverted principle that we maintain, by the Law of Nations, "as understood and acted upon, by most of the principal maritime powers of Europe, prior to the formation of the Treaty of Armed Neutrality, in 1780." And, in pursuing the investigation in this order, we shall begin with a controversy which took place between the Prussian and British governments, on the point in question, nearly half a century since: because the *ex-parte* decision of the latter, in that case, was founded on an official report of the great Law-officers of the British crown; which is declared, in England, to have been "ever since received, as the standard of authority in cases of that nature*."

In the year 1752, a memorial was presented to the duke of Newcastle, by the Prussian secretary of legation, at London; complaining of violations of the commercial and maritime rights, belonging to the subjects of Prussia, as a neutral nation. The causes which led to this complaint, had been previously heard and examined by, and the facts on which it was founded, fully established before, a board of Commissioners, constituted by the Prussian government: but, whether these Commissioners were appointed for the purpose of taking cognizance of this particular case, or formed a pre-existent tribunal, for acting on all cases of the same nature,....is not ascertained; nor is the fact material to the present

* See the proceedings at large, in this case, in *Collectanea Juridica*, No. 1. and 2.

inquiry: it is sufficient to known, that they acted under the authority of the Prussian government.

It is laid down by these Commissioners, as the basis of the memorial, " That, by the Law of Nations, the goods of an enemy cannot be taken, on board the ship of a friend." In controverting the truth of this proposition, the duke of Newcastle, on the part of the British government, contends (in his answer to monsieur Michell, the Prussian secretary, dated February 8, 1753), that the contrary may be proved, by the rule prescribed by the Law of Nations;" which rule (he asserts) is clearly established by the constant practice of other nations, and by the authority of the greatest men." This " constant practice," it is there contended, is both ancient and modern; and it is observed, that " the General Rule cannot be more strongly proven, than by the exceptions which particular treaties* have made to it."

* The treaties that are cited in the duke of Newcastle's answer, as forming " the exceptions" therein mentioned, are the following:

Treaty between France and England, Feb. 24, 1677, art. 8.

Treaty of Utrecht, between France and England, 1713, art. 17.

In support of the objections advanced by the British secretary of state, against the principle recognized and contended for, by the Prussian government, in the proposition laid down by its commissioners,....sundry writers on the Law of Nations* are particularly cited, as authorities which seem to be greatly relied on. In order, also, to assist in supporting the doctrine, laid down in such books as are referred to, respecting the point in question,

Treaty between England and Holland, Feb. 17, 1668, art. 10.

Treaty between England and Holland, Dec. 1, 1674, art. 8.

Treaty between England and Portugal, July 10, 1654, art. 23.

Treaty between France and the States General, at Utrecht, April 11, 1713, art. 26.

* The books cited, as above, are the following; viz.

Il Consolato del Mare, cap. 273. (This is called, in the British Answer, "A book of geat authority.")

Grotius, de jure Belli ac Pacis; lib. iii. cap. i. sect. 5....and, lib. iii. cap. vi. sect. 6.

Loccenius, de jure maritimo; lib. ii. cap. iv. sect. 12.

Voet, de jure militari; cap. v. nu. 21.

Heineccius, de Navibus ob Vecturam vetitarum Mercium commissis; cap. ii. sect. 9.

Bynkershoek....Questiones Juris publici; lib. i. cap. xiv.

Zouch (an Englishman) in his book, *De Judicio inter Gentes*; pars. ii. sect. 8. nu. 6.

two Treaties* are adduced; in both of which, Great-Britain is a party.

The principle, therefore, of the Law of Nations, that free bottoms make free goods,.... as maintained by the Prussian government and judicature,....is attempted to be invalidated in this instance, by the British government and the expositors of the law on its part, on these grounds; 1st. The authority of "writers on the Law of Nations"....(some of which are cited for the purpose, as above mentioned;) 2d. the "constant practice," as is alleged, "both ancient and modern;" and, 3d. the general rule; which, it is asserted, "cannot be more strongly proved, than by the exception which particular treaties have made to it."....Such are the bases on which the British cabinet, in 1753, endeavoured to support their doctrine....that the goods of their enemy, found on board the ships of neutral powers, are not privileged, by the friendly flag, from seizure and confiscation. It is worthy of

* Treaty between Great-Britain and Sweden, Oct. 23, 1661. Art. 12, 13.

Treaty between Great-Britain and Denmark, Nov. 19, 1669. Art. 2.

remark, that the official letter of the duke of Newcastle to M. Michell, on this occasion, was grounded on a special report made thereon, to the crown, under the signatures of four of the great Law-Officers* at that time in its service: and it was then, and probably yet is, considered as "a standard of authority,"† by the Admiralty Court in England, in cases of that nature.

* Sir George Lee, Dr. Paul, Sir Dudley Ryder, and Mr. Murray.

† What kind of standard-authorities are sometimes permitted to govern the decisions of the British Courts of Admiralty, may be learnt from a very recent case.

A representation had been made to the British government, relative to the capture of American vessels by British armed vessels; and the documents on this head had been referred by that government to the Advocate General of the crown, in order to obtain his report thereon. The Report was accordingly made, bearing date May 23, 1801....In this paper....expressly purporting to be the "opinion" of his Bitannic majesty's Advocate General, and this on a question affecting the rights claimed by a neutral nation, that officer says; "It has been held by the tribunals of this country, that neutrals cannot be admitted by the enemy, under the pressure of war, to carry on his colonial trade, from which, in time of peace, they were wholly excluded. But this principle may be, and has been on account of special circumstances during the present hostilities, to a certain degree, relaxed. His majesty's instructions, of January 1798, only order, that vessels shall be brought in for legal adjudication, which are coming directly from the

Let us, then, examine what degree of strength the argument possesses, that is ad-

enemy's colonies to Europe, and not being bound to England, or a port of their own country. A trade between the neutral country and the enemy's colonies, is now clearly permitted. Colonial produce, actually imported into the neutral country, may also be re-exported from thence to any other place; even to the mother-country of that colony, of which it is the produce....His majesty's existing instructions are therefore the rule by which, at present, the judges of the Vice-Admiralty Courts ought to govern themselves."....It will be recollected, that by the "instructions" of the king of Great-Britain, of the 8th, January, 1794, to the commanders of his ships of war, his instruction of the 6th Nov. 1793, was revoked: and that, by the first clause of the former, it was directed...."That they shall bring in, for lawful adjudication, all vessels with their cargoes, that are laden with goods the produce of the French West-India islands, and coming directly from any port of the said islands to any port in Europe."

Here we observe, that the mere opinion of a Law-officer of the British crown....dependent for the tenure of his office on the will of his sovereign,....is assumed as the basis of a rule, to which the Admiralty Courts of that crown were commanded to conform their decisions: although the cases that were the objects of such rule involved rights of foreign states, derived from the Law of Nations;....Rights, the controversies concerning which can be no otherwise lawfully determined, than by the unerring rules prescribed by the Law of Nations. We find that the instructions issued to the British naval commanders, at different times, and founded on the basis of such opinions, were considered by the British government as the rules, "by which the judges of the vice-admiralty courts ought to govern themselves;" although these varying instructions involved principles attached to the Law of Nations,....consequently, such as

vanced by the British government, in this document, respecting a very important prin-

are invariable in their nature. Yet, seizure and condemnation of the property of independent neutrals, were inflicted, as a penalty for their non-conformity to the maritime regulations prescribed by these arbitrary ordinances of the British king, unwarranted by the Law of Nations....Thus, the royal ordinance (under the denomination of "instructions") of Nov. 6, 1793, declared it lawful "to stop and detain all ships loaden with goods, the produce of any colony belonging to France," &c. These instructions were revoked by those of Jan. 8, 1794; which restrict the power given to commanders of British armed ships, to the bringing in, "for lawful adjudication, all vessels with their cargoes, that are loaden with goods, the produce of the French West-India islands, and coming directly from any port in the said islands to any port in Europe." The course of proceeding in the English courts of admiralty ought, unquestionably, to be guided by the rules of the Law of Nations, in all maritime questions relating to the independent national rights of other states. The equity which generally prevailed throughout the system of the Roman Civil Law caused it to be received and allowed in all the admiralty-courts of Europe, as the rule for determining all rights, of maritime concern, derived from the Law of Nations. This code, which was chiefly composed of the ancient general laws of Rome, and also of Greece; and, professing to be founded on principles of natural justice, was considered as a compilation from the Laws of Nature and Nations: it was therefore adopted by the civilized nations of Europe, as a general rule; applicable to all such juridical cases of general polity, as did not become, by their peculiar circumstances or local concern, objects of municipal law. It is well known, that, in England, mercantile causes are left to be decided according to the rules of the Law-Merchant, which is a branch of the Common Law of that country; and the reason assigned for

ciple in universal jurisprudence. In doing this, we shall test each member of the argu-

this, is, that...."as a part of the Law of Nature and Nations, it is universal, and one and the same in all countries of the world: For, as Cicero says of that Law, *Non erit alia lex Romæ, alia Athenis, alia nunc, alia post hæc; sed et omnes gentes, et omni tempore, una eademque lex obtinebit.*" (See Zouch's jurisdiction of the admiralty of England asserted; Assert. 1.)....It is the obvious result, then, of these premises, that every ex-parte construction of the Law of Nations,....and all rules, arbitrarily prescribed by what are called "instructions," varying in their principles according to the dictates of a fickle and mutable policy,....are both unreasonable and unlawful. The king of Great-Britain has no authority to make Laws, even for the government of his own subjects: much less, can he have a right to prescribe rules, deriving any sanction from the Law of Nations, which shall be obligatory on other states or their people....And, in another view of the subject,....if it was not admissible by the Law of Nations, in 1793, for the people of any neutral state to navigate the ocean with their own ships, when loaden with goods the produce of any colony belonging to France....according to the tenor of the British instructions of that date; then the king of Great-Britain could possess no right, according to the same Law, to annul the prohibition contained in those instructions, as he actually did by the terms of his subsequent instructions, in January 1794. Because, had it been an injunction of legal obligation, that neutral ships should not carry, any where, goods the produce of any colony belonging to France....as it is implied to be, in the first instruction; the king of Great-Britain could not then rightfully permit Neutrals to carry such goods from the colonies of France in the West-Indies, to Asia, Africa, or the continent of America,....confining the former restriction to European ports, only. This, it is contended, he could not rightfully do; inasmuch as it would amount to a power of dis-

ment by such facts, admitted principles, and rational deductions, as, it is conceived, must completely overthrow the whole fabric of their doctrine.

In noticing the points advanced, in the British answer to the Prussian memorial, in support of the doctrine of the former, we shall pursue the order in which they stand, in their

pensing with the laws of his country (of which the Law of Nations is a part); and the exercise of which power would be a violation of his coronation oath. This power, however, it is well known, was assumed by the Stuarts, who exercised it as a branch of the royal prerogative; and this pretended right of dispensing with the execution of the law, was finally abrogated by the Bill of Rights, in the reign of William III. Even Mr. Hume, in his history of the reign of James II, styles it "a branch of prerogative, incompatible with all liberty and limitations;" and concludes his observation with the following remark:...."There needs no other proof of the irregular nature of the old English government, than the existence of such a prerogative; always exercised and never questioned, till the acquisition of real liberty discovered, at last, the danger of it."

The repeated violation of the rights of Neutrals, enjoined by the British instructions to the naval commanders of that nation, in addition to many other cases, were, in every instance manifest infractions of the Law of Nations. May we not, then, justly coincide with Dr. Ramsay's opinion of the conduct of that government; when....treating of the vexatious measures pursued by the British cruisers against the maritime rights of the neutral states, during the American revolutionary war,....he says, that, "having been in the habit of commanding on the sea, they considered power and right to be synonimous terms."

statement of the case, which they call "the standard of authority."

1st, The Authority of Writers on the Law of Nations.

Here a preliminary consideration naturally arises, which suggests this question.... What constitutes the authority of a book treating on the Law of Nations,....a subject of such vast magnitude and universal concern? It will not be pretended, that a private citizen of any country, however virtuous and enlightened he may be; or even any illustrious individual, possessed of the highest species of power and authority in any particular state, though he may be aided by superior talents;....has a right to prescribe rules, which shall bind to their observance, the members of any community whatever, in the one case; or any nation, besides that of which he is himself a member, in the other. No such right can appertain to any man, of either description. Because a law is, in its very nature, a rule of conduct prescribed by a superior, which the inferior is bound to obey: and all nations being considered as equal, independent and free, with respect to each other; those holding the supreme authoritative power of one state,....and, *a fortiori*, such persons as are invested with no legislative power, whatever,... cannot prescribe any rule, to which other states, or their citizens individually, are under any rightful obligation to conform. The political equality subsisting between separate and independent states, cannot comport, *ex vi termini*, with the superiority and inferiority, which, in the definition of law, respectively attach to those prescribing the rule and those bound by it.

It is evident, therefore, that no system of universal jurisprudence, emanating from such conceptions of right and wrong, formed by any man, as constitute mere opinions, unwarranted by reason, could ever possess the properties of a law; imposing an obligation of obedience on either a moral or physical person,....on one independent and equal, in a political view, relatively to himself.

Hence it becomes necessary to trace, to its origin, the legitimate source of those obligations, which constitute one of the essential properties of that extensive and important rule of human conduct, usually denominated the Law of Nations.

If, among nations, no ideas of relative superiority or inferiority are to be admitted, as is politically true,....then the rule that constitutes the Law of Nations, must derive its origin from an higher source than human authority. It is, in fact, a law founded upon,... and, as far as the precepts of Natural Law are susceptible of application to nations collectively, and the affairs of society, incorporated with, that unerring and invariable rule, prescribed to mankind by their great superior, Nature*, and which we, her inferiors, are

* St. Paul says....“ When the Gentiles, which have not the Law, do by Nature the things contained in the Law, these, having not the Law, are a Law unto themselves; which shew the work of the Law written in their hearts, their conscience also bearing witness;” &c. Romans ii. 14, 15.

“ Lex,” says Cicero, in his first book *de Legibus*, “ est *Ratio summa, insita in Natura*, quæ jubet eaa quæ facienda sunt, prohibetque contraria. Eadem *Ratio*, cum est in hominis mente confirmata et confecta, *Lex est*.” See Tom 4, of his works, p. 219, Hamburgh edit. of 1618....And afterwards, in p. 222, of the same volume, this author makes the following observation: “ Atqui nos Legem *bonam a mala*, nulla alia nisi *Naturæ Norma* dividere possumus. Nec solum *jus* et *injuria* a natura dijudicantur, sed omnino omnia honesta, ac turpia. Nam et *communis intelligentia* nobis notas res efficit, easque in animis nostris inchoavit, ut *honesta* in virtute ponantur, in vitiis *turpia*. *Hæc autem in opinione existimare, non in Natura posita, dementis est*.”

bound to obey;—that rule, corresponding with the natural precept which enjoins on all men the pursuit of their own happiness.

Man being destined by the Author of his Being for social intercourse with his fellow beings, he is endowed with those aptitudes and dispositions, which qualify him for maintaining the relations of Rights and Duties, required in that state. His natural incapacities produce wants; for the necessary supply of which, he is compelled to resort to the aid of others; and, the talents and powers of the species being infinitely diversified, such as possess the means of furnishing aid to others, are often under the necessity, in their turn, of claiming the assistance of those, whom, on other occasions, they had been enabled to benefit. Each individual of the society stands in need, in some way or another, of the protection, aid, or counsel, of its other members: whilst, on the other hand, each one possesses some means of promoting those benefits, which he can confer in such manner, as to augment the fund of general welfare. This mutuality of privations and deficiencies, of means and capacities, creates reciprocal Rights and Duties; and these become, by consequence, correlative obligations: Hence, he who is entitled, as a member of civil society, to receive from his fellow-member that species of succour, which the establishment of society was calculated by nature to bestow,....though such as is nugatory, if not altogether unattainable, in a state of existence independent of society;....he, we say, is under a natural obligation to claim it as a right, resulting from nature: and, in like manner, the other is equally bound to perform the obligation, thus imposed on him, as a natural duty.

Those kind and beneficent offices of humanity, that are dictated by the benevolent social affections of our nature, belong to that class of duties which are the correlatives of Rights of imperfect obligation. Such are, charity to the poor; aid and consolation to the helpless, the injured, and the afflicted; civility, and urbanity of manners towards all with whom we hold intercourse; good-will towards the whole human race; and the like beneficent conduct and dispositions. These are acknowledged duties; to the observance of which, mankind have a natural claim on each other. The manifestation and performance of these duties are enjoined by the divine precept...." Do unto others, as you would they should do unto you." Our legitimate claim to their fulfilment, which is sufficiently made known to all men, by the silent dictates of Nature's Law, implies a Right, in the claimants, to the benefits resulting from such fulfilment. The principal difference, therefore, between duties of imperfect obligation, and those whose obligation is perfect, seems to consist in this; that with respect to the latter, the laws of society, or municipal laws of particular states, may enjoin a discharge of them, and inflict penalties in case of default; whereas, in regard to the former, the mere authority of human laws cannot compel their observance: the obligation to it, being constituted by the dictates of Nature alone: neither, of course, can any penalty be exacted in this case, in the event of their non-observance. The distinction here taken, between perfect and imperfect Rights, with their correlative duties, is, in some measure, illustrated by the following cases, stated by Dr. Rutherforth*: "I have a perfect Right to keep my property; since my possession of what is

* Institutes of Natural Law, b. i. ch. i. sect. 4.

my own, does not violate the Rights of any other man. When my property is withheld, my Right to recover it is a perfect one; because no Law restrains me, or no person has any Right to hinder me from recovering it. My poverty may give me a Right to expect relief, from them that I have deserved well of; but I cannot carry this Right into execution, without breaking in upon the Right which they have to their own property: the Law, therefore, restrains me from carrying it into execution, and the Right is an imperfect one."

In the progressive improvement of civil society, wants of a more artificial kind than the bare necessaries of life, grow out of its refinements. The superior talents, activity, or good fortune, of some of its members, give them advantages over others, in acquiring not only the means of subsistence, but those things which contribute to the ease, the comfort, and the rational enjoyments of man. The means, thus acquired, become exclusively vested in the possessor, as his peculiar and appropriate Right. Being obtained by the exertion of his personal skill or industry, or gratuitously* vested in him, by the voluntary act of the prior rightful occupant; the distinction of *meum* and *tuum* results, with reference to the means so acquired by the respective members of the community, as a necessary consequence. Here we trace the origin of exclusive property, and hence discern the nature of its Rights.

These create a new and distinct class of obligations and duties; the compulsory performance of which, on failure of voluntary conformity thereto, is enjoined by positive rules, prescribed by independent communities or states; adapted, in each, to the peculiar nature or construction of its society, and the fundamental regulations of its institution; and these rules constitute a branch of the civil and municipal Law of every country, respectively.

But, as the refinement of manners, and improvement in science and the arts, which spring from a state of civilization, required

* This mode of acquiring property seems to imply some inherent, though dormant claim, in the nature of an imperfect right, attached to the donee; either on the score of actual merit, or, as a retribution for beneficent offices, previously rendered by him to the donor, by which the latter would have incurred, at least, a debt of gratitude.

that commercial as well as friendly intercourse of separate and independent nations with each other, which operate as the mutual cause and effect of civilization; so the Rights of property, originating from such intercourse, produced another species of obligations and duties, in relation to the members of those distinct and independent communities. Their equality, in their character of separate moral persons, admitted, as a necessary consequence, of no superior among them, who could prescribe obligatory rules or regulations; yet such rules were, nevertheless, absolutely necessary, in order to direct a performance, when requisite, of the reciprocal obligations arising from the nature and objects of their intercourse.

The necessity of recurring to the Law of Nature, in this case, is obvious. This Law is founded on the principles of immutable justice.

By the unerring index of right Reason, the mind is directed to a knowledge of those various duties, the performance of which is enjoined by the Law of Nature; and that portion of them which man is bound to perform towards his species, is divided into classes, of a primary and secondary grade. To the first of these, it has been noticed, belong those duties that are the correlatives of perfect Rights, and are therefore denominated duties of perfect obligation: they rest on the foundation of natural equity. And, under the other are arranged such as form the correlatives of imperfect rights; thence termed duties of imperfect obligation: the bases of these are the principles of universal benevolence. The Law of Nature imposes on mankind an indispensible obligation to obey the precepts which enjoin an observance of both these classes of duties.

Now the Law of Nations, the "*Jus Naturale Societatum*, is neither more nor less, as we have already seen, than the "Law of Nature applied to social life, the affairs of societies, and of independent political bodies." The latter does not differ from the Law of Nations, as Heineccius justly observes, either in respect of its foundation and first principles, or its rules; but solely with regard to its object. Nay, says this writer, "the Law of Nations is the Law of Nature itself, respecting or applied to social life, and the affairs of societies and independent states."

Both must, then, derive their origin from the same unerring source; therefore, the maxim of Natural Law "that no right can be founded on an injury*," is, in consequence, a maxim of the Law of Nations, also.

The fair and obvious deduction, then, from the premises, is, that no allegation of any writer on the Law of Nations, in support of any doctrine or theory that purports to be a part of that Law, is a valid authority in that particular; unless such doctrine or theory be strictly conformable to the principles of natural justice: because, "no right can be founded on an injury." Besides, as Vattel observes, "The first general Law, which the very end of the society of nations discovers, is, that each nation ought to contribute all in its power to the happiness and perfection of others†."

In this view of the subject, we discern certain and invariable tests,....by the application of which, to the principles maintained by any writer, whatever, on the Law of Nations, we are enabled to ascertain the soundness or fallacy of any particular doctrine in question. These tests are infallible in their nature;

* Rutherforth's Institutes, b. i. ch. ii. sect. 31.

† Vattel, prelim. sect. 13.

whereas all human authorities, deduced from factitious systems of every kind, are liable and prone to error.

As such authorities, however, are cited, in support of the principle now controverted, we shall, in this place, adduce some proofs of their contradictory testimony and erroneous doctrines, by way of example.

The celebrated Wolfius asserts (in his *Jus Gentium*, sect. 878.) that we are naturally allowed to make use of poisoned arms, in war.... "This decision (says Vattel, in his preface,) shocks me, and I am sorry to find it in the work of so great a man. Happily for the human race (continues this writer) it is not difficult to shew the contrary, even from M. Wolfius's principles, themselves."....Here are Wolfius and Vattel at variance; and farther, M. Wolfius at variance with himself!

The emperor Justinian says*....the exigencies and necessities of mankind have induced all nations to constitute certain rules of right: for wars have arisen, and produced captivity and servitude, which are contrary to the Law of Nature; since, originally, all men were born

* Instit. lib. i. tit. ii. sect. 2.

free.....Yet, a modern writer on Natural Law*, in defining slavery, has these words....“ Perfect despotism seems, in the common notion of it, to be an unalienable Right to direct all the actions of another: and, consequently, perfect slavery is an obligation to submit to be thus directed.”....Besides the inconsistency of these two “ authorities” with each other, in this instance,....Dr. Rutherforth is also at variance with himself; for, how does his definition of rightful slavery comport with the maxim of Natural Law†....“ That no right can be founded on an injury,”....quoted by himself!

* Rutherforth, in his institutes.

† “ *Servitus* autem est constitutio Juris Gentium, qua quis dominio alieno, *contra Naturam*, subjicitur.” Justin. Instit. lib. i. tit. 3....Slavery (servitus) is defined in almost the very words of Justinian, by Bracton; lib. i. cap. 6....Fleta, lib. i. cap. 3.... And by Cowell, in his Institutes, tit. 3....If, therefore, that condition of man, which is denominated slavery, be repugnant to Nature, (as Justinian, Bracton, Fleta, and other jurisconsults have affirmed), it can never be sanctioned by such pretended right of holding him in bondage: notwithstanding this pretended right is attempted to be engrafted upon the Law of Nations, by the arbitrary and erroneous decisions of such civilians, and writers on the Law of Nations, as have assumed the sovereign power of legislating; and that, too, in a matter of such high concern. Surely, if slavery be contrary to Nature, no man can rightfully possess, under any other Law, whatever, than that of Nature herself, “ an unalienable Right,” as Dr. Rutherforth affirms, “ to direct all the actions of another.” Well may he

Dr. Turnbull (the able translator and annotator of Heineccius's system of Universal

apply the term "perfect slavery," to the condition of any human being, subjected to the exercise of such a dominion over him, by another fellow-mortal!....Dr. Rutherforth admits (sect. 4.) that slavery is not the natural state of any man; yet says, it "may be introduced, consistently with the Law of Nature"....And he also asserts, in the same section, that "slavery may arise from a man's own consent."....Let us see, however, what is the language of the 9th Article of the Constitution of Pennsylvania, (commonly called the Declaration of Rights.)...It is declared by the first section of that Article..."That all men are born equally free and independent, and have certain inherent and indefeasible Rights; among which, are those of enjoying and defending life and liberty; of acquiring, possessing, and protecting property and reputation, and of pursuing their own happiness."

But Dr. Rutherforth, who is a dignitary of the church, in England, affords not a solitary instance of the avowal of such tenets, even by persons of his profession. The learned and philanthropic Mr. Granville Sharp, of London, published, many years since, an answer to the Rev. Mr. Thompson, who had written in favour of the African slave-trade....Ecclesiastics may be presumed to derive their notions on this subject from the ancient Jewish writers. But Mr. Sharp observes, "that the Jewish constitutions were not strictly consistent with the Law of Nature, in all points; and, consequently, that they are not to be considered as the rule by which lawyers and casuists may safely determine what is, and what is not, according to Nature." (See Sharp's Tract on the Law of Nature and principles of action in man, page 3.)....And in confirmation of this observation of the truly pious Sharp, we refer to a passage, extracted from Mr. Barbeyrac's historical and critical account of the science of morality, sect. 7....prefixed to baron Pufendorf's

Law) remarks....that the disputes about the dominion of the sea, between Grotius and Selden, Rob. Johnston, Petr. Bapt. Burgus, Guil. Welwood, Jo. Isaac. Pontanus, Theod. Graswinckelius,....and, more lately, between Pufendorf, Huber, Jac. Gothofredus, Jo. Hen. Boeclerus, Corn. van Bynckershoek, and Christ. Thomafius, and others,.....are well known; although the same learned commentator expresses his opinion, "that no one can doubt that the sea is under the dominion of none." He justly observes, that navigation to

treatise on the Law of Nature and Nations; and which we have quoted in another place.

The false and unnatural doctrines, propagated by such writers as Mr. Thompson and Dr. Rutherforth, on the subject of slavery, are notable examples, among others, of the erroneous and interested bias, which has not unfrequently actuated men, against the dictates of Nature and of Religion.

We have dwelt the longer on the subject of this note, which is merely incidental to the main point in controversy,....not solely on account of the enormity of the principles it opposes; but to shew, in addition to other instances which will be adduced, how very fallible is the authority of writers on the Law of Nature and and Nations,....even on points that involve the unalienable natural Rights of Man; when their interpretation of that great Law is unsupported, both by Reason and Religion: For, the condition of unlimited bondage....such as Dr. Rutherforth has defined "perfect slavery" to be....is equally repugnant to both: And yet it merits notice, that this gentleman is a writer of Institutes of Natural Law, as well as a teacher of Christianity!

the territories not belonging to us, for the sake of Commerce, is as unjustly denied by us, as the use of a public road;....unless (says he) this navigation be hindered by pacts and treaties*."

We have already noticed Barbeyrac's censure of Grotius's pretended distinction between the Law of Nature, and a certain arbitrary Law of Nations, which he conceives to be founded on the tacit consent of the people: and it has also been observed that Pufendorf frequently refutes the opinions of Grotius.... Finally, by recurring to the note on page 60, we have another proof of the incongruous tenets of writers on universal Law, manifested in their doctrines concerning private slavery.

The foregoing, independently of numerous instances of the same kind, serve to shew, how little reliance ought to be placed on the authority of authors, who have treated on subjects of universal jurisprudence; unless in those cases, wherein the principles they advocate are manifestly supported by Reason and Natural Equity.

Some observations, however, of another nature, naturally occur, on the authorities (as

* See Heineccius, book ii. chap. viii. sect. 175, in note.

they are styled) cited in the British document now under consideration....But we shall first premise, that so late as the year 1782, the treaty which was concluded between Great-Britain and the States General of the United Netherlands, in the year 1674, was made the basis of a treaty of peace proposed by the British crown to that Republic: And, by this treaty of 1674, "the principles of the Armed Neutrality are established, in their widest extent, to all the contracting parties*."....His Britannic majesty then offered to accept, "as the basis of a separate peace between him and the States General, a free navigation, according to the principles demanded by her imperial majesty (the empress of Russia,) in her declaration of the twenty-sixth of February, 1780†."

Here, then, is incontrovertible evidence on the part of Great-Britain herself, manifested by public acts of her government, at two several periods, viz. in 1674 and 1780,....of her acquiescence in those principles of a free

* Mr. Secretary Fox's letters, of the 29th of March, and 4th of May, 1782, to M. Simolin.

† Mr. Fox's letter, of the 4th of May, 1782, to M. Simolin.

navigation to neutrals, on which the treaty of Armed Neutrality was founded.

This celebrated League....which comprehended almost the whole of the great maritime powers of Europe, either as the original contracting parties, or such as afterwards publicly avowed their accession to its fundamental principles and stipulations, ...may be justly considered as fixing the æra that consummated the establishment of the *modern* Law of Nations*.

* This phraseology is used, merely in compliance with the practice of some modern writers. The great and fundamental principles of the Law of Nations are unchangeable; therefore, the ancient and the modern Law of Nations, with respect to them, must be the same. All that is meant, then, by the modern Law of Nations, is the modern construction of those principles. We have said, that the Treaty of Armed Neutrality, in 1780, may be considered, " as fixing the æra that consummated the establishment of the modern Law of Nations." We have, however, referred to the year 1674, as the period at which that æra may, on the present occasion, be supposed to have its commencement. And that period has been fixed upon, because the British government did so unequivocally recognize in 1782, the principle with respect to Neutrals, contained in their treaty with the States General, concluded in that year. But, perhaps, it would be more proper to date the modern Law of Nations (that is, the modern interpretation or construction of that Law) from the year 1647; since which time almost every maritime treaty concluded in Europe has expressly declared that free ships make free goods; contrary to the doctrine

When books, therefore, are cited, as authorities on the Law of Nations, concerning points settled in the treaty of Armed Neutrality; they are no authority, nor have the speculative opinions or arbitrary decisions of their authors any weight or validity, farther than as they comport with the general principles and rights maintained in that treaty, in conformity with the dictates of Natural and Universal

of Grotius, and one or two others, who wrote before that period. This was the idea of Mr. Fauchet (late minister of France to the United States) on this subject. "The prerogative (says he) which neutral nations enjoy in time of peace, is the portion of the Law of Nations most subject to dispute. Neutrals having a great interest in enjoying the most extensive liberty for their commerce, belligerent powers, who have not a maritime force to give convoys, having an equal interest that their commerce may continue under a neutral flag during hostilities,....it is clear, that those two kinds of powers must, necessarily, have constantly endeavoured to give to the trade of neutrals the utmost latitude of freedom: Therefore do we see all the treaties concluded for a century and an half back, by either or one or other of the two kinds of powers which we have designated, contain principles extremely liberal in this respect. Authors (continues Mr. Fauchet), who have written on the Law of Nations, have laid down the maxim, that enemy's property does not cease to be so, under a friendly flag; and, consequently, may be seized. The Treaties, of which we speak above, establish, on the contrary, that the friendly flag protects enemy's property, and places it beyond violation. This is what is commonly called the modern Neutrality." See Fauchet's Sketch, &c. published after his return to France.

Law. And, if this observation be just, with respect to authors whose works were written prior to 1780,...though subsequently to 1674; how much more forcibly does it apply to those writers on Universal Law, who died prior even to the year 1674; when the principles of a free navigation to neutrals were "established, in their widest extent" (to all those who afterwards became the contracting parties of the treaty of Armed Neutrality), by the treaty between Great-Britain and the United Provinces, in that year.

In the counter memorial, or answer of the British minister, in 1753, to the Prussian memorial concerning neutral ships,....a book entitled *Il Consolato del Mare**, is cited, as "a book

* The *Consolato del Mare*, which is sometimes cited as an authority, is but a rude and mis-shapen mass, and pretty ill chosen collection of positive Maritime Law, and particular ordinances of the middle ages, or of ages little enlighted:.... But no part of it can be of any assistance to those who wish to discuss the rights of belligerent nations, on the subject of the Navigation of Neutrals....All the fruit that may be expected from perusing that collection, is to gratify curiosity, by comparing the maxims and policy of those ages with those of the present times, to the advantage of the present state of things; and learning, as it were, from the mouth of those sovereigns, the profound ignorance in which they then were, as well as those of their subjects, who enjoyed the greatest reputation for ability and learning....Hubner; Preface to his work *De la Saisie*, &c.

of great authority," in support of the British construction of the principle, which was the subject of controversy between the parties. This antiquated Italian production, which, by a few dashes of the compiler's pen, makes a Law by which nations are to be bound,....in which he pronounces, in the authoritative style of a legislator, that "if the vessel, or fleet, which shall have been taken, belongs to a power at peace, but the cargo, with which she is laden, to an enemy,....the admiral of the armed vessel, or fleet, is at liberty to force the master of the ship, or fleet, which shall have been taken, to carry the goods of the enemy where he (the admiral) shall think proper;"....this book, we say,....whose compiler appears to be anonymous,....is cited by Grotius, as his authority for maintaining a similar doctrine: And Grotius, thus supported as to the point in controversy, is then cited in the British counter memorial, as an additional authority, in support of the same principle!*

* It is a fact that Grotius, in his work *De Jure Belli ac Pacis*, appears to favor the system of seizing enemy's goods on board of Neutral Vessels; yet afterwards, when he had more maturely considered the subject, wrote a formal Treatise in which he maintained the opposite doctrine....This Treatise has never been published; but the proof of its existence has been preserved, in an original letter of Grotius to his brother,

But let us examine what this work really is, which is such a favourite of the British government and their admiralty courts; and we shall then be enabled to decide, how far it deserves to be considered as "a book of great authority."....Giannono gives the following account of it, in his history of Naples, viz. "The articles of which the *Consolato del Mare* is composed, were approved by the Romans, the Pisanians, Lewis king of France, count Jolosa, and by many other princes and nobles; the kings of Arragon and the counts of Barcelona added new ones; and Arnoldo Vennio does not depart from the opinion of those who assert, that this compilation was made in the times of St. Lewis, king of France."

Louis IX of France, usually styled St. Lewis, reigned from the year 1226 to 1270; and was the cotemporary of Henry III of England*. Now, every person, in the smallest

which M. Burigny has inserted in his Life of that celebrated Author....This letter was written in the year 1629, and Grotius informs his brother, in it, "that he had written a Treatise in order to prove that war between sovereigns ought not to impair the freedom of the trade of Neutral Powers." See Hubner, *De la Saisie des Batimens Neutres*, &c. vol. i. Introduction sect. 10.

* In order that we may be able to form some ideas of the fitness of that period, for the formation of a code of maritime

degree acquainted with history, must know, that, within that period, maritime commerce

and commercial laws, we present to our readers the following extract (which is indeed somewhat ludicrous) from Mr. Hume's reign of Henry III, in his History of England.

"Interest had in that age amounted to an enormous height, as might be expected from the barbarism of the times, and men's ignorance of commerce. Instances occur, of fifty per cent. paid for money."...."Commerce must be in a wretched condition, where interest was so high, and where the sole proprietors of money employed it in usury only, and were exposed to such extortion and injustice. But the bad police of the country was another obstacle to improvements; and rendered all communication dangerous, and all property precarious. The Chronicle of Dunstable says, that men were never secure in their houses, and that whole villages were often plundered by bands of robbers, though no civil wars at that time prevailed in the kingdom. In 1249, some years before the insurrection of the barons, two merchants of Brabant came to the king, at Winchester, and told him, that they had been spoiled of all their goods by certain robbers, whom the knew, because they saw their faces every day in his court; that like practices prevailed all over England, and travellers were continually exposed to the danger of being robbed, bound, wounded, and murdered; that these crimes escaped with impunity, because the ministers of justice themselves were in a confederacy with the robbers; and that they, for their part, instead of bringing matters to a fruitless trial by law, were willing, though merchants, to decide their cause with the robbers, by arms and a duel. The king, provoked at these abuses, ordered a jury to be enclosed, and to try the robbers: The jury, though consisting of twelve men of property in Hampshire, were found to be also in a confederacy with the felons, and acquitted them. Henry, in a rage, committed the jury to prison, threatened them with severe

between nations had scarcely an existence among those European powers, who are now

punishment, and ordered a new jury to be enclosed, who, dreading the fate of their fellows, at last found a verdict against the criminals. Many of the king's own houshold were found to have participated in the guilt; and they said, for their excuse, that they received no wages from him, and were obliged to rob for a maintenance. Knights and Esquires, says the Dictum of Kennelworth, who were robbers, if they have no land, shall pay the half of their goods, and find sufficient security to keep henceforth the peace of the kingdom. Such were the manners of the times!"

Other parts of Europe did not, at the period referred to, exhibit a more favorable aspect. It was in the reign of St. Lewis, that the Crusade was carried on against the Albigenses, in the South of France, under the sanction of Pope Innocent III, who denominated them heretics, because they opposed the rites of the church, and the power and influence of the clergy: and, after a war of twenty years continuance, these sectaries....who, according to Mr. Hume, were "the most innocent and inoffensive of mankind,"....were exterminated, with all the circumstances of extreme violence and barbarity, by the crusaders, who flocked from all parts of Europe. The count of Toulouse, who headed the persecuted and discomfited Albigenses, was compelled by the Pope to cede his hereditary dominions to Lewis, and to pay a considerable sum of money to different churches and monasteries: "But no sooner," as Mr. Gifford observes, "did he consent to resign a great part of his dominions, than he became a good Catholic; his sentiments were declared to be orthodox; and not the smallest abjuration of his errors was required! So dreadful (continues this historian) was the infatuation, under which men laboured at this disgraceful period, when the practice of Christianity was, by designing priests and interested monarchs, made to consist in a

its great conductors. It was more than two centuries before either the discovery of America, or of the nautical passage to the southern and eastern coasts of Asia, round the Cape of Good-Hope. Commerce, in general, was then in a very rude and uncultivated state; and maritime trade, particularly, was carried on, within bounds as well as in a degree, extremely limited....Such portion of it, as was at that time cultivated, was principally in the hands of the Venetians and Genoese. Indeed, the Venetians alone, prior to the discovery of the Cape of Good-Hope, monopo-

violation of its precepts!" The same heroic and enthusiastic prince engaged in two expeditions, which he conducted in person, for the recovery of the Holy Land out of the hands of the Infidels; in which undertaking, he fell a victim to his pious but mistaken zeal....And, in the latter part of the same reign, the Flagellants made their appearance in Europe; a frantic sect, who, as Mr. Gifford observes (in his History of France), were actuated by a singular species of fanaticism, which was neither ordained by authority nor excited by eloquence:.... "When all Italy was sullied by crimes of every kind," says the monk of St. Justina, in Padua, "a certain sudden superstition, hitherto unknown to the world, first seized the inhabitants of Perusa, afterwards the Romans, and then almost all the nations of Italy."......Such (in the exclamation of Mr. Hume) were the manners of the times!....not in England merely; but in France, Italy, and indeed throughout all Europe!

lized the only maritime commerce in the world, that was then of any great importance*....At the æra of Louis IX, the state of society and manners, throughout Europe, was not many degrees removed from barbarism. Ignorance was the characteristic of the age. Most of the arts were in the rudest possible state. No beams of true science had yet dawned upon the mind; and just principles of the great business of legislation and jurisprudence were totally unknown. How preposterous, then, is it, to set up a compilation of arbitrary rules and regulations....made five centuries and an half since, and under such circumstances,.... as a standard of right, respecting navigation and commerce, at the present day! It is ridiculously absurd!....Yet such is the "book of

* About the time that commerce revived on the European shores of the Mediterranean, the ancient league of the Hanseatic Towns commenced. This was in the year 1164. But this association comprised, at first, only the towns situated on the Baltic sea, and some of those that were little distant from thence. The most flourishing times of this alliance, were not, however, until the end of the 14th, and the beginning of the 15th, centuries....Their maritime trade must have been very inconsiderable, at the time that the *Consolato del Mare* was compiled: and yet they then carried on, as well as long afterwards, almost the whole naval commerce of the northern parts of Europe.

great authority," which seems to serve as the fundamental support for that construction, which is given by Great-Britain, to one of the most important principles in the Law of Nations.

This, too, is such an authority as Grotius thought proper to build upon. Yet even Grotius died so long since as 1645; which was twenty-nine years before the treaty (between England and Holland) of 1674; and his treatise *de jure belli ac pacis* was published twenty years before his death.

We have dwelt the longer on this part of the argument, not only to evince the absurdity of bringing forward such authority under such circumstances,....and, consequently, the invalidity of the authority itself; but because the *Consolato del Mare* has been principally relied on, as their fundamental support on this occasion, by the English law-officers;... .having been considered by them as a kind of standard authority, and so styled in their report to the crown.

We shall, however, proceed to offer some observations on the other authors, cited in the British report on the same occasion.

Loccenius, a Swedish writer, flourished at Upsal in 1670: but his book must have been published several years prior to that date; as it is referred to, by Zouch, in his treatise entitled, " The Jurisdiction of the Admiralty of England asserted;"....and this work was put into the hands of T. Baldwyn, to be printed, before the year 1663....Zouch himself, who was a doctor of the civil laws, was also a judge of the high court of Admiralty in England, prior to that year. It cannot therefore be doubted, that his construction of the Law of Nations, with relation to the principle that free ships make free goods, would be perfectly consonant to the interested maxims of his nation.

Bynkershoek appears to have published his *Questiones Juris Publici* in 1737....Yet, on examination, what is the sum of this writer's testimony, as to the point in question? In book i. chap. xiv. he has this passage, concerning enemy's effects found in the ship of a friendly power:...." We must rather consider Reason itself than Treaties. I cannot see any cause why it should not be lawful to take enemy's goods, though found in the ship of a nation not at war; for I consider it as the property of the enemy, and belonging by the right of war to the conqueror." ....Here we are told that Reason ought to be our guide, in construing litigated points of the Law of Nations: and we entirely coincide with Bynkershoek, in that opinion. But, when he lays down a principle of public Law, as the result of his own Reason;....another, who interprets the Law differently, has an equal right to make the result of his Reason, the standard of legitimacy. Both, in such case, amount to no more than the opinions of the respective parties. If these opinions relate to the same principle, derived from the Law of Nature....and they oppose each other,.... those on one side, at least, must necessarily be erroneous. The opinions, that conform to natural justice and right reason, can only be right;....there being no other infallible standard of truth, in this instance: But no speculative opinions of the most ingenious writer, are entitled, merely as such, to the weight of *authorities*. We proceed, however, to the remaining authors, cited in support of the same principle.

Voetius (John) most probably wrote his treatise *De Jure Militari*, since 1674; but, the work not being in our possession, the precise time is unknown: We find, however, that he died in 1714.

Heineccius was born in the year 1681; and probably wrote his treatise *De Navibus*, &c. about forty years after, when he was made professor of civil Law, at Halle.

Thus it appears, that of the several books ....cited, as authorities, in the report of the British Law-officers, in the case which is the subject of the Prussian memorial,....the greater part of them were written before (one of them, between five and six hundred years before!) the date of that Treaty, by which the British secretary of state, in 1782, declared....that " the principles of the Armed Neutrality, are established, in their widest extent, to all the contracting parties;"....that another of them was written nearly about the time of forming the same Treaty;....and, that the authors of the remaining ones, Bynkershoek and Heineccius, compiled their treatises, from about sixty-four to eighty years since. And, with respect to this last writer, who appears to be one of the most modern of the seven,....a very striking observation naturally suggests itself, on the present occasion. The British law-officers, in citing him as one of their authorities, style him a "learned Prussian." But they seem to have forgotten, that the Prussian commissioners, acting judicially, and under the authority of the Prussian government, maintained a doctrine directly opposed to that of "the learned Prussian" author! It cannot, surely, be contended that the mere *dictum*, or opinion, of any unauthorized individual, however "learned," can invalidate the solemn decision of a national judicatory. On the contrary, it must be admitted, that the authority of the board of Prussian commissioners (merely as such), in their decision of the controverted question, was more than a counterpoise in the weight of authority, to the contrary decision of the law-officers of the British crown, on the same question.

Under these circumstances, how can the authors, here mentioned, be cited with any kind of propriety, in support of that construction of the Law of Nations, which was not only adopted by England, in her treaty with Holland in 1674....as well as in some preceding and many subsequent treaties, to which England was a party; but, which was further sanctioned by the British government, so late as the years 1782* and 1786? Such authorities are, certainly, irrelevant to the point in question, for the reasons arising out of those circumstances; even if the principle they maintain, in relation to that point, could be deemed admissible on other grounds†.

* See, in the Appendix, the State-papers relative to the treaty of Armed Neutrality.

† There are some judicious observations on this subject, contained in that letter from Mr. T. Pinckney to Lord Grenville, which we have quoted in another place. Mr. Pinckney remarks, that, as his Lordship had adverted to an observation he had made in a preceding letter, he would take the liberty of briefly stating the principal reasons which suggested his remark that " some of the measures of this" (the British) " government will be considered by the United States, as infringements on their Natural Rights." He then mentions, that " the measures alluded to, are particularly those which contravene the principles, that free ships make free goods,....and, which prevent certain articles of Provision, the produce of the United States, from being carried, in their own vessels, to the unblockaded ports of France."

" With respect to the first (says Mr. Pinckney,) it is conceived, that as commerce has been more diffusively cultivated, and its principles better understood,....the Law of Nations, relating thereto, has secured material improvements, since the publication of the most modern and most approved writers on that subject; and, whatever doubts may formerly have existed on this point, that the sense of a considerable majority of the maritime powers of Europe has, within the last twenty years, been clearly expressed, in favour of the principle of free ships making free goods; which has been manifested, by their prac-

Before we dismiss this part of our observations, we are led to remark, that the cele-

tice, in the latter years of the American war,....by the stipulations entered into at that time,....and by their having inserted the same in their latest treaties. Of these, the treaties entered into between the United States and several European powers are among the most recent; all of which support this doctrine, by express stipulation."...“ The right contended for (continues Mr. Pinckney,) appears not only supported by modern practice, but to be conformable to reason: for if two nations have the misfortune of being engaged in war against each other, it is evidently contrary to the dictates of reason, that a third, who has no concern in the quarrel, and has offended neither party, should be injured thereby, or be debarred from that intercourse with either, which is not immediately connected with military operations."

Mr. Pinckney seems to have been sensible, that the interpretation of Public Law, which has resulted from the opinions of Writers on the subject....and which is generally denominated the Law of Nations, itself....is less consistent, as a rule of Right, with the present state of maritime commerce, and less consonant to reason,....that what he styles the late improvements in the Law of Nations, and in another place the modern Law of Nations.

In Mr. Jefferson's letter (of the 16th August, 1793) to Mr. Morris, the American minister at Paris,....the “ inconvenience" of the principle, that an enemy's goods are lawful prize in the vessel of a friend, (although stated by our administration, on that occasion, to have been long an established principle of the Law of Nations,) is expressly noticed :....“ a principle (continues his letter) which subjects merchant vessels to be stopt at sea, searched, ransacked, led out of their course ;" a principle, which is expressly declared to be “ oppressive to commerce." Notwithstanding, therefore, that construction of the Law of Na-

brated Pufendorf does not touch on the subject of Neutrality, throughout the whole of his extensive and inestimable work on the Law of Nature and Nations, which he published in 1669.* But, notwithstanding this omission, the sentiments of that great man, on the subject of the present dissertation, may be collected from the following assertion, in his letter to M. Groning, written in 1692. Speaking of free Navigation....concerning which, M. Groning then proposed writing a treatise,....M. Pufendorf says:....“The Laws of Humanity and Equity between Nations do not extend so far as to require, without any apparent necessity, that one people should give up its profit, in favour of another. But, as the avarice of merchants is so great, that, for the smallest gain, they make no scruple of exceeding the just bounds of commerce*;....so, nations that

tions which the administration then maintained, respecting the principle in question, Mr. Jefferson's letter shows, that the principle of maintaining, is in its operation injurious to the interests of commerce; and, consequently cannot be founded on a Right.

* We think M. Pufendorf has departed from his usual candor, in this unqualified censure of merchants. Too many of them are, without doubt, chargeable, at the present day, with

are at war, may certainly visit neutral ships; and, if they find prohibited goods on board, have a full right to confiscate them."....These expressions....." apparent necessity"...." just bounds of commerce"...and "prohibited goods" ....have an evident reference to such articles, alone, as are excepted....out of the general Right of Neutrals to enjoy the benefits of a free navigation,....under the denomination of Contraband of war. With regard to all other objects of just commerce, " navigation to the territories not belonging to us, for the sake of commerce (in the words of Dr. Turnbull), is as unjustly denied to us, as the use of a public road; unless this navigation be hindered by pacts and treaties." (See note in page 63). For, as Gerard Malynes remarks, " according to the common right of mankind, *Jure Gentium*,....the navigation through all the world is

that species of " avarice;" which impels them to transgress " the just bounds of commerce;" as they are not unfrequently detected in carrying on such illicit trade, as subjects themselves to discredit and loss, and the community to dishonor, even though it should not disturb the public peace. But there is nevertheless, we trust, a great body of the American merchants, whose honor and probity place them above the imputation, which, perhaps, too justly attached to the majority of men of that profession, in Europe, in the time of M. Pufendorf.

no less free, and open to every one, than the use of the air*."

Having shewn, that the writers on the Law of Nations....cited as authorities on the part of the British government, in the case of the Prussian memorial,....are not competent to support that principle, contended for by them, which goes to the disfranchisement of neutrals, in the prosecution of their fair and equitable maritime trade; we now proceed to the next point, on which they relied for that purpose; viz.

2d. "The constant practice"....which, it is alleged, is "both ancient and modern."

The most indubitable testimony of what has been the (warranted) practice of nations, in this particular, consists of their several treaties. We shall therefore examine what has been such practice, under the stipulations of various treaties.

The practice, or custom of nations, must be either voluntary, or conventional. But, in both cases, if the practice be repugnant to the natural rights of mankind, it is not obligatory under the Law of Nations. We have shewn

* See his Ancient Law-merchant, cap. 33....N. B. Malynes wrote in 1622.

that Grotius's notion of a kind of Law of Nations, to which the epithet of *arbitrary* has been attached....considering it as proceeding from the will or consent of nations,....is unfounded in Reason and in Nature. And, with respect to those customs that are prescribed by pacts and treaties, it is equally clear, that if they either tend to disfranchise men of their unalienable rights,....or enjoin, as duties, the performance of those things which are incompatible with moral rectitude; they possess not the legitimate properties of a Law, and have no obligatory force*. There are many things,

* What, then, are we to say to the treaty of peace and commerce (where there was not the stale pretence of the pressure of war) between "his most sacred majesty George I." &c. "and the most excellent lords Ali basha, Hassain Ben Ali, bey, Cara Mustafa, dey, the aga, and the divan of the most noble City of Tunis?" the 13th article is in these words...."That in case any ships of war belonging to the kingdom of Tunis, shall take, in any of their enemies' ships, any Englishman serving for wages, they are to be made *slaves*; but if merchants or passengers, they are to enjoy their liberty and effects, unmolested".... This, we believe, (for the honor of human nature) is the only instance in the annals of mankind, of a civilized nation, professing Christianity, consigning their compatriots to slavery among an herd of barbarians, by the sanction of a solemn treaty, entered into with a piratical state!....Will it be pretended, that this stipulation possessed the obligatory force of a law,......because it was inserted in a treaty, clothed with all the solemnities of a

indifferent in themselves, which may justly become objects of stipulation in treaties; independently of any obligation of natural Law. But, says Heineccius's annotator (Dr. Turnbull*), "it is manifestly contradictory, that the Law of Nature should confirm pacts contrary to itself; that it should at the same time prohibit a pact, and command it to be fulfilled; or that a pact should be, at one and the same time, null and yet obligatory. And therefore a pact is departed from, without perfidy; which could not be fulfilled, without committing a crime. Nor does he deserve the character of faithful, who performs what he cannot do without incurring guilt." Hence, it may be justly inferred, that the "practice" of nations....though it be "constant," and "both ancient and modern,".....can neither abrogate an inherent right, nor dispense with the obligation of a primary natural duty.

Having laid down these principles, which it is conceived are consonant to reason and

national pact?...No....We trust no modern expositor of the Law of Nations will have the hardiness to defend so detestable a principle; adopted in the reign of a "most sacred" king, to suit the purposes of state policy!

* See Heineccius's System of Universal Law, book i. cap. xiv. sect. 398, in note.

the nature of things,....we shall go on to shew, that the doctrine maintained by the law-officers of the British crown is not warranted by the "practice" of nations; but that such practice is directly opposed to their construction of the Law of Nations,....though with some exceptions. And in discussing this point, we shall consider the question of practice, or usage of nations, only; merely for the purpose of invalidating the argument, which the British government have rested on this ground. Let the observation already made be recollected: namely, that the practice of nations, respecting matters of commercial and maritime concern, cannot be ascertained from a truer source, than the treaties of navigation and commerce, that have been concluded between the principal maritime states.

From the discovery of America in the western hemisphere, and of the Cape of Good-Hope in the eastern....towards the close of the fifteenth century,....may be dated the commencement of a new æra, in the annals of naval commerce. The vast extension of navigation, consequent on those events, greatly multiplied the commercial relations of nations, and increased the importance of the objects, to which those relations applied. Hence, treaties for the regulation of their respective maritime interests, and leagues for the protection of the rights on which those interests depend, soon became necessary. The collision of various nations with each other, when engaged in the pursuits of gain from foreign commerce ....especially when a prosecution of objects of the same nature produced a direct competition among them,....readily led to a violation of the weaker states, by the more powerful: And, by an easy transition, resulting from the natural progression of injustice, even those states whose relative strength was more equal, were stimulated by the thirst of lucre, to commit infractions of their mutual rights. The desire of acquiring distant colonies was produced by the same incentive; and the wealth and power, flowing from the extension of commerce and acquisitions of foreign territory.....aided by their natural concomitant, ambition,....became fruitful sources of contention and wars. Thus, an augmentation of the mutual commerce of nations...by being pursued under the influence of some of the most unworthy passions of our nature,....became an additional source of strife, injustice, and hostility among men: although the Author of all Good had pointed out such intercourse, as a mean, under the direction of equitable and benevolent principles, of promoting the happiness of mankind. Such, however, was the actual state of things; produced less, perhaps, by the errors of our reason, than the vices of our nature.

The misunderstandings and disagreements arising between nations, from these causes, involved either real or supposed interests: and it is an obvious dictate of common sense, that an appeal to the sword, in national as well as private disputes, can never be an eligible mode of deciding a question of Right*. Even when war ensues between nations, as a consequence of either an actual or alleged violation of rights; the matters in controversy are ultimately decided by pacific adjustments, in the form of treaties.

* "Those who run to arms, without necessity, are the scourges of the human race, barbarians, enemies to society, and rebels to the Law of Nature, or rather to the Common Father of mankind."....Vatt. book ii. cap. xviii. sect. 354.

"A single robber or a few associates," as Mr. Gibbon observes, "are branded with their genuine name; but the exploits of a numerous band assume the character of lawful and honorable war." Hist. of Decl. and Fall of Rom. Emp: vol. ix. cap. 50.

But in all amicable decisions of disputes between nations, concerning their respective Rights, some common and invariable standard of national justice must necessarily be resorted to. This, we have seen, is only to be found in the Law of Nations.

If the principles and maxims of this Law were perfectly and generally understood, little difficulty would attend the settlement of national controversies, where there existed a disposition to do justice. Unfortunately, however, for the repose of mankind, an uniform construction of the Law of Nations, in some points of the highest importance, has not been given by the various writers on that subject. This observation has been abundantly verified, by the instances that have been adduced of the disagreement of such writers, concerning questions of the greatest magnitude. The prodigious extension and rapid increase of maritime commerce, within the last century and an half*, have vastly multiplied the ob-

* In the course of the debate on the French commerical treaty of 1786, in the British house of commons, Mr. Alderman Watson asserted; that, in the year 1677, England had "but one vessel with lingering sails, a single solitary bottom, that went to the Baltic"...." In 1786 (continued Mr. Watson)

jects, to which an application of the Law of Nations now becomes necessary. Yet, prior to that period, some of these objects that were considered as being of little importance....and therefore scarcely contemplated as a subject meriting much attention, by the writers of those days,....have since become matters of the most weighty concern. Thus, when Grotius wrote his treatise *de jure belli ac pacis*, the principle....that free ships make free goods, had scarcely afforded occasion for controversy. We do not observe any stipulation respecting that right, in any league or treaty before Grotius's time. This principle is, however, believed to have been *considered* as having its foundation in the Law of Nations, ...so early, at the least, as the year 1613: for we find that the memorable league into which the States General entered, in that year, with the republic of Lubeck*, was declared to be

we had several hundred sail; with a vast number to Groenland"....See Parliamentary Debates, for 1787.

* This league was solemnly confirmed about two years and eight months afterwards, and strengthened by the accession of most of the other Hanse-Towns. That between Lubec, Bremen and Hamburg, was concluded in 1640...between the Dutch, Bremen and Hamburg, in 1645....and between the Dutch and the king of Denmark, in the same year. The ostensible object

"for the defence and vindication of the liberty of navigation, trade and commerce,....and of

of the league between the Dutch and the Hanse-Towns, was the protection of their maritime Rights in relation to the trade of the Baltic and the waters of the German ocean; but the quotations, from the two first of those treaties, we think, prove, that the real design of the league was more general and extensive.

Mr. Hume (in his history of the reign of Edward VI.) remarks, that the trade of England had anciently been carried on altogether by foreigners, chiefly the inhabitants of the Hanse-towns, or Easterlings, as they were called; and in order to encourage these merchants to settle in England, they had been erected into a corporation by Henry III, had obtained a patent, were endowed with privileges, and were exempted from several heavy duties paid by other aliens. "So ignorant," continues Hume, "were the English of commerce, that this company, usually denominated the merchants of the Stil-yard, engrossed, even down to the reign of Edward (that is to say, until about the year 1547), almost the whole foreign trade of the kingdom: and, as they naturally employed the shipping of their own country, the navigation of England was also in a very languishing condition. It was therefore thought proper by the council (in 1551) to seek pretences for annulling the privileges of this corporation."...."Several remonstrances were made against this innovation, by Lubec, Hamburg, and other Hanse-towns; but the council persevered in their resolution," &c. And, in Appendix III, to the fifth Volume of the History of England, we find these observations of the same author, on this subject. "The merchants of the Hanse-towns complained loudly, in the beginning of Elizabeth's reign, of the treatment they had received in the reigns of Edward and Mary. She prudently replied, that as she would not innovate any thing, she would still protect them in the immunities of which she found them possessed. This answer not contenting them, their commerce

the rights and privileges belonging thereunto." And, by the 6th article of the treaty

was soon after suspended for a time, to the great advantage of the English merchants, who tried what they could themselves effect for promoting their commerce. They took the whole trade into their own hands; and their returns proving successful, they divided themselves into staplers and merchant adventurers. This success so enraged the Hanse-towns, that they tried all the methods which a discontented people could devise, to draw upon the English merchants the ill opinion of other nations and states. They prevailed so far as to obtain an imperial edict, by which the English were prohibited all commerce in the empire. The queen, by way of retaliation, retained sixty of their ships, which had been seized in the river Tagus with contraband goods of the Spaniards. These ships the queen intended to have restored, as desiring to have compromised all differences with those trading cities; but, when she was informed that a general assembly was held at Lubec, in order to concert measures for distressing the English trade, she caused the ships and cargoes to be confiscated."

Hence it appears, that although England was obliged, so late as the time of Henry VIII, to hire ships from Hamburg, Lubec, Dantzic, Genoa, and Venice, in order to fit out a navy; as Mr. Hume tells us, in another place; although, down almost to the middle of the sixteenth century, the navigation of England was in "a very languishing condition;" and although in a very few years afterwards, they had so far learnt the arts of navigation and commerce from the foreigners, who had settled among them, at various times, in consequence of privileges granted to them during the course of three centuries (since the reign of Henry III); it was, nevertheless, the unjust policy of the English, in perhaps fifteen or twenty years after their marine trade had been in this miserable state, to deprive those, to whom they were under obligations for its recent revival and rapid

of alliance between the States General and the Hanse-Towns (concluded December,

growth, of their ancient chartered privileges. In the course of the same century too, and in the same reign,...when the Easterlings with their compatriots in the Hanse-towns were pursuing measures for securing the rights of their common maritime trade, from farther injury by a nation who had acted towards them with so much injustice, if not ingratitude; those rights were again violated by a most atrocious act of hostile perfidy.....Whilst they were at peace with England, their merchant ships were seized by that nation, in the port of a belligerent power, with whom they were, themselves, in amity; and the vessels, as well as their cargoes, confiscated, under the pretence of their having "contraband goods of the Spaniards" (within whose sovereignty the Tagus then was); in direct violation of the rights of a Neutral Power.

These outrages on the rights of the Easterlings, and particularly the Hanse-towns, occurred in the reign of Elizabeth. That powerful and enterprizing princess died in 1603: And the modern Hanseatic league, originating in the treaty between the Dutch and the Lubeckers, took place only ten years after Elizabeth's death, during the reign of her pacific successor.

Do we not, then, perceive an obvious connection between these events?....And does not the league of the Hanse-towns, commencing in 1613....in its stipulations "for the defence and vindication of the liberty of navigation, trade, and commerce, and of the rights and privileges thereunto belonging"... "according to the Law of Nations,"...does not that maritime confederacy, it is asked, bear an evident aspect towards the antecedent infractions of the rights appertaining to the confederates?....That it does, can scarcely be doubted.

If, therefore, this league had a retrospective view to the seizure and confiscation of their ships with their cargoes, by the English, in the Tagus, the constituted authorities of the Hanse-

1615, in consequence of the foregoing), it is declared to be the design of the Union, "to assure the liberty of commerce and navigation." Now, although neither of these clauses contain an express recognition of the principle ....that free ships make free goods,....it seems to be implied: Because, it cannot be conceived as comporting with consistency, that several states should enter into an alliance,...avowedly "for the defence and vindication of the liberty of navigation, trade and commerce,....and of the rights and privileges belonging thereunto"....and, "to assure the liberty of commerce and navigation;"....and yet, that they should not contemplate, as one of the "rights and privileges" of a neutral nation, the "liberty" of navigating to the port of any nation in amity with them,....unless actually blockaded; and of carrying thither in time of war, in their own ships, any goods they should please,....except such as are contraband of war.

towns must have deemed such seizure to be a breach of neutral rights, under the Law of Nations; when attempted to be justified by reason of the goods on board those free ships being the property of an enemy.

The first treaty, containing a renunciation of the principle, that free ships make free goods, is that concluded between Great-Britain and Sweden, Oct. 23, 1661, (art. 12).... And the next, in order of time, is the one between Great-Britain and Denmark....November 19th, 1669. But it is remarkable, that by two treaties prior to the earliest of these, (as well as by three others between those dates, ...and in all of which, England was one of the contracting parties;) the right of protection to enemies' goods in the ships of neutrals, is expressly stipulated. These were, the treaty between England and Holland, of the 1st of December, 1647....that between England and Portugal, of the 10th of July, 1654....that between England and Spain, of the 13---23 of May, 1667....and two between England and Holland, of the 21st---31st of July, 1667, and the 7th---17th of February, 1668.

Thus, at a period commencing upwards of one hundred and fifty years ago, England had five times, in the course of twenty-one years, recognized the right of neutrals to protect, in their own ships, the goods of an enemy; and twice, within the same time, renounced the principle to which they themselves had given their sanction, by the solemn stipulations of five treaties;....two of which were several years antecedent to both of those that stipulated the adverse principle.

Within this same period, namely, in the year 1666, the principle, that free ships make free goods, was further recognized, by a treaty then made between France and Sweden.

We find then, that, by recurring to the period when the first conventional stipulation appears, respecting either the affirmative or negative side of the proposition in question, and within the short term of twenty-one years; six treaties were concluded, that recognized the controverted right of neutrals,....and only two that furnish instances of the abandonment of that right. It cannot therefore be said, that, during this period, the "constant practice" of nations....and this, too, referring to a period which may be styled "ancient"....in relation to the controverted principle, warrants that construction of the claim of neutrals, which has been contended for, by Great-Britain.

The earliest stipulation, by treaty, providing for the exemption from capture, by belligerents, of enemy's goods in the ships of neutrals,....was in 1647; as has been noticed. Before that time, this right does not appear to have been controverted; though it had been actually infringed*. It was then, as it now is, an established principle in the Law of Nations, that although a man, while he continues a citizen of a particular country, is considered as an enemy, by all those with whom his nation is at war,....he is, nevertheless, protected from personal injury or violence on the part of such enemy, when in the territory of a neutral state. Neutral territory also affords a rightful protection to the *property* of an enemy. And, by an application of the same principle, it seems to have been understood, from a parity of reasoning, that an enemy's goods, on board the ship of a friend, were entitled to a similar protection: the ship being under the jurisdiction, while on the high seas, of the friendly power to whom it belongs,....is therefore, *quoad hoc*, neutral territory†.

* See note on page 90.

† A similar reasoning, founded on the analogy of the two cases, is adopted by Mr. T. Pinckney, in a letter to lord Grenville....“ Although (says Mr. Pinckney) people in a state of war, have, in general, a right to seize or destroy their enemy's property; yet they cannot be justified in going, for that purpose, upon neutral territory: (in conformity to which doctrine, the

Grotius published his treatise concerning war and peace, in 1625. And in that work, this

British ship Grange, captured by a French frigate in the bay of Delaware, was lately liberated by order of the American government:) and the distinction drawn between neutral territory and neutral vessels, does not appear to form a difference sufficiently substantial, to preclude the application of the same principles to both."....The letter of Mr. Pinckney, which contains the passage here quoted, is printed (among the State papers published by order of Congress) without a date; but a copy of it was enclosed in a letter from him to Mr. Jefferson, dated at London, August 28, 1793. Thus, while the administration...in their communications with the French minister here, and with our minister in France, in 1793,...were advocating the position, that a neutral flag shall not protect enemy-goods...upon the authority of writers on public law; they were at the same time, through the medium of their minister at the court of Great-Britain, supporting the legitimate doctrine... that free ships make free goods,...upon the just principles of the Law of Nations.

Besides, it cannot escape notice, that the well known case of Jonathan Robbins is in point. By the twenty-seventh article of Mr. Jay's treaty, it is agreed, that each party, respectively, shall, on due requisition, "deliver up to justice all persons, who, being charged with murder or forgery, committed within the jurisdiction of either, shall seek an asylum within any of the countries of the other;" &c. Upon an allegation, that Robbins had committed murder on board a British ship, on the high seas, and had taken refuge within the United States,...he was demanded by the British government, as a fugitive from justice, who had committed the crime, charged upon him, "within the jurisdiction"...and, as it were, the territory,...of that government. He was accordingly, surrendered up, by the government of the United States, who thereby recognized that doctrine;...and the catastrophe is too well known.

learned author has laid down one of his dogmas ....that neutral ships shall not protect enemy's goods, laden therein,....as Law: though unsupported by any other foundation, than his own theory of Right, in such case; and the theoretical opinions of, perhaps, one or two less distinguished authors. The great talents of Grotius....and his being the first writer on general Law, who had undertaken to systematize its elementary principles,....procured to him a celebrity of reputation, that gave an undue sanction to some of his erroneous theories. His principles were sometimes at variance with reason and natural equity, as we have already demonstrated: and it is conceived that the truth of this observation is, in no instance, more justly applied, than to his doctrine, that neutral ships do not rightfully protect the goods of an enemy, laden therein. Yet, has this opinion of Grotius, which has been implicitly adopted by many subsequent writers on the Law of Nations, served as an Authority, and been received as a Rule of Right by some states, who have believed it to be (at least occasionally) consistent with their national interests to conform to it. Is it, therefore, a matter of surprize, that thirty-six years after the publication of Grotius's book on war and peace,....at a period when the interests of maritime commerce became a primary object of attention, with the statesmen of a great commercial and maritime power;.... is it, we repeat, at all surprising, that England should have abandoned by treaty, that principle, which she had before recognized; merely because she then supposed, it comported more with her interest to do so?

We assert, that England abandoned the principle of free ships making free goods, when it suited her interest: Because, in prosecuting this subject, in order to shew that the general practice of the maritime states goes to support this principle,....it will appear, that she has frequently conformed to it in her treaties, since 1661, as well as before that period; and even so lately as the year 1786.

From the year 1669 to 1753, we trace no less than eleven treaties, wherein the principle is recognized....that free ships make free goods; and in eight of these, England was one of the contracting parties. Within the same period, comprehending eighty-four years, not one treaty is discovered, in which the opposite principle is stipulated.

This investigation has been brought down, for the present, to 1753; because the report of the British law-officers, in the case of the Prussian memorial (which is now the object of discussion), is dated on the 18th of January in that year.

From the year 1647, then, to 1753, making in the whole, one hundred and six years,.... we find seventeen treaties, recognizing the principle contended for; and only four, in which the opposite one is stipulated. So far, therefore, as the practice of nations is to be deduced from treaties, in this instance,....it appears fully to support our principle. But, as it is intended to commence the next section, with an inquiry into the sense of the principal maritime nations on this subject, from the epoch of the Armed Neutrality in 1780; if we prosecute our present inquiry down to that period, we shall find two* other

* The definitive treaty of peace between Great-Britain and Spain, concluded at Paris, February 10, 1763. The treaty of commerce between Great-Britain and Spain, concluded at Madrid, December 14, 1715, confirms the treaty of 1667.... This of 1667 was confirmed by the treaty at Madrid, between the same parties, concluded at Madrid, October 5, (N. S.) 1750...and these were farther confirmed by the second article of the treaty of 1763, first mentioned.

The Treaty of Amity and Commerce between the United States and France, concluded at Paris, February 6, 1778.

treaties....and in one of which, England was a party,....wherein the right of neutrals protecting enemy's goods in neutral ships, during a war, is further established. Yet, within this last mentioned period of twenty-seven years, we do not discover any adverse stipulation by treaty.

The " practice," here treated of, so far as it is considered as rightful by the British government, must depend either on the primitive principles of the Law of Nations, or the express stipulations of treaties. The former, it is apparent, do not warrant it; and it is very evident, that the latter enjoin an opposite course. That, in fact, almost all the treaties of navigation and commerce, which have been concluded in Europe, in the course of one hundred and thirty-three years preceding the establishment of the Armed Neutrality in 1780, have recognized the principle of free ships making free goods. The practice here referred to, considered with relation to at least a part of this period....and especially, if the term be extended thirty-four years farther back, to the league of the Hanse-Towns,.... may be called ancient. If, therefore, it shall be shewn in the following section, that a similar practice, *since* 1780, has generally prevailed, under the sanction of treaties, (and this shall be satisfactorily done); the position laid down by the British government, in the case before us, that "the constant practice, ancient and modern," militates against our principle, ...will be completely invalidated.

We now arrive at the third and last point, on which the law-officers of the English crown relied, in 1753, for the support of their doctrine. Having conceived that the negative of the proposition advanced by the Prussian commissioners could be proved, "by the authority of every* writer on the Law of Nations," ....and "by the constant practice, ancient and modern;" the British rest upon these two grounds, the supposed existence of a "general rule," contravening the principle of the Prussian proposition. The existence of this general rule being thus assumed, they assert,

* There is at least one most respectable writer on the Law of Nations, in the seventeenth century, who has not undertaken to establish the position maintained by the British government. M. Pufendorf, in his letter to M. Groning, mentioned in the preface...and written sixty-seven years after Grotius wrote his book on the Rights of War and Peace,...expressly says, "the question (concerning the rights of Neutrals to a free Navigation) is, certainly, one of those which have not yet been settled upon

that it cannot be more strongly proven, than by the "exceptions" which particular treaties have made to it. In this point of view, then, we shall examine what is here called, thirdly,

"THE GENERAL RULE."

This, indeed, seems to be a work of supererogation: Because, if neither the Law nor the Practice of Nations, support the principle contended for, on the part of Great-Britain; the supposed Rule, referring to such principle, cannot have any existence: if the foundation be removed, the superstructure must necessarily fall to the ground. It has been clearly shewn, we presume, that no such general Rule does in fact exist. If, however, the contrary be admitted, merely for the sake of argument; how can such general Rule be proven, by the exception of particular treaties to it? In the very document, in which that kind of reasoning is used, two treaties are cited in support of the supposed Rule; and six

any clear and undeniable principles, so as to afford a general rule to mankind."

In 1759, appeared M. Hubner's valuable work, *De la Saisie des Batimens Neutres;* vindicating the Rights of Neutrals,...and, particularly, the principle of free ships making free goods.

others, as exceptions thereto! In this way, the logical axiom.....*omne majus continet in se minus*....is completely inverted; for, the exception in this case is of larger extent than the Rule itself. If, however, it is meant, that an express stipulation in a treaty, of any particular principle, carries with it an implication that such principle would have no operation as a right, independent of the express stipulation; the argument is equally fallacious in that view: for by this mode of reasoning, both the negative and affirmative of the principle in question could be maintained, with equal validity. Thus, the British say, that free ships do not make free goods; and this, they assert, is a general Rule. Yet their government cite two treaties, wherein this principle is expressly stipulated; and these stipulations are adduced, in order to verify the Rule: whereas these, according to their mode of reasoning....being introduced into a treaty,.... form "exceptions" to a general Rule; and, consequently, this Rule must apply to the opposite principle.

It is an admitted point in the Law of Nations....a principle, equally founded in reason, with the one which we have been maintaining,

....that a neutral state shall not, in time of war, carry to either of the belligerent powers, any of those articles that are denominated contraband of war; under the penalty of their confiscation: and we know not any maritime treaty, in which this prohibition is not particularly mentioned. But it will scarcely be contended, that, because the prohibition is thus expressly in treaties, it is not consonant to the Law of Nations, independently of the stipulation*:

* The custom of Reprisals is considered, by the general acquiescence in the practice, as being warranted by the Law of Nations. It seems, indeed, to be a necessary consequence of what are called the Rights of war. Yet this custom, so deemed to be legalized, has been generally confirmed, under its proper restrictions and limitations, by an article in almost every treaty of peace, made in Europe for a long series of years past. If we admit, for the sake of argument...what is laid down by writers on the Law of Nations,...that the custom of making Reprisals became a law, by reason of the continued frequency of the practice, (though, according to Justinian, it was founded on the exigency of human necessities); its validity, in that character, could not be strengthened by what is termed its confirmation, in the subsequent stipulations of treaties. These treaties could amount to no more than an express recognition of a subsisting Law; and a declaration of the contracting parties, that they subjected themselves, in certain contingencies, to the operation of the powers conferred by such stipulations.

It was conformably to this view of the subject, that Mr. Randolph reasoned, when, as Secretary of State, he addressed

Though, according to the British doctrine, the very circumstance of its being so stipulated must imply, that the Law of Nations warrants a contrary principle; and that the "Rule," conforming to such principle, is "proven" by these "exceptions" to it.

We conceive it to be unnecessary to dwell longer on this point; because it must be evident, that the "practice" of nations does in

the French minister at Philadelphia, (under the date of July 6, 1795,) concerning Mr. Jay's treaty with Great-Britain. The extension of the list of contraband articles, yielded to by Mr. Jay, furnished to the French government a subject of complaint. It's minister, in his letter of June 30, 1795, had adverted particularly to the United States having admitted into the list of contraband of war, sundry articles of naval stores, and such as are used in the construction of ships; whereas, by their treaty with France, articles of the same description were not reputed contraband, but reckoned among free goods. The secretary of state asserts, in his answer, (though we peremptorily deny the truth of the doctrine),...that it never could be denied under the Law of Nations, and independently of a treaty, that materials for the building and repairing of vessels are contraband. Having, however, assumed this position (which is shewn, hereafter, to be erroneous), he observes...."the proposed treaty, then, does not grant, but recognizes only, a right to Great-Britain,...which, even without that recognition, she would have possessed and exercised. This recognition (continues the secretary) might have been omitted or inserted, without changing the nature of the subject; though it was more natural, in commercial arrangements, to particularize the articles of contraband."

no manner warrant the doctrine, contended for by the government of Great-Britain: On the contrary, it clearly supports the principle, contained in the Prussian proposition,....that free ships make free goods.

A DISSERTATION

ON THE

FREEDOM OF NAVIGATION

AND

MARITIME COMMERCE.

SECTION II.

SHEWING THAT THE POSITION....THAT FREE SHIPS MAKE FREE GOODS....WAS RECOGNIZED AS A PRINCIPLE OF THE MODERN LAW OF NATIONS, CONFORMABLE TO THE TREATY OF ARMED NEUTRALITY, IN 1780.

HAVING, in the preceding section, brought our inquiry, concerning the legality of the principle, that free ships make free goods, down to the year 1780; we shall now pursue the subject from that period.

The year 1780 constitutes a memorable epoch in the annals of maritime nations. It is from that point of time that we may properly commence the æra, in which the right of neutral nations to protect, in their ships, every description of goods, excepting those that are strictly contraband of war, was completely recognized by almost every great maritime power in Europe, as well as by the United States of America*,....in national acts of the highest solemnity.

It has been already shewn, that, prior to this period, the general practice of nations was conformable to the principle so decided; and that the numerous treaties, by which an adherence to this principle was stipulated, were so far from forming " exceptions" to a general rule grounded on the opposite doctrine, according to the allegations of the British government,....that they are strong evidences of the right of neutrals, as stipulated in those treaties.

The only remaining ground, therefore, on which the British can pretend to rest the de-

* " The principles of the armed neutrality, set on foot by the empress of Russia, in harmony with the other neutral powers,...and acceded to by all the powers then at war against England,...are extremely dear to us; because they are just in themselves, and in many respects very important to our welfare."...See letter from Mr. Monroe, minister plenipotentiary of the United States to France, to the French minister of Foreign affairs...dated March 15, 1796.

fence of their doctrine, is, what they call the "authorities" of writers on the Law of Nations. It has been demonstrated, that the speculative opinions of authors, who have treated on subjects of Universal Law, cannot possess the weight of authorities; so as to make such opinions, concerning matters of national right, a rule, obligatory on the conduct of nations: unless the rule itself be conformable to the natural and indefeasible rights of mankind. This observation, we have seen, is equally just, when applied to principles involving such rights, stipulated in pacts or conventions between different nations; as in the case of the mere opinions or theories of private men. For, "the Laws (says M. de Montesquieu) are the necessary relations that arise from the nature of things; and, in this sense, all beings have their Laws, &c. There is an original Reason; therefore the natural Laws are the relations which are found between that and the different beings, and the relations between these several beings themselves. Intelligent beings may have laws of their own making; but there are others that they have not made: before there were intelligent beings, they were possible; there were therefore possible relations, and consequently possible laws. Before there were laws made, there were relations of possible justice. To say that there is nothing just or unjust, but as it is commanded or forbidden by positive laws, is to say, that before a circle was ever drawn, all diameters of a circle were not equal."

We shall, in the next section, examine the natural foundation of that right belonging to neutrals, now contended for; which cannot be abandoned by any stipulation, without violating an essential principle of neutral equity,.... and one that embraces a right, relating to a benefit, in which all independent maritime nations have a common interest. It only remains for us, at present, to adduce on our part, "authorities" of such a nature, to support that right; as will completely invalidate those, relied on by the British government, for maintaining a contrary principle. To the unauthorized theoretical opinions of writers on the Law of Nations, on this point, we shall oppose the testimony of many and powerful nations, manifested by solemn public acts of their respective governments.

Although it is believed, for the reasons stated in the note on page 90, that one object of the Hanseatic league, of 1613, (with a special reference to England), was the maintenance of the right of the leaguers, in the character of neutrals, to protect in their ships enemy's goods, excepting those which were admitted to be contraband of war; yet, as that object was not particularly defined in the treaties constituting the league, we shall come down to a later period.

A treaty was concluded at Whitehall, on the 22d of August, 1689, between England and the United Provinces; whereby these powers agreed to notify all states, not at war with France, that they would attack every ship bound to, or coming out of the harbours of that kingdom; having previously declared all such to be lawful prize. There can scarcely be conceived a more palpable or more monstrous violation of the rights of neutrals*,

* This precedent, it has been observed by a late writer, was copied by the enemies of France, in the present war. The truth is, that the same inordinate ambition...the same rancorous and malevolent enmity to France,...influenced most of the crowned heads of Europe, in the present war, that actuated William III, in 1689. In the course of this same war, however, another instance...and as memorable an one...occurs, of the violation of Neutral Rights. Horatio Nelson, then second in command to Admiral Jarvis...while the British fleet lay

than that deliberately concerted in this treaty. This outrage upon the Law of Nations was projected by William III, soon after he had ascended the English throne; and by his connection, as Prince of Orange, with the United Provinces, he readily drew that government into the measure. Although this prince had been an instrument, in the hands of the English people, of rescuing their nation from the accumulated injuries they experienced, under the reigns of the Stuarts; he was, nevertheless, actuated by an ambitious and vindictive spirit, in his hostility towards France: And to that source, we trace this measure of his government, so derogatory from the splendor of his reign in most other respects. In consequence, however, of this treaty, Sweden and Denmark, from whom some ships had been captured by the English and Dutch, entered into a counter-treaty, on the 17th of March, 1693, "for maintaining their rights and procuring satisfaction."....." And the maritime powers (as Vattel* observes) perceiving that the com-

before the port of Cadiz, in the year 1797...published a proclamation or manifesto, in the absence of Jarvis, in which he declares..." It is found right that Spain should no longer have any trade"!!! So pronounced the present Lord Nelson.

* Book ii. cap. xii. sect. 192.

plaints of the two crowns were well grounded, did them justice." This was the first treaty of Armed Neutrality....if we except that between the Hanse-Towns, in 1613......until the celebrated confederation of the maritime powers, in 1780. Of this, we shall now proceed to give some account.

"The empress of Russia (says Dr. Ramsay, in his history of the American Revolution), took the lead in establishing a system of maritime laws, which subverted the claims of Great-Britain. Her trading vessels had long been harassed by British searches and seizures, on a pretence of their carrying on a commerce, inconsistent with neutrality. The present crisis (continues this respectable author) favoured the re-establishment of the Laws of Nature, in place of the usurpations of Great-Britain."

The principles and plan, on which the Armed Neutrality of 1780, was founded, were communicated on the 26th of February, of that year, in a declaration of the Russian government, addressed to the courts of London, Versailles and Madrid. In this state-paper it was observed, that though, from the conduct of her imperial majesty, it might have been hoped, that her subjects would have been allowed peaceably to enjoy the fruits of their industry, and of the advantages belonging to all neutral nations, experience had proven the contrary: her imperial majesty's subjects had been often molested in their navigation, and retarded in their operations, by the ships and privateers of the belligerent powers. Her imperial majesty therefore declared, that she found herself under the necessity of removing those vexations, which were offered to the commerce of Russia, as well as to the liberty of commerce in general, by all the means compatible with her dignity and the welfare of her subjects. But, before she came to any serious measures, and in order to prevent all new misunderstandings, she thought it just and equitable to expose to the eyes of all Europe, the principles which she had adopted for her conduct. After this, follow, in the empress's declaration, the principles referred to, which are reduced to five points: but, as the declaration is given, entire, together with other documents respecting this treaty, in the appendix, only the first and second points are here recited, viz.

First, " That all neutral ships may freely navigate from port to port, and on the coasts of nations at war."

Second, " That the effects belonging to the subjects of the said waring powers shall be free in all neutral vessels, except contraband merchandize."

In the answer of the king of Spain to this declaration, he says, that the principles, herein adopted by the empress, are " the same as have always guided the king, and which his majesty had for a long time, but without success, endeavoured to cause England to observe, while Spain remained neuter. These principles (continues the answer) are founded in justice, equity and moderation; and these same principles, Russia and all the other powers have experienced, in the resolutions formed by his majesty; and it has been entirely owing to the conduct of the English navy, both in the last and the present war (a conduct wholly subversive of the received rules among neutral powers), that his majesty has been obliged to follow their example*,

* According to Vattel, " when a sovereign is not satisfied with the manner in which his subjects are treated by the laws and customs of another nation, he is at liberty to declare, that

since the English, paying no respect to a neutral flag, if the same be laden with effects belonging to the enemy, even if the articles should not be contraband, and that flag not using any means of defending itself, there could not be any just cause why Spain should not make reprisals, to indemnify herself for the great disadvantages she must otherwise labour under."

The king of France (then engaged, as an ally of the United States, in a war with Great Britain), in his answer to the Russian declaration, asserts his "attachment to the freedom of the seas;" and declares, "he could not, but with the truest satisfaction, see the empress of Russia adopt the same principle, and resolve to maintain it. That (continues the answer) which her imperial majesty claims from the belligerent powers, is no other than the rules already prescribed to the French marine, the execution of which is maintained with an exactitude known and approved by all Europe. The liberty of neutral vessels, restrained only in a few cases, is the direct consequence of neutral right, the safeguard of all

he will treat the subjects of that nation in the same manner that his are treated."...Book ii. cap. xviii. sect. 341.

nations, and the relief even of those at war. The king has been desirous, not only to procure a freedom of navigation to the subjects of the empress of Russia, but to those of all the states who hold their neutrality; and that upon the same conditions as are announced in the treaty, to which his majesty this day answers. His majesty thought he had taken a great step for the general good, and prepared a glorious epoch for his reign, by fixing, by his example, the rights which every belligerent power may, and ought to acknowledge, to be due to neutral vessels."

The king of Denmark, in his declaration, observes, that " the neutral navigation has been too often molested, and the most innocent commerce of his subjects too frequently troubled; so that he finds himself obliged to take proper measures to assure to himself and his allies, the safety of commerce and navigation, and the maintenance of the inseparable rights of liberty and independence. If the duties of neutrality are sacred (continues this declaration), the Law of Nations has also its rights avowed by all impartial powers, established by custom, and founded upon equity and reason. A nation, independent and neuter, does not lose, by the war of others, the rights which she had before the war; because peace exists between her and all the belligerent powers. Without receiving or being obliged to follow the laws of either of them, she is allowed to follow, in all places (contraband excepted) the traffic which she would have a right to do, if peace existed with all Europe, as it exists with her. The king pretends to nothing beyond what the neutrality allows him. This is his rule, and that of his people; and the king cannot accord to the principle, that a power at war has a right to interrupt the commerce of his subjects."

The king of Sweden, in his declaration, announces, that ever since the beginning of the then existing war, "he had imposed unto himself the law of a perfect neutrality; that he had fulfilled all the duties thereof, with the most scrupulous exactitude; and, that in consequence thereof, he thought himself entitled to all the prerogatives naturally appertaining to the qualification of a sovereign, perfectly neuter. But, notwithstanding this, his commercial subjects had been obliged to claim his protection, and his majesty had found himself under the necessity to grant it to them." The declaration of the empress of Russia "was founded (says this memorial) upon such just principles of the Law of Nations and subsisting treaties, that it was impossible to call them into question. The king (continues the Swedish memorial) found them entirely concordant with his own cause, and with the treaty concluded in the year 1666, between Sweden and France."...."It is (says Sweden, in this memorial), the universal Law; and, when there are no particular engagements existing, it becomes obligatory upon all Nations."

In the treaty of Armed Neutrality itself, it is expressly stated, that, "by the declaration delivered to the belligerent powers, their contracting majesties have already challenged the privileges, founded on natural Right, whence spring the freedom of trade and navigation; as well as the right of neutral powers; and being fully determined not to depend, in future, merely on an arbitrary interpretation, devised to answer some private advantages or concerns, they mutually covenanted as followeth;" &c......Of the articles covenanted to be observed by this treaty, the first is...."That it will be lawful for any ship, whatever, to sail freely from one port to another, or along the coast of the powers (now) at war;"....and the second...." That all merchandize and effects, belonging to the subjects of the said belligerent powers, and shipped on neutral bottoms, shall be entirely free; except contraband goods."

Let it be remembered that this celebrated maritime treaty, which was concluded at Copenhagen, on the 19th of July, 1780, was acceded to, and signed by the plenipotentiaries of Sweden, at Petersburgh, 21st of July, 1780; accepted by the States General of the United Provinces, November 20th, 1780; and finally signed at Petersburgh, January 5th, 1781.... Portugal, as being a maritime state then at peace, was invited to join in the common cause; in order, it was said, that by the united care of the neutral maritime powers, the navigation of all the neutral trading nations might be established and legalized; and a system adopted, founded upon justice, and which, by its real advantage, might serve for a rule in future ages. But the queen of Portugal was the only sovereign, expected to concur in the measures of this just and honorable confederation, who manifested so temporizing a subserviency to the British cabinet, as to decline a co-operation.

In the "history of Europe" during the year 1780, contained in Dodsley's Annual Register of that year.....an historical detail of national events, much applauded for its correctness and impartiality,.....the writer, in speaking of the Russian declaration of neutrality, makes the following remarks...." The manifesto or declaration issued by the court of Petersburgh, has been the means of forming, under the name of an Armed Neutrality, that formidable naval and military alliance and confederacy, between the northern powers, to which most of the neutral states in Europe have since acceded; and which, Great-Britain not being in a situation directly to contravene, seems now to be settled as a part of the Law of Nations. The great principle of this piece, and of that confederacy to which it gave birth, is, that free bottoms make free goods;" &c.

We have seen that this confederation of the neutral maritime states originated between Russia and Denmark; and was immediately acceded to, by Sweden: indeed Dr. Gordon, in his history of the American revolution, asserts, that the idea of an Armed Neutrality was first suggested by the king of Sweden himself, to the Russian minister, count Panin. But, be that as it may, the league between those three northern powers was speedily concluded; and the principles on which it was formed, were as readily sanctioned by the decided approbation of two other great maritime states, France and Spain, though then engaged in the war. The accession of the States General, to this league, was, however, of great importance, to all the parties interested in the measure; and it was counted upon, by them, with moral certainty. England, on the other hand, was greatly interested in preventing it; and therefore pursued such bold and violent conduct against the Dutch, as she supposed would intimidate their government from becoming a party in this armed confederacy. It is not improbable, that the outrage upon the rights of neutrals, committed by the British squadron under commodore Fielding, at the commencement of the year 1780,....in the capture of a fleet of Dutch merchantmen, under a convoy commanded by count Beyland,....contributed to produce the Armed Neutrality. However, after that treaty had been concluded between Russia, Denmark and Sweden....and before Holland had notified those powers of her accession thereto, (viz. on the 9th of August, 1780,)....the British were guilty of another glaring infraction of the neutral rights of the Dutch. " At the island of St. Martin (say they*) his Britannic majesty attacked, and carried away by force, several vessels that lay at anchor under the cannon of the fort, where, according to the inviolable rights of mankind, the vessels ought to have found a secure asylum."...." If ever the annals of the world (continues the States General) have furnished an instance of a free and independent state being attacked by an enemy, in the most unjustifiable manner, and without the least appearance of right or equity, by a neighbouring power allied for a long time, and bound by ties founded on the basis of common interest,...it is, without doubt, the Republic of the United States of the Netherlands; which finds itself in that case, with his majesty the king of Great-Britain and his ministers."...." The differences between the courts of London and Versailles had scarcely broke out, when they beheld the ports of

* See the Answer of the States General to the Manifesto of the British Court, dated March 10, 1781.

England filled with Dutch vessels, which were unjustly seized and detained; these vessels navigated upon the faith of the treaties, and were not laden with any other merchandize than what the express tenor of the treaties had declared free and legal. They beheld those free cargoes forced to submit to an arbitrary and despotic authority. The cabinet of St. James's, knowing no other rule than an assumed right of temporary convenience, thought proper to appropriate those cargoes to the use of the crown by a forcible purchase, and to employ them in the service of the king's navy."....“ Affairs being thus situated, so that their high mightinesses had no other alternative left to them, but to see the navigation and commerce of their subjects, on which the ruin or prosperity of their republic alone depends, totally annihilated; or else, to adopt measures hostile to their old friend and ally: at this period, the empress of Russia, urged by a generous magnanimity of disposition, thought proper to interfere; and, with as much affection as humanity, invited the republic to take the justest measures, and such too as were entirely consistent with the treaty subsisting between the States and other powers, for the defending and maintaining, in conjunction with her imperial majesty, and the other northern powers, those privileges and immunities, which the Rights of Nations and the most solemn treaties allowed to neutral flags."

Such was the language of the answer given by the States General, on the 10th of March, 1781....and nearly four months after their accession to the Armed Neutrality,....to the manifesto issued against them by the British court. It appears to have been the determination of that court to prevent, if possible, the junction of the Dutch to that confederacy. Its formation was officially announced to the belligerent powers, by the Russian declaration of the 26th of February, 1780; and, from that time until the final accession of the States General to the treaty of the Armed Neutrality....comprehending a period of nearly nine months,....various measures were pursued by the government of Great-Britain, to provoke a war with the United Provinces; thereby to preclude the possibility of their becoming a party in a confederation of neutrals. The violations of the neutral rights of the Dutch, and the insults to their flag, already mentioned, (excepting the case of count Beyland's convoy, which occurred before the date of the Russian declaration), all tended to that end. But, besides these, the memorial presented to the States General by Sir Joseph Yorke, and dated the 21st of March, 1780; and the declaration of the court of London, dated the 17th of April, following, stating,....that from thenceforth the operation of their ancient treaty (of 1674) with the Dutch republic, would be suspended; spoke, in forcible terms, the language of hostility on the part of the former. Yet every act of the Dutch government evinced their earnest desire to maintain a just and honorable peace. Both Russia and Sweden had offered their mediation, before the States General had joined the Armed Neutrality (and the latter of those powers, so late as the 18th of September, 1780), to accommodate the differences then subsisting between the British and Dutch governments; but without effect: because terms were insisted on, by the former, incompatible with the rights, the welfare, and the independence of the republic. Finally, on the 20th of November, 1780, the States General formally acceded to the treaty of Armed Neutrality. Irritated by this decision of the Dutch, Sir Joseph Yorke addressed his second memorial to the States General, on the 12th of December following; in which he reiterated the former claims and pretensions of his government: though it is observable, that, on this occasion, the British minister did not think proper to notice the recent accession of the States General to the Armed Neutrality, as a cause of offence to his court. Only eight days, notwithstanding, after the date of this memorial, the hostile manifesto of Great-Britain was issued against the Dutch Republic; being exactly one month after the latter had joined the northern maritime confederation.

In the answer of the States General to the British manifesto, dated the 10th of March, 1781, they again explicitly avow their adherence to the principles on which the Armed Neutrality was founded. This they had previously done, in their memorial to the court of Stockholm, bearing date the 6th of the same month; wherein they say....“ That their high mightinesses having acceded, by their resolution of the 20th of November, 1780, to the treaty of Armed Neutrality, in conformity to the invitation of the northern powers; and placing the most perfect confidence in the power, magnanimity, and fidelity of their imperial and royal majesties, for the fulfilling of their engagements, and the maintaining of their dignity, by accomplishing a work so gloriously undertaken.....namely, the liberty of the seas, and freedom of navigation for all neutral nations,.....were not deterred by the consideration of the consequences, of which that accession and declaration might be productive, to the Republic, from the part of the belligerent powers."

On the 30th of April, 1781, the king of Prussia issued his "ordinance and declaration, concerning the navigation and maritime commerce of his subjects, during the (then) present war." This state paper expressly recognizes the treaty of Armed Neutrality, and is founded on similar principles.

Thus, the obligations of that treaty comprehended, either as direct parties thereto, or as states which explicitly acceded to its principles, all the great maritime powers of Europe; Great-Britain and Portugal excepted:.... Russia, Denmark, Sweden, and the United States of the Netherlands; together with France, Spain and Prussia. But we shall shew, that the United States of America did also, in the most unequivocal manner, adopt the principles of the Armed Neutrality; even before the Dutch republic. Mr. J. Adams's*

* On April 19, 1781...more than six months after the Congress of the United States of America had adopted the principles of the Armed Neutrality,...Mr. J. Adams, then the American minister in Holland, presented a memorial to the Dutch government, urging reasons for inducing them to acknowledge the Independence of the United States of America. This manifesto contains some remarkable passages, respecting the principles of the Armed Neutrality; among which, are the following..." It is further submitted to the consideration of your High Mightinesses, whether the last maritime code of Laws, relative to the rights and privileges of neutral vessels, notwithstanding all the sentiments of equity and humanity which shine forth in the said code, can possibly be established without the Independence of America; as Great-Britain will certainly never adopt it, unless forced by necessity."..." Another matter to be submitted to the consideration of your High Mightinesses, is the system of the United States, maturely examined, scrupulously discussed, and unanimously adopted in Congress, in 1776, at the time of sealing the treaty afterwards proposed to France: a system according to which it was resolved to make treaties with all the maritime powers of Europe, and to yield to no individual power, the government or monopoly of this commerce; a system afterwards approved by the king of France, and which served as the basis of the treaties concluded with his majesty; a system to which the United States have since constantly adhered, and from whence they will never depart, unless some power, contrary to their expectation, should declare against them."...." The English are so well convinced of the truth of this assertion"...respecting the commercial advantages which the Dutch republic would derive from an alliance with the American,..." that they have ever consi-

letter from Holland, on this subject, dated the 10th of April, 1780, was read in Congress on the 1st of September, following. On the 5th of October, 1780, Congress took into consideration the report of the committee, on the motion relative to the proposition of the empress of Russia; on which they came to the following resolutions:

"Her imperial majesty of all the Russias, attentive to the liberty of commerce and the rights of nations, in her declaration to the belligerent and neutral powers, having proposed certain regulations, founded on the principles of justice, equity, and moderation, of which their most Christian and most Catholic majesties have already declared their approbation; Congress, anxious to demonstrate their regard for the rights of commerce, and their respect for the sovereign who proposed, as well as for the powers which have approved the said regulations, do resolve, 'That the

dered the Dutch as their rivals, in the commerce with America; and it is that conviction only, which has inspired them with the idea of publishing and maintaining that terrible act of navigation, equally detrimental to the maritime commerce and power of this republic, as to the commerce, and rights and privileges of the colonies. The opportunity now offers for both states to throw off, forever, those odious shackles."

'Admiralty-office shall prepare and report 'instructions* for the commanders of armed 'ships, bearing the commissions of the United 'States; which instructions shall be conforma-'ble to the principles contained in the declara-'tion of the empress of all the Russias, concern-'ing the rights of neutral bottoms: that the 'ministers plenipotentiary of the United 'States, in case they shall be invited thereto, 'shall be respectively authorized, as they are 'authorized by these presents, to accede to 'such regulations, conformable to the spirit 'of the said declaration, as shall be framed by 'the General Congress, which is expected to 'assemble (in Europe), in consequence of her 'imperial majesty's invitation."

Having demonstrated that the principles, designed to be supported by the Armed Neutrality....the chief of which is, that free ships make free goods,....were recognized and established in 1780 and 1781, by all the great maritime powers of Europe, excepting Great-Britain, and her obsequious ally, Portugal; we shall proceed to shew a farther acknow-

* An ordinance of congress, containing such instructions, was afterwards passed, on April 7, 1781: These instructions we shall further notice in another place.

ledgment of those principles, in the succeeding year.

By this combination of almost all the considerable maritime states, "the usurped authority of Great-Britain, on the highway of nature* (to use the words of Dr. Ramsay), received a fatal blow."

The principles, on which the armed association of neutrals was formed, were so manifestly just, and the attitude assumed by the confederates was so firm and imposing, that Great-Britain was obliged reluctantly to acquiesce in the measure. In fact, that government not only abstained from any hostile opposition to the powers composing the Armed Neutrality, as such; that, in two years after it was concerted, she formally assented to the very principles on which that confederation was established. The States General of the Seven United Provinces, one of the members of the league, were neutral at the time of its formation; but, in the succeeding year, they

* "The ocean, either as to the whole, or as to the principal parts of it, does not admit of property; but remains still in common to all mankind, notwithstanding the institution of property in other things." Rutherf. inst. book i. cap. v. sect. 1.

became involved in the war. In the beginning of the year 1782, however, Russia, who was the principal in the Armed Neutrality, offered her mediation to the British government.... against whom that association was designed to operate,....for the purpose of effecting a cessation of hostilities between that nation and the Dutch republic, one of the members of the confederacy. The empress had made a recognition, by the British government, of the principles on which the Armed Neutrality was founded, a *sine qua non* of the proposed negociation for a peace, between the court of London and the States General: yet these terms were acceded to, by the British ministry; and the proffered mediation accepted. Accordingly, Mr. Fox; then secretary of state, addressed a letter, on the 29th of March, 1782, to Mons. Simolin, the Russian minister; in which the British secretary declares, that his king "is ready to enter into a negociation, for the purpose of setting on foot a treaty of peace, on the terms and conditions of that which was agreed to, in 1674, between his majesty and the republic; and that, the better to facilitate the execution of a plan which his majesty has so much at heart, the king is willing to give immediate orders for a suspension of hostilities, if, on their part, the Lords the States General should think such a measure suitable to the object in view."....In the second letter from Mr. secretary Fox to the same minister, dated the 4th of May, following, this passage is remarkable...." The king promises himself that her imperial majesty understands with pleasure, that he has anticipated her counsels, in having offered to the Hollanders, the entire liberty of navigation, according to the treaty of 1674, between Great-Britain and the republic; a treaty by which the principles of the Armed Neutrality are established, in their widest extent, to all the contracting parties. His majesty, then, does not make any difficulty to say, that he will accept, as the basis of a separate peace between him and the States General, a free navigation, according to the principles demanded by her imperial majesty, in her declaration of the 26th of February, 1780*. The

* In the course of debate in the British house of commons, on the French commercial treaty of 1786, Mr. Wilberforce threw out some insinuations, reflecting on Mr. Fox's conduct, with respect to the negociation with the States General, proposed by him in 1782. Mr. Fox, in his reply, observed; that, if there was any blame to be affixed to that measure, he was

Dutch had, themselves, made a concession by Great-Britain, of the indubitable rights of neutral nations, as claimed by the confederated neutrals, an indispensible condition of their entering into any negociation with that court, for a peace: For, in the memorial wherein prince Gallitzin and monsieur de Marcoff communicated to the States General, on the part of the Russian government, the official letter of Mr. Fox to monsieur Simolin, they say...." it will convince your high mightinesses of the intentions of his Britannic majesty to be sincerely reconciled to the republic, on the conditions by yourselves established, in your resolution of the 14th ultimo, by which you again accept of the empress's mediation: the prelimary concession made on the part of Great-Britain, concerning the principal article of the treaty of 1674, seems to level all the obstacles, which had hitherto prevented your entering upon a negociation for a final peace. If, in the interim, the proposal made in the said letter, of a suspension of hostilities, should be thought conformable

willing to take his share of it; though it had been done with the unanimous consent of his majesty's council."...See Parliamentary Debates, for 1787.

to the interest of the nation, nothing could be more so to the principles of humanity in general, which actuate the empress, and to her private sentiments of benevolence and affection for this state; especially, as such a measure has the double advantage of preventing the useless effusion of blood, and from this instant restoring to the republic the enjoyments of the rights of freedom in trade and navigation, which fall to the share of neutral nations, and particularly those that have acceded to the principles of the Armed Neutrality."....And when, in the commencement of this negociation, the vice-chancellor of Russia, count de Ostermann, communicated the information to the Dutch ambassador at Petersburgh, of his having transmitted to the Russian minister, at London, the conditional overture of the States General for peace, before mentioned, he observed....that " the motives by which this minister will endeavour to influence his Britannic majesty to admit the proposal, which is to be the basis of pacification, will be founded on the perfect knowledge which his majesty possesses of the impartiality professed by her imperial majesty, and the fidelity and constancy with which she has adhered, in the face of all Europe, to the principles adopted by her, and which are founded in justice."

Having considered the treaty of Armed Neutrality, of 1780, as being, what Mr. Adams styles it, a "maritime code of Laws, relative to the rights and privileges of neutral vessels,"...."founded (in the words of Congress) on the principles of justice, equity and moderation,"....and having demonstrated, that all the considerable maritime states of Europe, including Great-Britain....Portugal alone excepted,....and that also, the United States of America,....had, in the year 1782, either directly or indirectly acceded to the principles of that treaty; we shall now shew that the provisions of that "maritime code" are obligatory on all nations.

With this object in view, we shall lay it down as a *postulatum*, at present....the truth of which will be more fully manifested in the following section,.....that this code is, as the Congress of the United States have declared it to be, "founded on the principles of justice, equity, and moderation."

"If treaties are valid," says Vattel*,.... that is, if the stipulations contained in them are founded on the principles of justice, equity, and moderation, and be not repugnant to the essential and indefeasible rights of mankind,.... "they have, in their own nature, a perpetual and irrevocable effect." Great and important principles, recognized in the pacts or treaties of different nations, acquire the sanction and force of National Law, if such principles are established on the foundation of natural justice; although the pacts themselves may afterwards be annulled, and become extinguished, by the subsequent hostility of the contracting parties: and this is more especially true, where such pacts....instead of professing to extend the natural rights of mankind, in behalf of the parties concerned in the pact, beyond those limits within which they are necessarily contracted, in time of war, between the belligerent parties themselves,....do no more than express a confirmation of those fundamental rights, which have been incorporated into the Law of Nations, for promoting the general weal of the great community of neutrals, un-

* Book ii. cap. xii. sect. 192.

der the sanction of perfect justice. If the thing stipulated by treaty, to be performed, be, in itself, lawful and right, and such as the party, by whom it is to be performed, is under a pre-existing obligation to do; the moral obligation imposed on him, previously to the treaty, to do that act, is not enhanced in *foro conscientiæ*, by his express engagement to do it: and, consequently, it cannot be inferred, that, because a duty is thus expressly stipulated to be performed, its obligation did not previously exist;....no more than it can be justly said, that, because a man has given his creditor a bond, by which he binds himself to pay the obligee the amount of a simple-contract debt, that he had antecedently contracted, no obligation to pay existed, prior to the date of the bond. Human laws may attach penalties to the non-performance of contracts; but the inherent force of the obligation to perform, is not thereby changed. Thus, too, a public treaty may enjoin upon the parties the fulfilment of certain specified duties, on stipulated terms and conditions: yet, if those duties be correlatives of such unalienable rights as are sanctioned by the Law of Nature, the obligation to fulfil them does not result from the stipulations of the treaty; but has a permanent existence, independent of it. Particular privileges, resulting wholly from the artificial institutions and arrangements of society, and not being founded on the natural and unalienable rights of man, may rightfully become objects of stipulation in treaties between independent nations; if they respect the performance of such acts, as are, in their own nature just: and privileges of this description may be abrogated, by mutual consent of the contracting parties, without any breach of moral obligation. But, when the unalienable natural rights of mankind are attempted to be either invalidated or restricted by the provisions of a public treaty; the stipulations, tending to that end, have no lawful obligatory force, whatever. Hence, when two or more nations, either by engaging in a state of warfare, or otherwise, restrict among themselves the enjoyment of those natural rights, which are the common property of all nations; such restrictions ought not to affect....and cannot do so, in reason or in justice,....those nations, who are neither parties to their acts nor in their hostility. On the other hand, every recognition in a public treaty, of the natural rights appertaining to the intercourse of all nations in amity with each other, is not only obligatory on the parties to such treaty; but the principles so recognized, though having their foundation established on a pre-existing and independent authority, which no human laws can invalidate,....acquire by such express recognition, when once made, that kind of general and permanent establishment, of which every nation (not otherwise incapacited) may rightfully claim the benefit. The recognition of the principle, is evidence of its admission by the party making it; and, notwithstanding the measures and conduct of nations between whom treaties subsist, may, from various causes, eventually differ from the stipulations of the contracting parties,....the recognized principle becomes permanent, and retains its original obligation and lawful force.

There are innumerable facts, evincing the truth of the doctrine just stated. Almost every modern treaty refers to some principle, contained in a preceding treaty between the same parties, as remaining in force; even where repeated wars have intervened between the periods of the several treaties. Indeed, this is a point so well established, that we shall content ourselves with adducing a very few prominent cases for its illustration. A war of thirty years continuance, which was occasioned by an acceptance of the crown of Bohemia by the elector Palatine, Frederick, (who married Elizabeth, daughter of James I, of England), terminated by the peace of Westphalia, in 1648. The famous treaty by which this pacification was effected, settled the constitution of the German empire, by establishing the rights, privileges and authority, of the Germanic body. This treaty, says baron Bielfeld (in his elements of universal erudition), " is a fundamental Law of the empire; and, perhaps, the principal of all its laws, seeing that it regulates the state of Germany. Its tenor was fixed by a double instrument; one part made at Munster, with France,....and the other at Osnabrug, with Sweden." Yet, notwithstanding this treaty " is a fundamental Law of the empire"....and as Mr. Thompson (in his spirit of General History) remarks, " is still* the foundation of the Germanic

* The celebrated Oxenstiern, the minister of Sweden, and M. D'Avaux, the French plenipotentiary, were the principal negociators of the treaty of Westphalia; and their conduct, on that occasion, affords a laudable example to all negociators.

constitution, and the basis of the rights of one part of Europe,"....the parties to that treaty have since been opposed to each other in hostilities; and an elector of Brandenburgh, a member of the Germanic body, has since violated the imperial constitution, by erecting his electorate into a kingdom, *actually* independent of the empire. The peace of Nimeguen, concluded between the emperor and France, in 1679....that of Ryswyck, in 1697.... that of Baden, in 1714....that of Vienna, in 1725....and likewise those of the Pyrennees and Aix-la-Chapelle, &c. have all, according to M. Bielfeld, acquired the force of Laws, so far as they relate to the state, to the affairs and interests, of the German empire*....

Mr. Thomson (in his Spirit of general History) observes... that, "deaf to the solicitations of the emperor, they consulted only the interests of the German states. Their conduct was open and free. They employed none of those subterfuges, none of those intrigues, none of those deceptions which are too often decorated by the name of politics."

This great constitutional treaty cannot, however, be considered as now having the same force and operation, which it heretofore possessed. The recent treaty of Luneville...produced by the consequences of the French Revolution,...has operated such a change in the organization of the Germanic empire, as amounts to a virtual repeal (at least in part) of the treaty of Westphalia.

* Element of Erudition, Vol. I. chap. 14.

It is, nevertheless, unnecessary to mention, how often most, if not all of the parties to these several pacifications, have been engaged in mutual wars, since the dates of the treaties by which they were respectively concluded. To the cases here adduced, in support of our assertion, we shall mention but one; the treaty between Great-Britain and the States General, in 1674. This is acknowledged, by Mr. Fox, the British secretary, in the year 1782, to be "a treaty by which the principles of the Armed Neutrality are established, in their widest extent," &c.

It is wonderful, that, after this subject is viewed in the light in which it presents itself to an inquiring and unprejudiced mind, the permanent effect of the principles settled by the Armed Neutrality, should have been controverted, in 1798*, by the American envoys to France: yet such is the fact!...." A new Law of Nations, it is contended (say those envoys, speaking of the Armed Neutrality), was introduced by that confederation.

* See the letter addressed "to the minister of Foreign Affairs? of the French Republic;" dated, Paris, January 27, 1798, and signed "Charles Cotesworth Pinckney, J. Marshall, E. Gerry."

But who were the parties to that federation, and what was its object? The northern powers of Europe united to protect by force, in their own bottoms, during the then existing war, the goods of either and of all the belligerent powers. The compact in its own nature was confined, with respect to its objects and its duration. It did not purport to change, nor could it change permanently and universally, the rights of nations not becoming parties to it. It did indeed hold forth the promise of future and more permanent and more general engagements for the same object; but such engagements were never formed. How then can this temporary and partial convention be considered as altering, radically and generally, principles which have been universally adopted, and in the modification of which all have an interest?"

We hesitate not to say, that every sentence of this quotation from the letter of our envoys, contains an erroneous and unwarranted assertion; and it is believed, that a recurrence to the arguments and facts already adduced on this subject, will fully justify this declaration on our part. We shall however notice, in this place, one of their assertions....

"The compact" (of the Armed Neutrality,) say the envoys, "in its own nature was confined with respect to its objects and its duration." The treaty of the Armed Neutrality was undoubtedly limited as to its objects, with regard to their extent or description: but, that no limits either were or could be assigned to the "duration" of the *principles* and *rights*, which that confederation was instituted to assert and defend, will appear from official documents of the parties thereto. Prince Gallitzin, the Russian minister at the Hague, in his Memorial to the States-general, dated April 3, 1780, inviting them to accede to the confederation, says;...."The same invitation has been made to the courts of Copenhagen, Stockholm, and Lisbon; in order that, by the united endeavours of all the neutral maritime powers, a natural system, founded on justice, might be established and legalized in favor of the trade of neutral nations, which by its real advantages might serve for *a rule for future ages*." In the Declaration of Russia to the courts of London, Versailles and Madrid, the empress states, that she finds herself obliged to exonerate commerce from those hindrances which infringed upon the liberty of trade in general and of Russia in particular; "but, before she puts this into execution, and with a sincere intention to prevent any future infringements, she thought it but just to publish to all Europe the principles she means to follow, which are the properest to prevent any misunderstanding or any occurrences that may occasion it. Her imperial majesty does it with the more confidence (continues the Declaration), as she finds these *principles* coincident with the *primitive right of nations*, which every people may *reclaim*, and which the belligerent powers cannot invalidate, without violating the Laws of Neutrality, and without disavowing the maxims they have adopted in the different treaties and public engagements." The king of Denmark, in his Declaration to the same courts, says...."he thinks it due to himself, and his subjects, faithful observers of the rules (of Neutrality), and to the powers at war, themselves, to declare to them the following *principles*, which he *has always held*, and which he *will always avow and maintain*, in concert with the empress of all the Russias, whose sentiments he finds entirely conformable with his own," &c....The king of Sweden, in his

Declaration to the same courts, sets forth, that the empress of Russia's Declaration "was founded upon such *just principles of the Law of Nations*, that it was impossible to call them into question:"....And the States General, in their memorial to the court of Stockholm, dated March 6, 1781, style the treaty of Armed Neutrality (then ratified by the four powers we have mentioned) a work gloriously undertaken, for maintaining "the liberty of the seas, and freedom of navigation *for all Neutral Nations*." Although Prussia was not one of the contracting parties to the treaty of neutrality, that court fully and explicitly acceded to the principles and regulations adopted thereby, in its Ordinance and Declaration concerning the commerce and navigation of Prussia, dated April 30, 1781. By this instrument, regulations are prescribed for protecting, in conjunction with the confederated powers of the north, the maritime rights of Prussia, as a neutral nation; and, after reciting sundry arrangements for that purpose, these words follow...."the king's intention is merely to secure, by the above arrangements, the lawful commerce of his subjects, and not to cause any prejudice to the different powers at war, with whom he lives in perfect harmony, nor to favor any contraband dealings whatever; all the subjects of his majesty who traffic by sea, or practice navigation, are hereby enjoined to observe the most exact neutrality, conformable to the Laws of Nature and the rights and privileges of nations, almost universally acknowledged. But as the different treaties, respecting the maritime commerce, which several powers have concluded between themselves, might create some difference in these rights and privileges, it is principally to the known Declaration which her majesty the empress of Russia has caused to be presented, last year, to the belligerent powers; and to the ordinance which her majesty has afterwards issued on March 8, 1780, for the regulation of her colleges of commerce; to which the subjects of the king are to conform, with regard to their maritime commerce; the *principles* set forth therein, being such as his majesty finds the most coinciding with the *rights and privileges of nations in general*, and with his own in particular." Thus we find Prussia concurring in *the establishment* of the same *principles*, respecting the maritime rights of neutrals, in 1781, which she asserted against Great-Britain, in 1752.

It is true, that *one* object of the treaty of Armed Neutrality was the *protection* of the maritime trade of the parties to that treaty, during the then existing war; and the measures thereby adopted, for that purpose, were accordingly limited to the continuance of that war: but it is equally certain, that it was the design of the confederates *to establish*, by that alliance, *a permanent system of neutral maritime rights, grounded on the Law of Nations; to serve as a law in future times.* If any doubt is yet entertained on this head, the ninth article of the treaty of Armed Neutrality, itself, cannot fail to dissipate them, entirely. It is in these words...." This convention shall remain in force, for and during the continuance of the present war; and the obligation, enforced thereby, will serve as the ground-work of all treaties that may be set on foot, hereafter: according to future occurrences, and on the breaking out of any fresh maritime wars which might unluckily disturb the tranquillity of Europe. Meanwhile, all that is hereby agreed upon, shall be deemed as binding and *permanent*, in regard both to mercantile and naval affairs; and shall have the force of *Law*, *in determining the rights of Neutral Nations*."....The obvious result, therefore, of these several views of the subject, is a demonstration, that the American envoys to France were egregiously mistaken (independently of their errors on other points), in declaring, that the treaty of Armed Neutrality, "in its own nature was confined, with respect to its objects and its duration."*

* On January 15, 1801, Lord Grenville presented to the Danish and Swedish Ambassadors, at the Court of London, a note on the subject of the convention, then recently concluded by the Northern Powers, for the defence of their Neutral Maritime rights. In this, Lord Grenville affects to believe, (as the American envoys did, in their letter of January 27, 1798, to the French minister for foreign affairs,) that the measures adopted for the same purpose, in the armed neutrality of 1780, had been "completely given up." In order to support this assertion, his lordship goes on to say thus..."At the beginning of the present war, the Court of Petersburg, which has taken a most active part in the establishment of the former alliance, entered into articles with his majesty, which are not merely incompatible with the convention of 1780, but which are directly in the face of it; engagements which are still in force, and the reciprocal execution of which, his majesty is entitled to demand, upon every principle of good faith, during the continuance of the war."

In the answer, on the part of Denmark, to this Note...after adverting to the hostile measures that had been recently adopted by Russia against England,...the Danish ambassador

It is evident, then, that there is not a state in the civilized world, possessing an extensive navigation and considerable maritime commerce, that has not directly,* at some period within the last two centuries, testified its assent to the principle, that free ships make free goods; and who have not all (the dependent† monarchy of Portugal alone excepted), either expressly or virtually, recognized the same principle, as established by the treaty of Armed

proceeds thus..."A difference which arose between the courts of Petersburg and London, during the negociation destined solely to the protection of a perfect neutrality in the North, has no relation whatever with that; and as his imperial majesty of all the Russias has caused to be published a formal declaration, on the subject of the motives of the measures adopted on his part, Denmark finds, in it, a complete refutation of the argument advanced by the British minister. With respect to the *principles* of the Northern powers, *respecting the sacred Rights of Neutrality, they have not been abandoned.* Russia, in her belligerent quality, has only suspended the application; and Denmark and Sweden have, by their convention of March 27, 1794, (officially communicated to all the belligerent powers,) declared in the face of all Europe, that their system of protection, in favor of innocent commerce, was *invariable.*"

* By Treaty....Even Portugal agreed to the principle, that free ships make free goods, by the twenty-third article of her treaty with England, dated July 10, 1654.

† Mr. Postlethwayt, in his Dictionary of trade and commerce, treating of Portugal, has one head in express terms... "Of the dependency of Portugal on Great-Britain."

Neutrality, in 1780. Numerous public treaties, and other national acts of equal notoriety, abundantly testify in favour of the legitimacy of that principle, which became finally established in consequence of the Armed Neutrality. They constitute, collectively, what Lord Somers called, on a different occasion, the judgment of whole kingdoms and nations. To such " authorities" as these, who will oppose the speculative opinions....or, more properly, the mere *dictums*, of writers on the Law of Nations? What weight is due to the opinions of Grotius, Loccenius, and others....even the antiquated *Consolato del Mare* (that " book of great authority!") considered *as authorities;* when opposed to the decisions of many great and enlightened nations? The candid inquirer after truth will readily determine, that, in such case, they are entitled to none;....without being biassed by influential names or traditional prejudices.

Although further proof is not requisite, to shew, that the sense entertained by Nations, of the justness and ligitimacy of the principle, that free ships make free goods, tends directly to its support; we shall proceed, in pursuance of our plan, to notice the treaties that have been concluded since 1780, wherein the observance of that principle is stipulated. They are as follow, viz.

The treaty of amity and commerce, between the United States of America and the Dutch Republic. October 8th, 1782.

The treaty of amity and commerce, between the United States and Sweden. April 3d, 1783.

The treaty of amity and commerce, between the United States and Prussia. September 10th, 1785.

The treaty of peace and friendship, between the United States and the emperor of Morocco. January 1st, 1787.

The treaty of friendship, limits and navigation, between the United States and Spain, of the 27th October, 1795.

The treaty of peace and amity, between the United States and the Dey of Algiers, concluded the 28th November, 1795.

The treaty of peace and friendship between the United States and Tripoli (of Barbary), concluded the 10th February, 1797.

The treaty of peace and friendship, between the United States and the kingdom of Tunis.....of August 1797,.....as altered, and finally concluded with the Bey and Regency of Tunis, on the 26th March, 1799.

The convention between the United States and the French republic. September 30th, 1800.

And besides these....in which the United States are one of the contracting parties,.... there are the following, viz.

The treaty between France and Great-Britain. September 26th, 1786.

The convention between Russia, Denmark and Sweden, (afterwards acceded to, by Prussia),....concluded at St. Petersburgh, December 16th, 1800:....And

The treaty of amity, commerce and navigation, between Russia and Sweden....definitively ratified on the (30th May, O. S.) 11th June, 1801.

Thus have the United States, in nine maritime treaties since 1780, stipulated an observance of the principle, that free ships make free goods;....a principle, which they adopted in that year, by the resolution of Congress approbating the Armed Neutrality; which they again recognized, in the succeeding year, by the memorial of their minister in Holland; and by the ordinance of Congress, of the 7th

April, in the same year; which they had engrafted upon their virgin-treaty with France, two years before the formation of the maritime confederacy of the north....(a treaty which, as Mr. Adams declared to the States General, had for its basis, that marine system, unanimously adopted by Congress, in 1776, from which the United States would never depart*);....yet finally, that very princi-

* In the case of Derby and others, appellants, against the brig Erstern and others, (after the cause had been solemnly argued during three days, in the Court of Appeals of the United States) the court declared, that, " if the Erstern had been employed in a fair commerce...such as was consistent with the rights of neutrality,...her cargo, though the property of an enemy, could not be prize; because congress have said, by their ordinance, that the rights of neutrality shall extend protection to such effects and goods of an enemy. But if the Rights of Neutrality are violated, congress have not said that such a violated neutrality shall give such protection: nor could they have said so, without confounding all the distinctions between right and wrong." (N. B. This decision took place in February 1782.) see 2d. Dall. Rep. 34....See also, in the some book, the case of Miller et al. libellants and appellants, versus the ship Resolution &c. claimant and appellee...decided in the federal Court of Appeals, at August Session, 1781.]

The ordinance of congress, here referred to, was passed on April 7, 1781,...containing a set of instructions, for commanders of private armed vessels sailing under the authority of the United States; the fourth of which is in these words...." You shall not seize or capture any effects belonging to the subjects of the belligerent powers, on board neutral vessels, excepting

which the administration had put into operation, according to the plans they had formed.

construction of the Law of Nations, concerning the principle in controversy, which is to be found in most writers on public law; and it became the duty of Mr. Jefferson...as the proper organ of the government, in such case, to announce their decisions and their will, to the public functionaries of the powers concerned. Thus we find, that these letters were considered, in England, as acts of the American government: and, accordingly, the author of "Letters of Sulpicius, on the Northern Confederacy," makes the following remark...."The law itself (meaning the Law of Nations, the British interpretation of which, the writer of those letters endeavours to support,) cannot be more satisfactorily, or unequivocally established, than by the express avowal of the American government, at a period of manifest partiality to the enemies of this country; and, through the channel of Mr. Jefferson, whom they, at least, must acknowledge as an unexceptionable witness, in favor of any British claim."...The author of this British publication knew perfectly well, that Mr. Jefferson's private opinion, however adverse it may have been to the principle which the administration of this country then thought it expedient to adopt, could not be asserted by him, in his official capacity, in opposition to the decision of the administration....The secretary of state was, in that instance, merely "the channel" (in the words of Sulpicius,) "through" which the sense of the presidential cabinet-ministers (decided by a plurality of voices) was to be made known. It has been the practice in the American government to convene, occasionally, the heads of departments, including the attorney-general; in order to consult them collectively, as a sort of cabinet-council, on those measures of the government, the duties of which are devolved, by the constitution, on the president. The execution of the measure, decided upon in such council, became the duty of the officer

In this momentous conjuncture, a patriotic mind could scarcely hesitate, on which side of the

to whose department it belonged: the measure itself was the act of the government. Thus, Mr. Jefferson's successor in the department of state, (in his letter to Mr. Monroe, of June 1, 1795,...respecting Mr. Genet's proposition in May, 1793, to negociate a new treaty of commerce with the United States) ....after noticing the dissatisfaction expressed by Mr. Genet, on Mr. Jefferson apprizing him, that a definitive answer to his proposition could not be given, until the meeting of the Senate,....adds these observations....“ It is of no consequence to inquire, whether it was or was not more agreeable to Mr. Genet, that the negociation should lie over; when he heard that a definitive answer must be delayed, until the meeting of the senate. Notwithstanding it has the appearance of being the voluntary act of both;....yet let it be conceded to have been, on the part of Mr. Jefferson, an act of the government,....and on the part of Mr. Genet, a respectful submission.”

To the like effect, Messrs. C. C. Pinckney, Marshall and Gerry....in their letter of the 27th of January, 1798, to the French minister of Foreign affairs,....observe; that “ the letters from Mr. Jefferson, already quoted,” (the letters before mentioned) “ had stated to the world the perfect conviction *of the United States*, that, by the Law of Nations, a belligerent power, not restrained by particular treaty, might rightfully take out of the bottoms of a neutral, the goods of its enemy;” &c.

If the opinions of writers on the Law of Nations, are to be considered as the Law of Nations itself,....then, it is admitted, the principle asserted by the American government in 1793, through the medium of Mr. Jefferson's two letters above cited, is conformable to the general Law of Nations: and, in that case, the American administration would have been right, in their avowal of such principle. But it may be inferred, from the second of the letters cited (that to Mr. Morris), that the very

alternative to decide; painful as the situation must have been, that impelled to the adoption

principle so avowed, was not considered as being derived from the rightful Law of Nations; for, says the letter, "the inconvenience of this principle....which subjects merchant-vessels to be stopped at sea, searched, ransacked, led out of their course, ...has induced several nations latterly to stipulate against it by treaty, and to substitute another in its stead, that free ships shall make free goods,....and enemy-bottoms, enemy-goods; a rule equal to the other in point of loss and gain, but less oppressive to commerce."...."We have introduced it into our treaties with France, Holland and Prussia."...."It is our wish to establish it with other nations."....And further; Mr. T. Pinckney, then the American minister at London, in his letter of the 9th of January, 1794, to Mr. Jefferson,....stating a conversation between himself and Lord Grenville,....says; "I reminded him, that our ideas differed materially from theirs, on this subject; and, without repeating the arguments I had before addressed to him, both verbally and in writing, in support of our position, it was only necessary to say, that we did not admit the right of the belligerent powers to interfere further in the commerce between neutral nations and their adversaries, than to prevent their carrying to them articles, which, by common usage, were established as contraband, and any articles to a place fairly blockaded: that, consequently, the two first articles, though founded upon their principles of not suffering, in war, a traffic which was not admitted by the same nations in time of peace, and of taking their enemy's property, when found on board of neutral vessels, were nevertheless, contrary to what we contended to be the just principles of the modern Law of Nations."

Thus it appears, that the American government, in 1793 and 1794, conceived, that "the just principles of the modern Law of Nations" warranted the position, that free ships make

of either the one or the other. The extreme importance of the precept....*Salus populi suprema Lex esto*....must have been powerfully experienced, on such an occasion; and a friend to his country could not fail to act in conformity with it.

But the period to which we have alluded, was past; and about a year and an half elapsed, before the signature of Mr. Jay's treaty. In the meantime, the actual state of public affairs, between the United States and the principal belligerent powers, respectively, became greatly changed. At no time, was this country under any obligation whatever, either

free goods;....yet that, in the former year, they adopted the contrary position, as a principle of the Law of Nations; according to the interpretation of jurists, and the writers on public Law.

We profess to be unacquainted with....and, in fact, do not know....Mr. Jefferson's own, uncontrouled opinion, respecting the point in question;....further, than as it is deducible from that diplomatic correspondence, which he conducted, while secretary of state, with acknowledged great talents, in conformity to the policy of the administration,....and wherein he has ably vindicated such neutral rights as the government then thought proper to assert. Nevertheless, the general tenor of his political conduct and principles....his extensive erudition....and the force and correctness of his mind....are ample guarantees for the justness of his sentiments, on those points of public Law, which involve important natural Rights of Nations.

moral or political, to accede to the least dereliction, in favor of Great-Britain, of Rights which our government had solemnly and repeatedly recognized: and, at the latter period, we had not even the plea of imperious necessity to offer, in justification of any concessions in her favor. On the contrary, her injurious conduct towards the United States loudly demanded redress. We professed, by the mission of Mr. Jay, to seek it: and it was then in our power to have obtained justice from the British crown; or, in case of failure to procure it by amicable negociation, to have completely indemnified ourselves against its depredations on our commerce, and infractions of its conventional stipulations at the peace,....by means honorable, just, and lawful. We had the Law of Nations on our side....practicable means of redress were fairly within our reach....and, as yet, we had neither yielded to our adversary those means of security and defence, which we lawfully possessed; nor surrendered to him those rights, which it was our duty forever to retain, sacred and inviolable. Mr. Jay, however, thought otherwise: his treaty was dictated by different considerations; and it was the policy of the American government, finally to give it their sanction of legitimacy*. It stands recorded on our national statute-book,

* The treaty arrived at Philadelphia, on the evening of the 7th March, 1795....Mr. Randolph, then secretary of state, asserts, that scarcely a day passed, on which the President saw him, that he did not enumerate many objections to it;....“ objections, going not only to the commercial part, but also to the Canada article, which though seemingly reciprocal in words, would as he thought, want reciprocity in practice ; to the omission of compensation for the negroes and property plundered; and to some other parts of less consequence. When the message, which was to accompany the treaty to the senate, was about to be prepared, at the latter end of May, 1795, I observed to him (continues Mr. Randolph) that it was necessary for him to make up his mind, to ratify or not; and he answered, that although the treaty was so exceptionable to him, yet he would not separate from the Senate.”....The president writes thus to Mr. Randolph, from Virginia, on the 22d of July, 1795....“ My opinion respecting the treaty, is the same now, that it was; that is, not favourable to it;....but, that it is better to ratify it, in the manner the Senate have advised,....and with the reservation already mentioned,” (namely, “ if the late order”....that of November 6, 1794....“ which we have heard of, respecting provision-vessels, is not in operation,”)....than to suffer matters to remain as they are,....unsettled. Little has been said to me, on the subject of this treaty, along the road I passed; and I have seen no one, since, from whom I could hear much concerning it:....but, from indirect discourses, I find endeavours are not wanting to place it in all the odious points of view, of which it is susceptible, and in some which it will not admit.”

Such was the opinion entertained of this treaty, by president Washington, four months and an half after it came to his hands! ....It was almost universally reprobated by the people of the United States:....But Mr. Jay, by concluding such a treaty,

as a memorial....though a solitary one of the kind*....of the United States having been seduced into a conventional surrender of great and important interests, appertaining to them as neutrals,....and of rights and privileges, inherent in them as an independent nation.

We shall here subjoin a catalogue of such public treaties, as recognize and establish the legitimate principle, that free ships make free goods. In their chronological order, they stand thus, viz.

1. Treaty marine between England and Holland, London, Dec. 1, 1647, art. 1, 2.

had placed the government of the country in a most embarrassing situation, at an awful crisis in our affairs;....such a situation, as induced the great and patriotic character, then at the head of our government, to suppose it necessary to ratify the treaty, on certain conditions; notwithstanding "all the odious points of view," of which even then, he deemed it "susceptible."

* In a letter of the 7th of July, 1796, from Mr. De la Croix, the French minister of Foreign Affairs, to Mr. Monroe, the American minister at Paris....on the subject of Mr. Jay's treaty,....are the following observations:...."The abandonment of the principles, consecrated by this treaty" (referring, in this place, to our treaty of commerce with France, mentioned just before), "has struck us with greater force, from the consideration that all the other treaties, which the United States have made, contain them; as from the further one, that these principles are since so generally acknowledged, that they now form the public Law of all civilized Nations."

2. Treaty between England and Portugal, July 10, 1654, art. 23.

3. Treaty between France and Sweden, 1666.

4. Treaty of peace, commerce and alliance, between England and Spain; Madrid, May 13---23, 1667: art. 22, 23.

5. Treaty between England and Holland, July 21---31; 1667.

6. Treaty between England and Holland; Feb. 7---17, 1668: art. 10.

7. Treaty between England and Denmark; July 11, 1670.

8. Treaty between England and Holland; Dec. 1, 1674: art. 8.

9. Treaty between France and England; St. Germaines en Laye; Feb. 24, 1677: art. 8.

10. Treaty between Denmark and Holland, (for 20 years); June 15, 1701.

11. Treaty between France and Great-Britain; Utrecht, March 31, 1713: art. 17.

12. Treaty between France and Holland; Utrecht, April 11, 1713: art. 26.

13. Treaty between Great-Britain and Spain; Utrecht, Nov. 28---Dec. 9, 1713.

14. Treaty of commerce between Great-Britain and Spain; Madrid, Dec. 14, 1715.

15. Treaty of amity, commerce and navigation, between Russia and Great-Britain; St. Petersburgh, Dec. 2, 1734: art. 11, 12.

16. Treaty between France and Denmark; (for 15 years), dated at Copenhagen, Aug. 23, 1742.

17. Treaty between Great-Britain and Spain; Madrid, Oct. 5, (N. S.) 1750.

18. Treaty of peace (definitive) between Great-Britain and Spain; (signed at Paris), Feb. 10, 1763.

19. Treaty of amity and commerce, between the United States of America and France; Paris, Feb. 6, 1778.

20. Treaty maritime, between Russia an Denmark; and acceded to, by Sweden and the States General of the United Provinces, (the treaty of Armed Neutrality); signed at Copenhagen, July 9, 1780.

21. Treaty of amity and commerce, between the United States, and the States General; Hague, Oct. 8, 1782: art. 10, 11.

22. Treaty of amity and commerce, between the United States and Sweden; Paris, April 3, 1783: art. 7, 10.

23. Treaty of amity and commerce, between the United States and Prussia, (for 10 years); Sept. 10, 1785: art. 12.

24. Treaty between France and Great-Britain; Versailles, Sept. 26, 1786.

25. Treaty of peace and friendship, between the United States and Morocco; Jan. 1, 1787.

26. Treaty of friendship, limits, and navigation, between the United States and Spain, San Lorenzo el real, Oct. 27, 1795.

27. Treaty of peace and amity, between the United States and Algiers; Nov. 28, 1795.

28. Treaty of peace and friendship, between the United States and Tripoli (of Barbary); concluded Feb. 10, 1797: art. 2.

29. Treaty of peace and friendship, between the United States and Tunis; concluded March 26, 1799: art. 3.

30. Convention between the United States and the French republic; Paris, Sept. 30, 1800: art. 14.

31. Convention between Russia, Denmark, and Sweden, (acceded to, afterwards, by Prussia); concluded at St. Petersburgh, Dec. 16, 1800.

32*. Treaty of amity, commerce and navigation, concluded at St. Petersburgh, be-

* Our countryman, Mr. Joel Barlow, (in the appendix to his second letter to the citizens of the United States,....dated

tween Russia and Sweden, the 1st (13th) of March, 1801....and definitively ratified on the 30th of May, O. S. 1801....June 11, 1801: art. 24.

at Paris, 20th Dec. 1799), has exhibited a catalogue of treaties, in which it is stipulated that the flag shall protect the cargo, in all cases except the contraband of war. In this list are contained some, which are not stated in the above enumeration of treaties of that description; and many are omitted which we have given:....Those which we have omitted, appear to be the following; and, therefore, if Mr. Barlow's list be correct, as far as it goes, the addition of it to the one above stated, will render the catalogue complete.

Between France and	Holland,	in 1646
	Hanse-Towns, art. 2, 3.	1655
	England, art. 15.	1655
	Spain,	1659
	Holland, art. 35.	1662
	Idem,	1678
	Idem,	1697
	Idem,	1739
	Denmark,	1662
	Sweden,	1672
Between England and	Spain,	1670
Between Holland and	Portugal, art. 12.	1661
	Sweden,	1667
	Idem, art. 6.	1675
	Idem,	1679
	Naples,	1752
Between Spain and	Austria,	1725
	Denmark,	1742
Between Denmark and	Genoa,	1756
	Naples,	1749

And, in addition to these, Mr. Barlow has added (under the head of Armed Neutrality, in 1780), a treaty between Russia and *Naples.*

We presume Mr. Barlow's statement is accurate, as far as it extends; though we have had no opportunity of ascertaining this, ...as we did not see his list, until the present work was some time in the press. Such remarks, therefore, as have been suggested by the catalogue contained in the text, will be so modified by the reader, as to comprize both lists.

(No. 3.) See the declaration of the king of Sweden, to the courts of London, Versailles and Madrid, in 1780, respecting the northern confederacy of Armed Neutrality, formed in that year.

(No. 4.) This was ratified and confirmed by the treaty of of Navigation and Commerce, between Great-Britain and Spain, concluded at Utrecht, Nov. 28....Dec. 9, 1713: And by the 6th article of this treaty, of Utrecht, it is further declared.... that, " as the respective subjects of their majesties ought to enjoy an entire, safe, and unmolested use and liberty of Navigation and Commerce, whilst the peace and friendship entered into by their majesties and their crowns shall subsist; it is provided by their majesties, that for any little difference that may arise, their said subjects shall not be deprived of this security; but, on the contrary, they shall enjoy all the benefits of peace, until war be declared between the two crowns."....See also note, No. 14.

(No. 6.) In the month of August, 1685, James II renewed all former alliances with the Dutch; and, among the rest, this treaty of Feb. 17, 1668, and that of Dec. 1, 1674, more particularly.

(No. 8.) See note, No. 6.

(No. 13.) See note, No. 4.

(No. 14.) By the 5th article of this treaty, it was declared ...." that the said subjects" (of Great-Britain and Spain) " shall enjoy all the rights, privileges, franchises, exemptions, and immunities whatsoever, which they enjoyed before the" (then)

" last war, by virtue of the royal schedulas or ordinances, and by the articles of the treaty of peace and commerce, made at Madrid in 1667, which is hereby fully confirmed."....And, by article 7th of this treaty (of the 14th December, 1715), " the " treaty of commerce, made at Utrecht, the 9th December, 1713, shall," (it is declared) " continue in force;" excepting only such of its provisions as contravene the stipulations of this treaty. Mr. Beawes, who published his *Lex Mercatoria*,.... in 1751, remarks....that this treaty of Madrid, (of the 23d of May, 1667), was the basis on which the several subsequent treaties between Great-Britain and Spain, up to that time, were founded.

(No. 15.) There was another commercial treaty, afterwards entered into, between Russia and Great-Britain; viz. in 1765.... This was concluded for a limited time; but was in force, at the formation of the Armed Neutrality. It contained a specification of articles contraband of war,....comprising military stores only; to the exclusion of such materials, as serve for building or repairing ships of war. This, we presume, is the one referred to, in the treaty of Armed Neutrality,....and in the empress of Russia's declaration, concerning contraband: But, this being one of the documents, which we were unable to procure, so as to serve the present purpose,.....we cannot ascertain what stipulation it contains, respecting the security of enemy-goods under a neutral flag. Such of our readers, therefore, as can readily have access to the treaty itself, are referred to it. The provisions of this single treaty can, however, very little affect our present subject, be they what they may.

(No. 17.) The treaty of Madrid, of May 23, 1667,....excepting some new stipulations, which have no relation to the principle, therein established, of free ships making free goods,... was confirmed by this treaty of 1750: And these were again confirmed, by the 2d article of the definitive treatv of peace, signed at Paris, the 10th February, 1763.

(No. 18.) See note, No. 17.

(No. 20.) This treaty was acceded to, and signed by the plenipotentiaries of Sweden, at St. Petersburgh, July 21, 1780, ...and by the States General, accepted November 20, 1780; and signed at Petersburgh, January 5, 1781, with the addition of one article only.

(No. 25.) It is asserted in an anonymous pamphlet, entitled, *Principles of Trade*, (printed in London, in 1774), that "the trading subjects of any power, with whom the emperor of Morocco may be at war, are not liable to capture, when within sight of his land, going or coming; and have otherwise free liberty to trade and reside in his dominions."....If this assertion be well founded, it evinces a liberal policy in that government, deserving the imitation of more enlightened nations.

England, in happier days of her government than the present, manifested a similar indulgence towards such of the subjects of her formidable rival, as resided at the commencement of a war, within her territory. The king of England having declared war against France, at the period alluded to,....the declaration contained these words :...." And whereas there are remaining in our kingdom, divers of the subjects of the French king; we do hereby declare our royal intention to be, that all the French subjects, who shall demean themselves dutifully towards us, shall be safe in their persons and effects."

(No. 31.) The object of this convention is, "to re-establish, in their former shape, the engagements, which, in the years 1780 and 1781, constituted the system of the Armed Neutrality." That is....as we understand it,....to renew the engagements, stipulated between the parties, in 1780; for providing and organizing a combined armed force;....for the purpose of supporting the *principles* adopted by them, in the Armed Neutrality.

(No. 32.) The purport of this treaty was not known in the United States, until after the present dissertation had been completed: but we were enabled to add it to this list, before the work was put to the press.

The reader will be pleased to take notice, that the *numerical* references, in the notes to the catalogue of thirty-two treaties, given in the text, apply to the *numbers* of those treaties, respectively.

A DISSERTATION

ON THE

FREEDOM OF NAVIGATION

AND

MARITIME COMMERCE.

SECTION III.

OF NEUTRALITY, AND THE RIGHTS OF NEUTRALS, AS DEDUCED FROM THE NATURE OF WAR.

MAN is a free agent; and, in the words of the constitution of Pennsylvania, has an inherent and indefeasible right of pursuing his own happiness. His political liberty consists in his not being obstructed, by any positive regulation of society, from prosecuting that object, in such manner, and by such means, as he may think proper; provided they do not tend to infringe similar rights, appertaining to others.

Commerce is calculated to meliorate the condition of man, and to enlarge the sphere of human happiness: it has, consequently, its appropriate rights, founded in nature.

But, since those occasional conflicts of hostility, which occur between distinct and independent communities of men, seem to be inseparable from the condition of our species ....being, as it were, the necessary consequences of human imperfections and frailties ....a new class of Rights (as they are called) has arisen, as the necessary consequence of that state of things. These are denominated by civilians, the *rights of war.*

Although these are styled Rights, they cannot, in strict propriety, be considered as such. War is confessedly an evil. " Were men always rational (says M. de Vattel*) they would terminate contests by the arms of reason only: natural justice and equity would be their rule, or their judge. Force is but a wretched expedient against those who spurn at justice, and refuse the remonstrances of reason; but this is the ultimate method to which a nation must have recourse, when

* Book iii. chap. iii. sect. 24, 25.

every other proves ineffectual." The same author farther observes, that "the right of using force or making war, belongs to nations no farther than is necessary to their *defence*, and the support of their *rights*." There is a mutual connection between human felicity and the precepts of eternal justice: consequently, the Author of nature, to use the words of judge Blackstone, "has graciously reduced the rule of obedience to this one paternal precept; that man should pursue his own true and substantial happiness."...."This (he adds) is the foundation of what we call Ethics, or Natural Law*."

The enjoyment of life, liberty, and property, are human Rights of the highest order. Yet the destruction of these *rights*, is the effect that war is calculated to produce. Their infringement is punished by the laws of civil society. The violation of either, is an injury; and constitutes an offence, criminal in its own nature. Yet War authorizes the slaughter of the human species, the captivity and thraldom of our fellow-men,...and the robbery and plunder of their property! If, then, the maxim

* i. Bl. Comm. 41.

be just....as undoubtedly it is,....that *no right can be founded on an injury;* how can we speak, correctly, of the *rights* of war? Grotius treats "*de jure belli ac pacis:*" but Pufendorf observes, that the word *jus*, is a very wide and ambiguous term. Besides its being used to signify a moral right, it is also taken for Law, and for a system or body of municipal laws or constitutions; and likewise for a sentence* pronounced by a judge. What are called the rights of war, may, therefore, with more propriety be considered, as rules or regulations, adopted by the consent of nations; regarding the conduct to be pursued, in certain circumstances, not only by the belligerents themselves, but by neutrals. The progress of civilization, and the consequent refinement of sentiment and manners, have introduced, in the conduct of war, practices, tending to repress that ferocious, vindictive and exterminating spirit, which is excited by the natural impulse of the human passions, between na-

* This is only proper in Latin. *Prætor quoque Jus reddere dicitur, etiam quum iniqui decernit.* "The Prætor is said to pronounce Law, even when he gives an unjust sentence." Digest. lib. i. tit. i....See Pufend. book i. chap. i. sect. 20, in the text and note.

tions engaged in hostility:....And these practices, sanctioned by humanity, have acquired the force of laws. But there are also regulations of war, affecting Neutrals, as we have already observed. The very meaning of *Neutrality* imports, that the neutral nation does not intermeddle with the quarrel between the warring powers. It is to shew no preference to either, in regard to the matter in dispute; and, of consequence, it is bound not to yield any aid or succour, (unless previously stipulated by treaty), that can be immediately employed in war,...to one; whereby the comparative strength of the other would be diminished: nor to do any act, whatever, that would give a direct superiority to either*. Because, were the neutral power to do any of these things, it would cease to be neutral, and render itself liable to be considered as an auxiliary party in the war; thereby subjecting itself to the consequences of that situation. Hence, arms, ammunition, and such other ar-

* The impartiality which a neutral nation is to observe,.... relates solely to war. It is not to give any succours, when there is no obligation (that is, no obligation arising from a former defensive alliance), nor freely to furnish troops, arms, ammunition, or any thing of direct use in war. See Vatt. book iii. chap. vii. sect. 104.

ticles as serve for the immediate and appropriate purposes of war, are forbidden to be carried into the territories of a warring nation; being denominated Contraband of war:....and, because princes and states consider themselves justifiable, in endeavouring to reduce to their subjection, besieged and blockaded places, belonging to their enemy,...by depriving them of every thing necessary for their subsistence and support; it is also forbidden to all neutrals to enter places, so invested by the armed forces of another nation. With relation to such, all supplies whatever are considered to be contraband. Indeed this principle has been carried so far, during the recent war, that a powerful, extensive, and populous nation, was attempted to be held in a state of *blockade;* in order that thirty millions of men, women, and children, might be *starved* into submission. The measure, however, failed; and afterwards, the projectors of the plan were nearly overwhelmed by an actual famine, resulting from natural causes, unaided by similar interdictions on the part of any of their enemies.

Having noticed the only two cases, in which the natural rights of nations, not engaged in any existing war, are lawfully and reasonably restricted, in relation to their foreign commerce, by the operation of rights claimed by the parties in such war; it follows, that the neutral nations are justly entitled to the enjoyment of *all other* commercial rights, which would belong to them, if no war existed.

" Whatever a nation does, in a use of its own rights (says Vattel*), and solely with a view to its own good, without partiality, without a design of favouring one power to the prejudice of another; cannot, in general, be considered as contrary to neutrality, and becomes such only upon particular occasions, when it cannot take place without injury to one of the parties, who has then a particular right to oppose it. Thus, the besieger has a right to prohibit access to the place *besieged.*" In another place,† the same writer observes, that (what he calls) the Law of Necessity justifies the seizure of goods *contraband of war*, when going to an enemy, though belonging to a friend....“ If this law (says he) warrants me on occasion, to seize what belongs

* Book iii. chap. vii. sec. 110.

† Book iii. chap. vii. sect. 111.

to another, shall it not likewise warrant me to stop every thing *relative to war*, which Neutral nations are carrying to my enemy?"....On this head, Vattel appears, indeed, very liberal:.... for, in the same section he affirms, "that if a nation *trades* in *arms*, *timber*, *ships*, *military stores*, &c, I cannot take it amiss that it sells such things to my enemy, provided it does not refuse to sell them to me also*. It carries on

* The justness of this doctrine is maintained by Mr. Jefferson, as appears by the following extract from his letter, when secretary of state, to M. Ternant, minister plenipotentiary of France....dated May 15, 1793. Having stated, that several memorials were received from the British minister, on subjects arising out of the recent war; the secretary then proceeds thus...."In one of these memorials, it is stated, that arms and military accoutrements are now buying up by a French agent in this country, with an intent to export them to France. We have answered, that our citizens have always been free to make, vend, and export arms: that it is the constant occupation and livelihood of some of them. To suppress their callings....the only means, perhaps, of their subsistence,....because a war exists in foreign and distant countries, in which we have no concern, would scarcely be expected. The Law of Nations, therefore, respecting the rights of those at peace, has not required from them such an internal derangement of their occupations. It is satisfied with the external penalty pronounced in the President's Proclamation" (the proclamation of Neutrality, as it is generally called), "that of confiscation of such portion of these arms, as shall fall into the hands of any of the belligerent powers, on their way to the ports of their enemies. To this penalty our citizens are warned that they will be abandoned; and, that

its trade, without any design of injuring me; and, in continuing in it, the same as if I was not engaged in war, that nation gives me no just cause of complaint." But, continues our author, "I here suppose my enemy goes himself, into a neutral country, to purchase what he has occasion for. Let us now discuss another point, namely, the *trade* which neutral nations carry on, with my enemy's country. It is certain, that as they have no part in my quarrel, they are under no obligation to abandon their trade, that they may avoid furnishing my enemy with the means of making war. Should they refuse to sell me any of these articles, by taking measures for transporting great quantities of them to my enemy, with a manifest intention of favouring him; such a partiality would exclude them from the neutrality they enjoyed. But if they only continue their *customary trade*, they do not thereby declare themselves against my interest; they only exercise a right, which they are under no obligation of sacrificing to me."....The learned and ingenious writer of a tract, entitled, *Fea-*

the purchases of arms, here, may work no inequality between the parties at war, the liberty to make them will be enjoyed equally by both."

tures of Mr. Jay's Treaty, in like manner observes (page 14)....“It is a general principle of the Law of Nations, that, during the existence of a war, neutral powers shall not, by favor or by treaty, so alter the situation of one of the belligerent parties, as to enable him more advantageously to prosecute hostilities against his adversary.” But such alteration of the condition of the belligerent party, can only proceed from a *variation* in the commercial operations of the neutral power with the belligerents, manifesting a *preference* of one to the other. It is *this* that constitutes the breach of Neutrality*; for the neutral has a perfect right to continue his customary trade. This is a principle so conformable to reason and natural equity, that it would not appear to admit of a doubt, had it not been so often violated, and so grossly, in respect to this country; as in the case of some of the decrees

* Barbeyrac, observing that Pufendorf treats no where on the subject of Neutrality, borrows from Buddeus (in his *Elemens de la Philosophie pratique*) the following observation....“He who undertakes a just war, may oblige other nations to observe an exact and general neutrality; that is to say, not to favor his enemy more than himself. This then is, as it were, an abstract of the duties and obligations of Neutral Nations.”....See Pufend. Book viii. chap. vi. sect. 7. in note.

of the French Convention respecting the commerce of Neutrals, passed in 1793, and more particularly by the several instructions or orders issued by the British cabinet to their naval commanders, on June 8, 1793, &c....We shall therefore quote some farther authorities, in support of this point....They are at least evidence of the opinions entertained by others, on the subject. Vattel*, treating of the rules to be observed concerning the commerce of Neutral Nations, "and on which," he observes, "Europe seems to be generally agreed,"...proceeds thus...."The first is, carefully to distinguish common goods, which have no relation to war, from those peculiarly subservient to it. In the trade of the former, Neutral Nations are to enjoy an entire liberty; the parties at war cannot with any reason deny it, or hinder the importation of such goods into the enemy's country. In this, the care of their safety, the necessity of defence, does not authorize them, as by these the enemy does not become more formidable. An attempt to molest or destroy this trade, would be a breach of the rights of

* Book iii. chap. vii. sect. 112.

Neutral Nations*, a flagrant injury to them; necessity, as we have just observed, being the only reason, which can authorize a restriction of their trade and navigation to the ports of the enemy."....This quotation goes completely to establish the principle, that Neutrals have a right to protect, in their shipping, the goods of an enemy; and all other goods whatever,.... contraband of war (properly so called) alone excepted.

The reason of the principle is also well stated in the Danish Declaration to the courts of London, Versailles, and Madrid, in 1780.... "If the duties of Neutrality (says the declaration) are sacred, the Law of Nations has also its rights avowed by all impartial powers, established by custom, and founded upon equity and reason. A nation, independent and neuter, does not lose by the war of others, the Rights which she had before the war; because peace exists between her and all the belligerent powers. Without receiving or being

* On this point, however, Vattel is grossly inconsistent; because, after establishing the *principle*, on which the right of protecting enemy's goods in friendly ships is founded,....he afterwards declares such goods *seizable*.

obliged to follow the laws of either of them, she is allowed to follow, in all places, (contraband excepted) the traffic which she would have a right to do, if peace existed with all Europe, as it exists with her. The king pretends to nothing beyond what the Neutrality allows him. This is his rule, and that of his people; and the king cannot accord to the principle, that a power at war has a right to interrupt the commerce of his subjects."

We shall conclude our quotations, on this point, with an extract from the letter of the present illustrious chief magistrate of the United States, while secretary of state, to Mr. Thomas Pinckney our Minister at London,.... dated September 7, 1793;....a letter, which Messrs. Charles C. Pinckney, Marshall, and Gerry, acknowledge to contain "much justness of sentiment and strength of argument*". "Reason and usage (says the secretary) have established, that when two nations go to war, those who chuse to live in peace, retain their natural right to pursue their agriculture, manufactures and other ordinary vocations; to carry the produce of their industry, for exchange, to

* See the Commissioners' letter to the French minister of foreign affairs, dated January 27, 1798.

all nations, belligerent or neutral, as usual; to go and come freely, without injury or molestation; and, in short, that the war among others shall be, for them, as if it did not exist. One restriction on their natural rights has been submitted to, by nations at peace; that is to say, that of not furnishing to either party implements merely of war, for the annoyance of the other, nor any thing whatever to a place blockaded by its enemy. What these implements of war are, " that are forbidden to be carried by neutrals into the territories of a belligerent nation, " has been so often agreed, and so well understood, as to leave little question about them, at this day. There does not exist, perhaps, a nation in our common hemisphere, which has not made a particular enumeration of them, in some or all of their treaties, under the name of contraband. It suffices, for the present occasion, to say, that corn, flour, and meal, are not of the class of contraband; and, consequently, remain articles of free commerce. A culture, which, like that of the soil, gives employment to such a proportion of mankind, could never be suspended by the whole earth, or interrupted for them, whenever any two nations should think proper to go to war*." In the whole of this letter, the rights of neutral nations respecting their foreign commerce, are ably vindicated; and the agricultural interest of our country, in particular, is zealously supported. The letter is therefore given, entire, in the appendix. But it also contains....what is important to our present purpose,...a justification, by a very obvious deduction, of that principle in the Law of Nations, whereon is founded the right of neutrals to enjoy protection for all property whatever, laden in their ships, whether belonging to enemies or friends of belligerent states;....save only, such as is con-

* In the before mentioned letter of the American envoys to France, we find this passage, corresponding with the sentiments of Mr. Jefferson on the subject....“ The right of one nation to exchange with another the surplus produce of its labour, for those articles which may supply its wants or administer to its comfort, is too essential to have been ever classed among those admitted to be in any degree doubtful. It is a right, in ceding which a nation would cede the privilege of regulating its own interests and providing for its own welfare. When any two nations shall chuse to make war on each other, they have never been considered, nor can they be considered, as thereby authorizing themselves to impair the essential rights of those who may chuse to remain at peace. Consequently, these rights, the free exercise of which is essential to its interests and welfare, must be retained by a neutral power, whatever nations may be involved in a war."

traband of war; or, as is proceeding directly into a blockaded port. The right is, in truth, a natural one; and of that kind, which cannot be justly superseded by any positive or implied rules of human institution. The adverse doctrine rests on no other support, that has even the semblance of rightful authority, than the written opinions of certain civilians, and some few conventional stipulations. Even our envoys to France, in 1798, seem to rest the doctrine, that friendly ships shall not afford protection to enemy's goods, on no other foundations than these; though, on these grounds, they labour its vindication: For, in their letter of the 27th of January, to the minister of foreign affairs of the French republic, is the following passage...." The desire of establishing universally the principle, that neutral bottoms shall make neutral goods, is perhaps felt by no nation on earth, more strongly, than by the United States. Perhaps no nation is more interested in its establishment. It is an object they keep in view; and which, if not forced by violence to abandon it, they will pursue in such manner as their own judgment may dictate, as being best calculated to attain it: but the wish to establish a principle is essentially different from a determination that it is already established. The interests of the United States could not fail to produce the wish: their duty forbid them to indulge it, when deciding on a *mere right.* However solicitous America might be to pursue all proper means, tending to obtain for this principle the assent of all or any of the maritime powers of Europe, she never conceived the idea of obtaining that consent by force." Does it not appear from this quotation, that the *inexpediency* of attempting to establish, on the part of the United States, the principle in question, " by force"....that principle, which the envoys seem to admit is founded in " right," and which they say the United States will " keep in view"....“ if not forced by violence to abandon it;"....we ask, does not the *inexpediency alone*, according to the conception of the envoys, of thus attempting the establishment of a principle, predicated on a right, seem to have influenced them, in their support of the adverse principle on the authority of writers on the Law of Nations? We conceive it did: and, although it was not the " duty" of the United States to make such an attempt, under the existing circumstances; it most clearly was their duty, not to sacrifice by treaty, a principle, which it was their " interest" and " right" to retain, unviolated; and which they were " not forced, by violence, to abandon." Yet Mr. Jay, by his treaty with Great-Britain, in 1794, ceded to Great-Britain this very principle....this right, in which the United States have so great an interest: admitting, too, *ship-timber* and *naval stores* to be contraband of war, though contrary to the Law of Nations and our former treaties; and leaving it to Great-Britain to declare *provisions*, also contraband, that is, seizable, when going to France or her colonies, in American vessels, though only deemed to be contraband, when going into a blockaded or besieged place. The mischief is, however, done: It only remains for us to hope, that no American negociator will, in future, ever make, in favour of any foreign nation, even a temporary cession of the rights and interests of his country. Indeed, it must be extremely gratifying to an American, that our last commissioners to France were actuated by a more patriotic spirit: for, notwithstanding there is reason to believe, that at least two of those gentlemen adhered to that construction of the

Law of Nations, that militates against the just principle which we support; grounding their opinion on the authority of writers on the Law of Nations;....they nevertheless introduced into the convention between the United States and the French Republic, an express stipulation of the legitimate principle, that free ships make free goods.

When it is considered, that neutrals have a right of enjoying, during a war, all the commercial advantages which they were justly accustomed to possess in time of peace; excepting, only, the transportation to an enemy, of articles contraband of war; and of any kind of goods to a blockaded port;....it follows, that the principle of a neutral flag making free goods, results from a natural right necessarily attached to the free pursuits of commerce; For, as the neutral nation would have had an undoubted right to carry in its ships, in time of peace, goods, the property of any other nation that chose to lade them therein; and, as the commercial rights of the first can become no otherwise justly restricted by the subsequent event of war, than with respect to contraband goods and blockaded places;....it is such designation, only, of the goods, that can divest the owner of the neutral ship of his right of carrying them to the place of their destination. This is a privilege, appertaining to the condition of a neutral nation, as such, which it cannot surrender without a breach of its own rights and interest; and which no other nation can lawfully infringe.

A maritime nation derives important advantages from continuing in a state of Neutrality during a war. If two or more states engage in war, they subject their trade to all the injuries incident to that state. It is the penalty attached to warfare. On the other hand, those nations who are either so fortunate or prudent, as to continue in amity with other nations, are entitled to enjoy, without interruption from belligerent powers, the same freedom of trade with all the world, that they were accustomed and privileged to carry on, before the commencement of any hostilities: excepting ony the restriction from going into a blockaded port; and from carrying to any of the ports of a nation engaged in war, such articles as are properly contraband of war. Neutral Nations are the common friends to both the belligerent parties. The very condition of Neutrality implies that they remain such, during a war, "not favouring the arms of one, to the detriment of the other." Reason and justice do not, and therefore no law can, farther deprive them of the natural liberty of commerce: and accordingly, M. de Vattel* observes....that, "in whatever does not relate to war, a neutral and impartial nation must not refuse to one of the parties, on account of its present quarrel, what it grants to the other. This (continues Vattel) does not trespass on its liberty in negociations, connections of friendship, its trade, or of governing itself by what is most advantageous to the state."

If a nation, engaged in war, permit neutral ships to be carriers of its goods,....subject to the two admitted cases of restriction, under the Law of Nations; the right to do so, is complete, between the party owning the goods and the party carrying them: and, the goods being such as do not relate to war; and the trade being also of that nature, which does not favor the arms of one to the detriment of the other; no power at war can have a right to interrupt it. It is the natural right of enjoying this freedom of maritime commerce, that is recog-

* See Vattel, book iii. chap. vii. sect. 103, 104.

nized and established by the various treaties and leagues, (particularly that of the Armed Neutrality in 1780) which constitute what is now termed the Modern Law of Nations: and it is on this just and reasonable foundation, that the rightful exemption of enemy's goods from seizure, when laden in friendly ships, is rested.

The modern usage of nations, with respect to the maritime rights of neutrals,....which had been recognized by congress in 1780....and conformed to, in every American treaty, with the single exception of Mr. Jay's,....is expressly referred to, in the proclamation issued by the President of the United States, on April 22, 1793. By that act of the executive, our citizens are prohibited from carrying to any of the belligerent powers, those articles, which are deemed contraband by *modern* usage of nations. The very terms here used imply an usage (or, as it is sometimes called a Law) of Nations, recognizing a different construction of the Law of Nations with relation to the rights of neutrals, from that to which the ancient usage was conformable. It is well known, that, by the *ancient usage*, ship-timber, and naval stores, generally,....and even provisions,....were considered to be contraband. But the modern usage exempts them from that denomination; and, "at this day (as Mr. Fauchett* justly observes), the modern neutrality ranks as contraband, only articles fit to be used *immediately* for offence or defence; and those which must be *wrought*, before they can be used in this way, are excluded. Provisions are contraband, only in the case of their being carried to a besieged and blockaded place."

The United States have manifested their adherence to the modern usage of nations, in every instance, excepting Mr. Jay's treaty, from the commencement of the American Revolution to the present day. The first conventional transaction of our government, with a foreign nation, was their treaty of amity and commerce with France, in 1778; and the last, was the convention between them and the French Republic, concluded September 30, 1800. Both of these, as well as every intermediate maritime treaty made by the United States....with the single exception already mentioned,....adopt the modern construction of the Law of Nations. While

* See his pamphlet, entitled....*A Sketch*, &c. published after his return to France.

Great Britain adheres to the ancient construction (in theory at least,) as maintained by writers on the Law of Nations; the United States of America, and other maritime states, adopt the principles of that law, recognized in modern treaties, which have established an usage of nations, with respect to neutrals, infinitely more conformable to reason and natural justice. Whatever may be the ancient law, considered as a mere theory; we have in fact adopted the principles of the modern law (so to speak); conforming to the "modern usage of nations," to use the words of the proclamation of neutrality. Men in this country, of acknowledged abilities and patriotism, who have been induced to favor the ancient theoretical system, viewed merely in that light, have abandoned it in practice; seeing it to be clearly more consonant to natural equity and right reason, to conform, in their application, to the principles on which the modern usage is established. Now, as no principle of the Law of Nations is more unequivocally recognized by modern treaties and usage, than the one contained in the proposition....that free ships make free goods,....and as this principle is, in its own nature, just and equitable; the

United States are bound, by an obligation of the most sacred kind, stedfastly to adhere to the principle, in the formation of every maritime treaty hereafter. They are bound to do so, by the relation in which they stand to the great community of Neutral Nations; and it is, moreover, a duty that involves the rights and interests of the American people, as a free, independent, and great commercial nation.

A DISSERTATION

ON THE

FREEDOM OF NAVIGATION

AND

MARITIME COMMERCE.

SECTION IV.

DESIGNATING WHAT ARTICLES OUGHT TO BE CONSIDERED AS CONTRABAND OF WAR, AND DEFINING THE RIGHT OF SEARCH; ACCORDING TO THE TRUE INTERPRETATION OF THE LAW OF NATIONS, AS NOW ESTABLISHED.

HAVING shewn in the preceding sections, that the freedom of maritime commerce is no farther restricted with respect to neutrals, during a war, than, first....by the prohibition of their trading with ports actually blockaded; and secondly,....by the prohibition of their carrying to any of the ports of a state engaged in hostilities, articles contraband of war*; it becomes proper, now, to consider some other points, connected with the subject.

The principles adopted in the treaty of Armed Neutrality, of 1780, appear incontestibly to place the rights of neutrals on the just foundation of the Law of Nations. The restriction of those rights, in time of war, being confined to the two points just mentioned, it follows, that what is called the *right of Search*, as claimed and practised by belligerent powers, requires to be so modified, as

* In the letter of the 9th of January, 1794,....from Mr. T. Pinckney, the American minister at London, to Mr. Jefferson,....the writer states a conversation between himself and Lord Grenville, concerning the *Instruction*, issued on the preceding day, to the commanders of British ships of war, &c.... "I reminded him (says Mr. Pinckney), that our ideas differed materially from theirs, on this subject."...."That we did not admit the right of the belligerent powers to interfere farther in the commerce between neutral nations and their adversaries, than to prevent their carrying to them articles, which, by common usage, were established as contraband,....and any articles to a place fairly blockaded: that, consequently, the two first articles....though founded upon their principles, of not suffering, in war, a traffic which was not admitted by the same nations in time of peace, and of taking their enemies' property, when found on board of neutral vessels,....were, nevertheless, contrary to what we contended to be the just principles of the modern Law of Nations."

to be conformable to the freedom of commerce appertaining to neutrals. When an armed vessel of a belligerent power meets, at sea, with a private trading ship of a neutral nation; all that the former is entitled to examine into, is, whether the latter is carrying to an enemy-nation, articles contraband of war; or, whether he is going into a port actually blocked up. If, on due examination, either of these is found to be the fact, the neutral is subjected to the penalty inflicted by the Law of Nations, for the violation of his neutrality. But in either case, the *intention* of the neutral to commit a breach of his neutrality, must clearly appear: For, his navigating along the coast of a nation engaged in war, with articles contraband of war on board his ship, is not to be construed into a presumption, that his destination was a port of that nation; and, with respect to blockaded places, it must appear,....first, that the port towards which the neutral was proceeding, is actually and effectually blocked up...secondly, that at the time of his attempting to pass into a port, so blockaded, he had due notice of its being invested by an armed force of its enemy. In conformity with these principles, the treaty of Armed Neutrality declares....first, " That it will be lawful for any ship, whatever, to sail freely from one port to another, or along the coast of the powers now at war;....secondly, That all merchandize and effects belonging to the subjects of the said belligerent powers, and shipped on neutral bottoms, shall be entirely free; except contraband goods;.....and thirdly, that, " In order to ascertain what constitutes the blockade of any place or port, it is understood to be in such predicament, when the assailing power has taken such a station, as to expose to imminent danger any ship or ships, that would attempt to sail into or out of the said ports."....These stipulations are so consonant to reason and natural equity, that it is unnecessary to dilate, concerning them. But the subject naturally suggests two questions, for more particular consideration.

First; What articles ought, properly, to be deemed *Contraband* of war?....And, second; What is justifiable, in its nature and extent, under the denomination of *Search;* in the examination of neutral ships, at sea, by belligerents?

All independent states have an indubitable right to regulate their respective national concerns, in such manner as they may deem most conducive to their own interests, conformably with natural justice. The internal policy of each state is subject to the jurisdiction of its own government, only: It has, consequently, a right to subject foreign nations to such limitations and conditions, in their commercial intercourse with its *territories*, as to itself shall seem proper. In a time of universal peace, therefore, the commercial intercourse of the whole world is free from all other restraints, than such as are either imposed by the municipal laws of particular states; or voluntarily submitted to, by virtue of conventional stipulations between different powers. But when the repose of mankind is disturbed by war, the freedom of commerce between the states remaining at peace, and those engaged in hostilities with each other, is controuled, in the two particulars which have been mentioned: For, it would not comport with the essence of neutrality, that a neutral should carry to a belligerent nation, such things as could be immediately employed for the annoyance of its enemy, in war; or, that he should introduce into a blockaded port, succour, that might be employed, either for the relief of the invested place, or for the support of the besieging party. Thus, the restrictions to which the foreign commerce of neutrals is subjected, in these cases, necessarily result from the nature and condition of war. These, however, are the only two cases, in which the operations of war can rightfully affect the trade of neutral nations; because there are no other, wherein it is necessary to controul it. War is the concern of the belligerents, alone; and nations remaining at peace, can take no interest in it, consistently with their neutrality, whatever may be their opinions concerning its merits: On the other hand, the pursuit, by neutrals, of their lawful commerce, appertains to them as a natural right; and belligerent powers cannot interrupt them, without violating the Law of Nations. ....“ When any two nations shall chuse to make war on each other, (say the American envoys to France*, in 1798), they have never been considered, nor can they be considered, as thereby authorizing themselves to impair the essential rights of those, who may chuse

* See their letter (without date) in answer to one addressed to them, on the 18th of March, 1798, by the minister of Foreign Relations of the French Republic.

to remain at peace. Consequently these rights, the free exercise of which is essential to its interests and welfare, must be retained by a neutral power, whatever nations may be involved in a war."

In order then to ascertain, what articles are properly *contraband of war*, independently of their designation by treaties, it is only necessary to inquire, whether any particular article, under examination in that respect, be such as may serve either for the immediate annoyance or defence of an enemy, without being wrought-up, or otherwise materially varied in its form. If a different construction were to be admitted, a great variety of other things might be considered by a belligerent power, as contraband; and, among these, most of the staple articles of the American export-trade. Thus ship-timber, masts, iron, tar, hemp, &c. serving for the construction of vessels of war, might be deemed contraband. In like manner, corn, wheaten-flour, and meal of every kind,....with rice, salted provisions, &c. might be denominated contraband of war; because these things serve for the victualling of armies and fleets. Indeed, various commodities of a different nature, and such as constitute usual objects of traffic between commercial nations, in time of peace, may, by the same forced construction of contraband, be brought under that denomination, if carried by a friendly power to an enemy-nation, during a war. Thus, woolen cloths may be made into cloathing for soldiers and sailors....linen cloths, into under garments for them....and hats, boots and shoes, are also necessary for their accoutrement: Thus too, sail cloth, and other coarse fabrics of hemp and flax, serve for rigging vessels of war, and making soldiers' tents; and sheet-copper is employed, very generally, for sheathing ships of war. A powerful maritime nation could readily find a pretext, when involved in war, for considering all these articles, with many more that belong to free commerce, as contraband. Indeed, provisions and ship-timber have been attempted to be rendered such; particularly, by the 18th article of Mr. Jay's treaty. Yet, in that letter of Mr. Jefferson, which Messrs. C. C. Pinckney, Marshall and Gerry, say, "contains so much justness of sentiment and strength of argument," he observes....that "one restriction on their natural rights, has been submitted to, by nations at peace; that is to say, that of not furnishing to either party implements merely of war, for the annoyance of the other, nor any thing whatever to a place blockaded by its enemy.".....“ Corn, flour and meal, (continues Mr. Jefferson) are not of the class of contraband, and consequently remain articles of free commerce.".....“ The Right (say the envoys just mentioned) of one nation to exchange with another the surplus produce of its labour, for those articles which may supply its wants or administer to its comfort, is too essential to have been even classed among those admitted to be in any degree doubtful. It is a Right, in ceding which, a nation would cede the privilege of regulating its own interests and providing for its own welfare." These observations are certainly just; but the reasoning of Mr. Jefferson is so full and conclusive on this point, that we again refer to his letter, entire, in the appendix. We cannot, however, forbear reflecting on the inconsistency of Mr. Jay's conduct with the sentiments of both Mr. Jefferson and the envoys, on this subject; in admitting, among the articles contraband of war, by his treaty, “ timber for ship-building, tar or rosin, hemp and cordage, and generally whatever may serve directly to the equipment of vessels; unwrought iron and fir planks only excepted." Mr. Jay has, *in fact*, admitted provisions also to be considered *contraband*, by Great-Britain; though the clause respecting them is worded in ambiguous and covert terms. It is in these words...." And whereas the difficulty of agreeing on the precise cases, in which alone provisions, and other articles not generally contraband, may be regarded as such, renders it expedient to provide against the inconveniencies and misunderstandings which might thence arise: it is further agreed, that whenever any such articles so becoming contraband, according to the existing law of nations, shall for that reason be seized, the same shall not be confiscated, but the owners thereof shall be speedily and completely indemnified; and the captors, or in their default, the government under whose authority they act, shall pay to the masters or owners of such vessels, the full value of all such articles, with a reasonable mercantile profit thereon, together with the freight, and also the demurrage incident to such detention."....What is meant by " the precise cases, in which alone provisions, and other articles not generally contraband, may be regarded as such?"....It has been made apparent by Mr. Jefferson's letter....which has been cited *as an authority*, by the American envoys to France, in 1798,....that provisions remain, during a war, articles of free commerce: and ship-timber, with naval stores generally, are likewise such, "according to the existing Law of Nations." Mr. Jay was therefore guilty of violating the Law of Nations, in admitting, by the provisions of a treaty, that there was *any possible case*, in which those articles could be regarded as Contraband, other than that of their proceeding into a blockaded port: and, even in that case, they would not have been liable to confiscation, unless the party had previous notice of such port being in a state of effective blockade; for, the before mentioned envoys assert, that "claims for provisions seized in cases of a mere proclamation-blockade, have been actually made, and have been actually decided in favor of the claimants." The truth is, that if a neutral vessel were to be stopped by a belligerent, in the act of proceeding into a port effectively blocked up, after due notice of its being in that predicament; confiscation would be lawful penalty, of such contumacious endeavour to violate the rights of Neutrality: but in no other case*, would the neutral be justly liable to any penalty, or even interruption. In the first instance, the British government would never have consented to pay for a cargo, which accru-

* The Convention concluded between the United States and France, in September 30, 1800, admits the truth of this doctrine; as does, likewise, *even Mr. Jay's Treaty*....The second clause of the twelfth article of the Convention, is in the words following; viz....“ And whereas, it frequently happens, that vessels sail for a port or place belonging to an enemy, without knowing that the same is either besieged, blockaded or invested; it is agreed that every vessel, so circumstanced, may be turned away from such port or place: but she shall not be detained, nor any part of her cargo, if not contraband, be confiscated; unless, after notice of such blockade or investment, she shall again attempt to enter:....but she shall be permitted to go to any other port or place she shall think proper. Nor shall any vessel of either, that may have entered into such port or place before the same was actually besieged, blockaded or invested, by the other, be restrained from quitting such place, with her cargo; nor, if found therein, after the reduction and surrender of such place, shall such vessel or her cargo be liable to confiscation, but they shall be restored to the owners thereof.”

The third clause of the eighteenth article of Mr. Jay's treaty is nearly in the same words and of the same tenor, as the above; excepting, that the word “ actually”, as applied to places blockaded, is omitted,....leaving room for blockades by construction, or, “ proclamation-blockades;” and, that vessels which shall have entered blockaded places, are thereby restrained from quitting such places, during the blockade.

ed to them, rightfully, as a forfeiture; and in the other, no negociator on the part of a neutral state could be justifiable in stipulating, by treaty, to surrender into the hands of a belligerent power, on any terms or conditions whatever, articles of free commerce, destined by their owner to the port of another nation.... The substitution of *payment of the value*, in lieu of forfeiture, of such provisions as should be seized, under the clause of Mr. Jay's treaty that has been just quoted, does not render the concession of a right to make the seizure, less repugnant to the Law of Nations. The British instructions of June 8, 1793, to their naval commanders, did the same thing, precisely: and yet it was *this act*, of the British executive that became the subject of Mr. Jefferson's letter of the seventh of September following, to Mr. T. Pinckney, the American minister of London. The first article of it permits all vessels, laden wholly, or in part, with corn, flour or meal, bound to any port in France, to be stopped, and sent into any British port, to be purchased by that government; or to be released only on the condition of security given by the master, that he will proceed to dispose of his cargo in the ports of some country "in amity with his majesty". "This article (it is observed in Mr. Jefferson's letter) is so manifestly contrary to the Law of Nations, that nothing more would seem necessary, than to observe that it is so."....The National Convention of France had passed a decree on May 9, 1793, relative to the commerce of neutrals; the first article of which is of like import. When the American envoys to France, in 1798, take notice of this document, in their letter already quoted, they ask.... "Could this decree, citizen minister, be regarded otherwise than as *infringing the Law of Nations, the rights of neutrals, and the particular engagements subsisting between France and the United States?*" And then proceeding to notice the British instructions, they make these observations...."When on the eighth of June, in the same year, the British government issued a *similar* order, it's injustice produced a ferment throughout America, indicating strong dispositions immediately to oppose its execution by force. The letter of Mr. Jefferson, the then secretary of state, to the minister plenipotentiary of the United States at London, dated September 7, 1793, and remonstrating against the order of the eighth June, contains so much justness of sentiment, and strength of argument, as to have been quoted by your predecessor, in his letter to Mr. Monroe, of March 9, 1796."....Here we have the opinions of Messrs. C. C. Pinckney, Marshall, and Gerry, superadded to that of Mr. Jefferson,....bearing testimony to the " injustice" of the British instructions of June 8, 1793,....as well as of their " infringement of the Law of Nations," and " the Rights of Neutrals". Now, by recurring to the 1st article of the British instructions, it will be found to correspond with the second clause in the 18th article of Mr. Jay's treaty; by which, of consequence, the Law of Nations is infringed....the rights of neutrals violated...and injustice towards our citizens authorized.

Yet, strange as it may appear, the necessity which the envoys conceived themselves to be under, of justifying to a foreign nation, under delicate circumstances, measures already adopted by the government of their country, led them into palpable inconsistencies. In their communication with the French government, on matters of mutual controversy, and which had produced much irritation between the two countries, the envoys justly reprobate the indefensible principles usurped by the British king, in his instructions of the 8th June, 1793: and they as justly approbate those contained in Mr. Jefferson's letter, of the 7th of September following, to Mr. T. Pinckney, in which the rights of neutrals are ably supported. The main object of Mr. Jefferson, in that letter, was to maintain the inviolability of *provisions*, as an article of free commerce, and their consequent exemption from seizure. But, between the date of the letter, and the correspondence of the envoys with the French ministry, Mr. Jay's treaty had been concluded. This granted to the British, when engaged in war, permission to seize provisions in neutral ships,...contrary to the Law of Nations. It had gone even *beyond* the British instructions of the 8th June, 1793: They contemplated the seizure of a particular description of provisions, only....namely, corn, flour and meal; whereas, the treaty authorized the seizure of *every species* of "*provisions*," under that general denomination;....it attached to them, also, "other articles not generally contraband;" and, by these vague terms, left every thing to the mercy of construction! Nevertheless, as this treaty had been, long before, ratified by the American government, the envoys seemed to think it was their duty, in the character with which they were invested, and in their peculiar situation, to attempt a justification of this *chef-d'œuvre* of Mr. Jay's diplomatic skill: and, although they had virtually condemned some *principles* of an important nature, when those principles were discussed by them, *abstractedly from the treaty;* yet, when the *treaty itself* became the subject of their discussion, they vindicated the very stipulations that are predicated on those principles. Accordingly, we find them asserting, in their letter before quoted, that " the most approved writers on the Law of Nations are believed to class timber for ship-building, and naval stores for the equipment of vessels, among articles admitted to be contraband of war." They cite Vattel, to shew that he defines contraband goods to be " commodities particularly used in war; such as arms, military and naval stores, timber*, horses, and even *provisions* in certain

* The envoys place an asterisk at the word *timber*, referring to the words....*for ship-building*....in the margin: but Vattel has *timber*, only; without any words explanatory of its use or kind.

junctures, when there are hopes of reducing the enemy by famine*."

* Mr. Monroe justly remarks, that, by Mr. Jay's treaty, even by the admission of the American administration, "we have departed from the modern rule of contraband, with respect to many articles made free by modern treaties; have also made an arrangement, by which, whilst it professes not to have sacrificed the right, has actually and avowedly sanctioned the doctrine and practice of England, in seizing provisions at pleasure, as contraband of war; and have likewise yielded the principle, so important to America, that free ships shall make free goods."

In a letter from Mr. Pickering to Mr. Monroe (dated department of State, September 12th, 1795), the writer observes, that "the second clause of the 18th article (of Mr. Jay's treaty) clearly refers to the doctrine asserted by Great-Britain, that provisions *may* become Contraband, when destined to places *not* invested or blockaded. To this pretension (says Mr. Pickering....or rather the American administration), which is contrary to our interests, and, as we are inclined to believe, unwarranted by the Law of Nations, especially in the extent asserted by Great-Britain,....we could not accede: the opinions of our government on this subject, formerly expressed, and well known to you, being amply detailed in the correspondence of Mr. Jefferson and Mr. Pinckney, in the year 1793. Though we have not been able to induce Great-Britain to relinquish *her* construction, *we have not abandoned ours*." Yet, what says Mr. Pickering, in the same breath,....after acknowledging that the British "pretension" of a right to seize provisions as contraband, though not destined to a blockaded port, could not be acceded to? "The result (says he) has been a stipulation that whenever provisions, and other articles, not generally contraband, shall become such, and for that reason be seized, they shall not be confiscated; but paid for, with a reasonable mer-

As we have already shewn what description of articles of commerce ought to be considered as contraband of war, according to the just principles of the Law of Nations, it is un-

cantile profit, including freight and the expenses incident to the detention."

Such was the kind of reasoning, to which the American government was obliged to have recourse, in order to vindicate Mr. Jay's treaty! It had, in fact, abandoned provisions to the British construction of contraband. We admitted they *might* "be regarded as such"...."according to the existing Law of Nations;" although we contended, ten months afterwards, that the "*pretension*" of the British, in this respect, was "*unwarranted by the Law of Nations.*" The government of the United States still insisted that *right* militated against the British "construction" in this instance, and the accession thereto, by Mr. Jay:....and accordingly, Mr. Randolph had, a little time before Mr. Pickering's letter just quoted, declared, (in a memorial presented to Mr. Hammond, the British minister), that "it was not without regret, that the efforts were unsuccessful, in conforming to the current of modern treaties, the definition of Contraband. But, that the order of the 8th of June, 1793, was thus *repeated* upon the United States by the proposed treaty (Mr. Jay's), was as apparent from the rules of construction; as an acquiescence in that construction was remote from every opinion hitherto formed."....Is it in the least surprizing, after all these inconsistencies, into which the American government was driven by Mr. Jay's treaty,....that their envoys to France, in 1798, should fill up the measure of this inconsistency, by asserting that, among articles admitted to be contraband of war, there might be classed...."even *provisions* in certain junctures, where there are hopes of reducing the enemy by *famine*?"

necessary to repeat what has been said on that point. The envoys themselves have agreed to the exclusion of *provisions*, at least, from the list of contraband, *on principle;* though they contend the contrary, especially with respect to ship-timber and naval stores, on the authority of one or two authors and particular treaties. They cite the treaty between France and Denmark, concluded in 1742, which places tar, rosin, sails, hemp, cordage, masts, and timber for ship-building, on the list of contraband; and they quote Valin, a commentator on the marine ordinances of France, who says....that, " of right these articles are now contraband, and have been so from the commencement of the present century." Conceiving, as we do, that Valin's assertion has been fully manifested to be unfounded and erroneous, on the ground of " right;" we shall offer a few remarks to prove it contradicted by fact: In doing this, we shall introduce the authority of sundry treaties, wherein neither ship-timber, &c. nor provisions are rated as contraband of war; and in some of which, the latter are expressly excluded from that denomination,....contrary to the doctrine of M. Vattel.

By the fourth article of the treaty between Denmark and the States-General, concluded at Christianople, August 13, 1645, it is declared, that "the transportation of no goods, what name soever they bear, shall be forbid through the Baltic sea"....And, by the thirteenth article of the same treaty, the king of Denmark is bound that he "shall not, without the consent of the possessors, take out of the said ships"... belonging to the subjects of the United Provinces,..."any men, or warlike necessaries, or other things, under any pretence whatsoever.

The second article of the treaty between Sweden and Denmark, concluded on the same day, declares...."that it shall be lawful for the subjects of Sweden to navigate freely, whether in their own or hired ships, through the straits of the Sound and the Belt, and to transport therein, according to their power and pleasure, all sorts of merchandizes and effects, without distinction, exemption or limitation; whether it be, goods bought and purchased in other towns or kingdoms, or whether it be the product of the earth or manufactures: *more especially, all sorts of munitions of war, and every thing that may be useful therein;* and particularly brass or iron guns, great or small fusils, musquets and arms, by what name soever they may be called, without any impediment, detention, inhibition, charge or tax; whether such things be transported from Sweden, Finland, Ingria, Esthonia, Livonia, Pomerania, Mecklenburgh, Lubec, or from the towns of Prussia and Courland, into the lands along the ocean; or whether they be transported from the aforesaid places, through the Baltic-sea, into Sweden and the aforesaid provinces, or directly into Pomerania, Mecklenburgh, Lubeck, the towns of Prussia and Courland, or others."

Mr. Beawes, in his *Lex Mercatoria* (published upwards of fifty years,) cites six treaties, containing this stipulation:....“Ships may freely sail to and trade with all kingdoms, countries and estates, which shall be in peace, amity or neutrality, with the prince whose flag they carry, and who is at present at peace with us, and are not to be molested by us, on account of any hostilities that may at present subsist, or hereafter may happen, between his Britannic majesty and those estates; provided such ships are not bearers of Contraband goods"....“ And to avoid disputes about the understanding of the term of Contraband goods, they are expressly determined to be *only arms, pieces of ordnance with all implements belonging to them, fire-balls, powder, matches, bullets, pikes, swords, lances, spears, halberds, guns, mortar-pieces, petards, bombs, granadoes, fire-crancels, pitched hoops, carriages, musquet-rests, bandoliers, salt-petre, musquets, musquet-shot, helmets, corslets, breast-plates, coats of mail*, and the like kind of *armature, soldiers, horses*, and all things necessary for the *furniture of horses, holsters, belts*, and all other *war-like instruments*, whatsoever."

"*All other goods whatsoever* (continues Mr. Beawes) are, by the aforementioned treaties, permitted *freely* to be carried, *except to places besieged.*"

The following are the treaties, which contain this specification of articles contraband of war; viz.

The treaty of commerce between Great-Britain and Spain; concluded at Madrid, 13th May, 1667.

The treaty of commerce between Great-Britain and the States General....21st July, 1667.

The treaty of commerce between Great-Britain and the States General....7th February, 1667....8.

The treaty between Great-Britain and Denmark....11th July, 1670.

The treaty between Great-Britain and the States General; concluded at London, 1st December, 1674.

The treaty-marine between France and Great-Britain; concluded at St. Germains en Laye,....24th February, 1676....7.

In all these treaties, Great-Britain is a party; and yet in none of them, are either ship-timber, naval stores of any kind, or provisions, made contraband.

But prior to the earliest of these, is the treaty between Great-Britain and the States General, concluded the 1st of December, 1647. This contains, almost precisely, the same list of contraband, as before specified.

The treaty between Great-Britain and Spain, of a more modern date than any of the above, viz. December 14th, 1715,....confirms that, between the same parties, of the 13th of May, 1667: Consequently, it establishes the same rule of contraband.

The enumeration of contraband articles, in the treaty of amity, commerce and navigation, between Russia and Great-Britain....concluded at St. Petersburgh, December 2, 1734, is still more limited.

The commercial treaty concluded between Russia and Great-Britain, in 1765, (since expired by its own limitation), enumerated, as contraband, military stores, alone; excluding those articles, which serve for building or repairing ships of war.

And a much more recent treaty,....namely, that between France and Great-Britain, concluded at Versailles on the 26th of September, 1786,....declares, that all implements of war, of what kind soever they may be, are alone to be considered as contraband.

Besides all these, the American envoys must have had in contemplation, not only the treaty of Armed Neutrality, of 1780; but the treaty of amity and commerce between the United States and France, dated the 6th of February, 1778, and every subsequent treaty which this country had then concluded; in no one of which, (Mr. Jay's excepted), will either any description of naval stores, or provisions, be found in the list of contraband articles. On the contrary, they might have readily discovered seven treaties, in which it is *expressly* declared that such articles of naval stores and provisions shall *not* be reckoned among prohibited goods. These are....the treaty-marine between England and the States General, of December 1, 1647, (S. V.)....that between France and England, of February 24, 1676...7....the treaty of navigation and commerce between France and Great-Britain, of the 31st of March, (O. S.) 1713....the treaty of amity and commerce between the United States and France, of February 6, 1778....that between the United States and Sweden, of the 3d of April, 1783....the treaty of navigation and commerce between France and Great-Britain, of the 26th of September, 1786....and the treaty of friendship, limits and navigation, between the United States and Spain, of the 20th October, 1795.

The first and second of these, class among free goods, iron, lead, copper, hemp, pitch, ropes, sails and anchors, masts and planks, boards and beams, of what sort of wood soever, and all materials requisite for the building or repairing of ships; also, wheat, barley, and all other kind of corn or pulse, salted and smoaked flesh, salted and dried fish, butter and cheese, &c. "and in general, all provision which serves for the nourishment and sustenance of life."

The other five of those treaties declare, that the same merchandize already enumerated, (among others), shall not be reckoned among prohibited goods. After specifying sundry articles, "proper either for building or repairing ships," these treaties liberally add.... "and all other goods whatever, which have not been worked into the form of any instrument or thing prepared for war, by land or by sea, shall not be reputed contraband; much less such as have been already wrought and made up, for any other use: all which shall be wholly reckoned among free goods." There is the same clause in all of them*, respecting provisions; expressly exempting from the denomination of contraband, all things which serve

* The treaty of navigation and commerce, concluded between England and the States General, 7....17th February, 1667....8, also expressly declares (art. 4.) that provisions shall not be comprehended under the denomination of contraband. But this treaty was not placed among the others, above mentioned; only because it does not in express terms exclude timber for ship-building, &c. as is done by the others; though it leaves them entirely out of the catalogue of contraband.

for the nourishment of mankind and the sustenance of life. Besides these, the treaty of amity and commerce between the United States and the Dutch, of October 8, 1782, comprehends in the list of contraband, only warlike stores and arms, as in the others. All other effects and merchandizes, not therein specified *expressly*, are declared to be free. Provisions, consequently, are exempted from contraband, though not named. "Even all sorts of naval matters (says this treaty), however proper they may be for the construction and equipment of vessels of war, or for the manufacture of one or another sort of machines of war, by land or sea, shall not be judged contraband, neither by the letter; nor, according to any pretended interpretation whatever, ought they, or can they, be comprehended under the notion of effects prohibited or contraband."

With these clear and explicit evidences from fact, before the envoys,....of the construction given to the Law of Nations, with respect to provisions, ship-timber, naval-stores, &c....it is inconceivable how they could think it proper to adduce the treaty concluded between France and Denmark, August 23,

1742; in order to support their assertion, that "timber for ship-building, and naval stores for the equipment of vessels," are admitted to be "contraband of war!" It is true, that treaty did place tar, rosin, sails, hemp, cordage, masts, and timber for ship-building, on the list of contraband: But the envoys must have known, that this treaty was made for fifteen years, only; and therefore, at the time they were treating of its stipulations, it had ceased to be a treaty for more than forty years. Thus they are left with one solitary treaty, as an authority in support of Valin's doctrine respecting contraband, to oppose the various treaties that establish the doctrine, for which we contend. This is the treaty concluded, July 10, 1670, between Great-Britain and Denmark; or, more properly, what is called an explanation of the treaty by a subsequent convention between the parties. The treaty itself describes...."any provisions of war, as soldiers, arms, machines, cannon, ships, or other things of necessary use in war, to be contraband;" and the convention explains this clause, so as to include "timber for ship-building, tar, rosin, copper in sheets, sails, hemp and cordage, and generally whatever serves directly for the equipment of a vessel, unwrought iron and fir-planks excepted."

From the view of the subject then, here taken, it is very evident, that the envoys were not supported, even by facts, in the notion they had formed on the authority of Vattel's *dictum* and Valin's assertion, concerning contraband articles. And Mr. Fauchet is perfectly correct, when he says....“ At this day the modern neutrality ranks as contraband only articles fit to be used *immediately*, for offence or defence*; and those which must be *wrought*, before they can be used in this way, are excluded. Provisions are contraband only in the case of their being carried to a blockaded and besieged place†."

In fact, the United States have, in the latest conventional act of their government, acted with regard to this point, as we have already observed they did, respecting the principle that free ships make free goods.... They have sanctioned, anew, those just prin-

* These are such as are denominated, in treaties, Utensils or implements of war; and are called in French, *Assortissemens servant a l'usage de la guerre.*

† See his pamphlet, published after his return to France from America,....entitled *A Sketch of the present state of our political relations with the United States of North-America.*

ciples of the Law of Nations, maintained by the first treaty with a foreign nation, which they ever concluded*.

* The thirteenth and fourteenth articles of the Convention between the French Republic and the United States....concluded September 30, 1800,....are in these words :....

Article 13....In order to regulate what shall be deemed contraband of war, there shall be comprised under that denomination, gun-powder, saltpetre, petards, match, ball, bombs, grenades, carcasses, pikes, halberts, swords, belts, pistols, holsters, cavalry-saddles and furniture, cannon, mortars, their carriages and beds, and generally all kind of arms, ammunition of war, and instruments fit for the use of troops. All the above articles, whenever they are destined to the port of an enemy, are hereby declared to be contraband, and just objects of confiscation : but the vessel in which they are laden, and the residue of the cargo, shall be considered free, and not in any manner infected by the prohibited goods, whether belonging to the same or a different owner.

Article 14....It is hereby stipulated, that *free ships shall give a freedom to goods ;* and that every thing shall be deemed to be free and exempt, which shall be found on board the ships belonging to the citizens of either of the contracting parties, although the whole lading, or any part thereof, should appertain to the enemies of either; contraband goods being always excepted. It is also agreed, in like manner, that the same liberty be extended to persons who are on board a free ship; with this effect, that although they be enemies of either party, they are not to be taken out of that free ship, unless they are soldiers, and in actual service of the enemy.

SEARCH.

ALMOST all regulations made by states, imposing restrictions on the natural freedom of commerce, tend to destroy its just equilibrium, by the introduction of exclusive privileges and monopolies. Yet, it being admitted that every independent nation has a *right* to regulate its own commercial concerns, in such manner as it may choose; the *policy* and *expediency* of perpetually trammelling trade with impositions, exclusions, and burdens of various kinds, are alone proper objects of discussion. It belongs to *states* to judge of such policy and expediency, in their own cases, respectively: therefore, we shall not attempt to interfere with their exercise of *that right*. The jurisdiction, however, of a nation, in the affairs of its trade, extends only over its own citizens, and foreigners trading within its territories.

But, since war gives to the belligerent nations a right to controul, to a certain extent, the free commerce of neutrals, on the high seas; we shall offer some additional observations, on the just extent of that right.

It has been seen, that the only cases wherein the maritime commerce of neutrals may be interrupted by belligerents, are....1st, where the neutral is carrying, in his ship, *goods contraband of war*, to an enemy-nation; 2d, where the neutral is proceeding, with even a free cargo, into *a port actually blockaded.*

In both these cases, some kind of *examination* is obviously necessary....In the first, for the purpose of ascertaining the contents and quality of the cargo:....and in the second, in order to discover what port was truly the place of the neutral-ship's destination. The privilege of searching neutral vessels, for *these purposes*, is generally exercised by belligerents.

A *search* of any sort in a neutral ship, merely to find *enemy's goods*, is altogether unwarrantable by the Law of Nations: It is contrary to natural justice and the rights of free nations; and, although it is submitted to, under conventional stipulations, by some states, we conceive the grant of such a privilege can never be *legalized.* The *right*, therefore, of *Search*, is confined to the two other cases, only, that are specified.

Such being the *objects* of the Search;.... what ought to be the nature and extent of the *Search itself?*

If this question were to be considered, abstractedly from the practice and authorities, it is conceived, that justice would dictate an answer not strictly corresponding with either. The maritime commerce of nations should be as free as possible from vexatious interruptions and hindrances. It is the duty and policy of every maritime state to take care, that its merchant-ships be provided with fair and regular ship-papers, exhibiting a true and faithful specification of the cargo, its destination, &c....All illicit and irregular trade ought to be discountenanced, and rendered liable to severe penalties. On the other hand, full faith and credit should be given by one nation, to the acts and proceedings of another, duly attested and verified, according to known and established rules of the government. It is certainly derogatory from the dignity of a free and respectable nation, that the official attestations of certain facts and truths, *bona fide* made by the public agents of its government, should be deemed unworthy of credit, by those acting under the authority of another state. The deportment of states towards each other, ought to be fair and honourable....It is presumed to be so, unless their conduct manifest the contrary. Sea-papers, therefore, relating to the shipping and marine trade of a particular country, and verified in due form by officers of the customs, admiralty, or other proper agents of that government, should justly meet with full faith and credit from the public agents of other nations. The exhibition of such documents, by the neutral to the belligerent party, ought to be deemed satisfactory. An *examination of this kind*, would answer all the *honest* purposes of a search; without injuring the party examined, or dishonoring his nation. But, as the mode of Search is now conducted,....honor, good faith, and common honesty, seem to be little regarded: nor will it be otherwise, until a spirit of magnanimous justice shall induce nations to abolish the infamous business of *privateering*. M. de Vattel observes, that "without *searching* neutral ships, the commerce of contraband goods cannot be prevented;" and, from this necessity, he infers the *right* of searching. The necessity of *examining* neutral ships, is readily admitted: and, if the examination be so made, as not to detain or otherwise injure the neutral property, and not reflect any indignity on the neutral nation; we shall *so far* acknowledge the right of searching.

It is by no means to be wondered at, that, as Vattel remarks, some powerful nations have, at different times, refused to submit to this search. Grotius tells us, that "after the peace of Vervins, queen Elizabeth continuing the war with Spain, desired the king of France to *allow* that all French ships on their voyage to Spain might be *searched*, in order to discover whether they did not secretly carry military stores: but this was *refused* as an *injury to trade*, and *a favorable occasion to pillage**."

* If it had been understood, two centuries ago, that an *actual search* of the neutral ships was warranted, by the Law of Nations, as a *right*,....is it to be presumed that so powerful and haughty a princess, as Elizabeth, would have asked *permission* of the king of France, *to exercise that right?* Undoubtedly, it is not. The permission desired, implied the demand of a *favor;* excluding, altogether, the idea of a right. The reason assigned by the king of France, for refusing to comply with Elizabeth's request, was a just and proper one; and the queen's acquies-

"At present (resumes Vattel) a neutral ship refusing to be searched, would, from that proceeding alone, be condemned as lawful prize. But to avoid inconveniencies, violence, and every other irregularity, the *manner* of the search is settled in the treaties of navigation and commerce. *According to the present custom, credit is to be given to certificates and bills of lading, produced by the master of the ship; unless any fraud appear in them, or there be very good reason for suspecting their validity.*"....This was the mode of searching, or rather of examining friendly ships, under many ancient treaties. Thus, the third article of the treaty between Denmark and the States General, August 13, 1645, directs....that "the *searching* of the ships and goods belonging to the inhabitants of the United Provinces, and passing through the *Baltic* sea, shall *cease;* and entire credit shall be given to the mariners that produce their *Cockets*, &c. who thereupon, paying the toll, shall be dismissed without molestation," &c.

sence in the refusal, strongly corroborates the presumption, that she herself believed she had asked an *indulgence*,....and not the consent of the French monarch to exercise a right.

The 5th article of the treaty between England and the States General, 7th....17th February, 1667....8, is in these words...." It hath been agreed, for the execution of what is above said, that the ships and barques of the English, laden with merchandize, being entered into any port of the said States General, and purposing to pass from thence into the ports of their enemies, shall be only obliged to shew unto the officers of the port of the said States, out of which they would go, their *passports*, containing the specification of the lading of their ships, attested and marked with the ordinary seal of the officers of the admiralty of those places from whence they first came, with the place whither they are bound, all in usual and accustomed form: After which shewing of their passports in the form aforesaid, they may not be disquieted nor *searched*, detained nor retarded in their voyages, upon any pretence whatsoever." The provisions of this article are made reciprocal by the one that follows it.

The treaty between France and Great-Britain, 24th February, 1676....7, in art. 5, 6, and 7....is full, on this head. The *passport* or *sea-brief* of either party is required to be shewn, in the ports of the other, or at sea, in ordinary cases: but if either of them be met at sea, *making way into any port in enmity with the other*,....such one, "shall shew not only a *passport* (or *sea-brief*,)" &c...." but also her *cocquets*, expressing the contents of the goods on board, given in the usual form by the officers of the customs, in the port from whence she came; whereby it may be known, whether she is laden with any merchandizes prohibited by the third article of this treaty," &c.

The 21st article of the treaty concluded at Utrecht, between France and Great-Britain, the 31st of March, (O. S.) 1713, directs, that in case either of the contracting parties should be engaged in war, the ships of the other party must be furnished with *sea-letters or passports*, &c. and likewise with *certificates*, containing the several particulars of the cargo, the place from whence the ship sailed, and whither she is bound; so that it may be known whether any forbidden or *contraband* goods, as are enumerated in the treaty, be on board the ship. All the stipulations of this celebrated treaty, respecting contraband goods, are extremely liberal:....Those respecting the examination, or kind of search, that is prescribed, are so entirely conformable to our ideas of what is right and proper, on this subject; that we wish the reader to recur to the 21st, 22d, 23d, 24th, 25th, and 26th articles of the treaty, which contain the stipulations concerning the kind of proceedings to be substituted in place of an actual *Search*. We shall content ourselves with mentioning, in this place, that the master of a merchant-ship of one of the parties, that should be met by an armed vessel of the other, was to *exhibit his passport*, or *certificate*, which was to entitle the party shewing it, to free passage; and, on *this* being done by the vessel so stopped, it was declared to be " wholly unlawful any way to molest her, *search*, or compel her to quit her intended course."

The same just and liberal conduct that is stipulated, in this particular, by the treaty of Utrecht, is prescribed by almost all those of more modern date. The 27th article of the treaty of amity and commerce, of February 6, 1778, between the United States and France, directs, that the ship of either of the contracting parties, when she shall have exhibited her *passport*, " shall be free and at liberty to pursue her voyage, so as it shall not be lawful to molest or *search* her in any manner, or to give her chace, or force her to quit her intended course."

The treaties, also, concluded between the United States and France, Holland, Sweden, Prussia, Spain, Morocco, Algiers, Tripoli, and Tunis,...*all* prohibit an *actual* search; conforming to the principles adopted, in this respect, by the two above mentioned. Indeed, some of these treaties go still farther....That with Sweden, declares....that "the exhibition of *papers* shall not be demanded of merchant-ships *under the convoy of vessels of war;* but credit shall be given to *the word of the officer commanding the convoy*."....By the treaty with Prussia, it is declared....that, "if the (said) vessel be *under convoy of one or more vessels of war*, belonging to the neutral party, *the simple declaration of the officer commanding the convoy*, that the said vessel belongs to the party of which he is, shall be considered as *establishing the fact*, and shall relieve both parties from the trouble of farther examination."....The treaty with Morocco directs.... that "a signal or pass shall be given to all vessels belonging to both parties, by which they are to be known when they meet at sea;

and if *the commander of a ship of war* of either party shall have other ships under his convoy, *the declaration of the commander* shall alone be sufficient to exempt any of them from examination."....A comparison of the passports (commonly called Mediterranean passes), between American and Algerine vessels, precludes all *search*, or farther examination of any kind,.... under one treaty with Algiers:....and the third article stipulates, that "the vessels of both nations shall pass each other without any impediment or molestation; and all goods, monies or passengers, of whatsoever nation, that may be on board of the vessels belonging to either party, shall be considered as inviolable, and shall be allowed to pass unmolested."....The recent convention between the United States and the French Republic, corresponds, respecting the exemption from search, with all the other maritime treaties entered into by the United States,...*Mr. Jay's excepted:* And, by the 18th article of the convention, "it is expressly agreed, that the neutral party shall, in no case, be required to go on board the examining vessel, for the purpose of exhibiting his papers, or for any other examination whatever." In fact, Great-Britain herself, by her commercial treaty with France in 1786, gave up all pretensions of a right to *search* French vessels; having adopted, in that treaty, just and liberal principles respecting the rights of neutrals.

The evident result of an investigation of this subject, is, that the manner of searching neutral vessels at sea, as practised by Great-Britain under the pretence of its conformity to the Law of Nations, is an odious usurpation of power, wholly unwarranted by the true principles of that Law; an outrageous violation of the rights of neutrals; a gross and humiliating indignity offered to the nation, whose flag is thus insulted and whose citizens are thus injured and abused*. It has been shewn,

* We have already noticed, that the English courts of Admiralty appear not to guide their decisions, in cases of maritime captures, by any uniform, steady, or permanent principles:.... That, in fact, the judges of those courts have been commanded by the crown to conform their decisions, in such cases, to the royal instructions, issued from time to time to the commanders of British armed ships of war....Those decisions have, therefore, been various and contradictory.

Sir William Scott, the present judge of the English Admiralty, has laboured to establish the right of Search, upon principles corresponding with the recent practice of the British ships of war. Yet we find, that in the year 1785, three of the judges of the court of king's bench, in England, (justices Willes, Ashurst, and Buller, Lord Mansfield being absent), delivered

that the freedom of navigation and maritime commerce, between independent nations, is

it as their opinion, "*that a neutral ship is not obliged to stop to be searched;*"....and, "*that the searcher stops a neutral ship at his peril.*" [See the case of Saloucci v. Johnson, in Park's law of Marine Insurances, p. 79, 80, 364, 365.] This was in an action brought upon a policy of insurance on the ship Thetis, a Tuscan ship, warranted neutral, and bound to London. This ship had refused to be searched; and resisted by force, having fired at the Spanish ship, by which she was, in the event, taken; ....and this resistance was one of the grounds of her condemnation. On argument, the three judges, already mentioned, gave their opinions on the case, severally. Willes said...." If a ship be neutral, and she be stopped, those who stop her must pay for the detention. But if it is said, she *must* stop to be searched;...I find no authority for such a position."....Ashurst said,...." I do not find, that a neutral ship must submit to be searched. It is rather an act of superior *force*, always resisted when the party is able; and the right falls within this position, that he does it at his peril."....Buller said,...." The answer given to the claim of Search is conclusive, that the party does it at his peril; just like the case of Custom-house officers. The practice of the Admiralty confirms it; for they give costs, in cases of improper detention: which they would not do, if neutral ships were, at all events, liable to be stopt."

It is true that afterwards, in the case of Garrells v. Kensington, in B. R. [see 8 Term R. 230, and Park's M. I. 365.] the court said, that, though they did not mean to overturn the case of Saloucci v. Johnson, the general point there mentioned.... that a neutral ship need not submit to be searched,....could not be supported:...." for (say they) it is laid down in *Vattel* (book iii. chap. vii. sect. 114), that this right clearly exists, without which the commerce of contraband goods could not be prevented."....Let it, however, be remembered, that the case of

lawfully subjected, in time of war, to very slight restrictions. Those respecting *contraband*, have been fully pointed out: and, with reference to *search*, the right extends no farther, according to the legitimate principles of

Saloucci v. Johnson was decided in 1785,....in time of peace, and but five years after the treaty of Armed Neutrality;.... whereas the other case was determined in the year 1799,.... whilst the French revolutionary war was raging throughout Europe, and at a period when all the maritime rights of neutrals were most shamefully violated. The English Admiralty court had adopted, in this latter period, a set of principles, suited to the unjust policy on which Great-Britain conducted her maritime war, so far as it respected neutrals: It was therefore to be expected, that the judges of their Common Law Courts would conform their opinions to the new doctrines maintained in the Admiralty. Yet it is ludicrous to find the Court of King's Bench gravely quoting Vattel, in 1799,....for the purpose of overturning a principle maintained by the same court, in 1785; as if Vattel's authority (such as it is, in this case), were not of equal validity at both periods. We contend, however, that the opinions of the judges quoted, in 1785, were right; and we trust it has been shewn, that M. Vattel's *dictum*, as to the point in question, is unsupported by the true principles of the Law of Nations.

It is worthy of remark, that, in the case of Garrells and Kensington, the following language is made use of:....“ That, as to the question concerning the right of searching neutrals, is was *said* by the Court, that *before the late Armed Neutrality*, it was *considered* in *this* country, and *so decided in many cases*, that the right of searching neutrals was part of the *Law of Nations*, and that such right was *supposed* to be founded on *Reason*.”....Such are the decisions on such a subject!

natural justice (even under the *existing practice* of war, which tolerates privateering), than that recognized in the treaty between the United States and Sweden. Indeed this treaty, and that with Prussia, concluded in 1785, for ten years, are infinitely more consonant with humanity and sound policy, as well as the essential rights of independent nations, than any other, ancient or modern. The latter exempted from confiscation, even articles contraband of war; and its twenty-third article declared, that if war should arise between the two contracting parties, "all *merchant* and *trading vessels*, employed in exchanging the products of different places, and thereby rendering the necessaries, conveniencies and comforts of life more easy to be obtained, and more general, shall pass free and unmolested; and neither of the contracting powers shall grant or issue any commission to any *private* armed vessels, empowering them to take or destroy any *trading* vessels, or interrupt *such commerce*." The whole of this article contains stipulations equally just, humane, and liberal; and there are various provisions in both of these treaties, in the same spirit, reflecting the highest honour on the contracting parties.

They are worthy of the venerable and philanthropic statesman and philosopher, by whom, solely, the former was projected, and the latter, in concert with his colleague* at the court of France: Nor can it fail to give the highest satisfaction to every true American, that their present chief magistrate justly shares in the renown, which the illustrious name of Franklin acquired, in addition to his previously well-earned fame, in being the first to interdict, by a national pact with a great and powerful state, the plundering of unoffending merchant-ships, by *public* ships of war, and the barbarous dishonesty of *privateering* against them....It is

* The Swedish treaty (which is permanent) was concluded at Paris, April 3, 1783, between Dr. Franklin, on the part of the United States, and the count de Creutz in behalf of Sweden.

The Prussian treaty was concluded between Dr. Franklin, Mr. Jefferson, and Mr. J. Adams, plenipotentiaries on the part of the United States, and the baron de Thulemeier, plenipotentiary for the king of Prussia. It was signed and sealed by these ministers, at the places of their respective residence, and at the dates expressed under their several signatures. Dr. Franklin signed at Passy, July 9, 1785....Mr. Jefferson, at Paris, July 28....Mr. Adams, at London, August 5....and M. de Thulemeier, at the Hague, September 10....all in the same year. The power of *renewing* this treaty with Prussia, on the *same principles*, devolved on Mr. Adams's son, J. Q. Adams, the late American minister at Berlin:...this, however, *was not done*.

greatly to be regretted, that a similar treaty to the extinct one, has not been renewed with Prussia. There is, however, ample reason for hoping, that, under the present administration of the United States....and impressed as all maritime powers, with a single exception, now are, of the necessity of establishing effectually the freedom of navigation and commerce,....this may yet be readily accomplished.

The assumed right of *searching* (in the strict sense of the word) Neutral Vessels, is carried to very extraordinary lengths by the British ships of war; the government of Great-Britain professing to pay no respect to neutral vessels sailing under convoy of public armed ships of the neutral nation. Of this, the case of admiral count Beyland's ship and convoy, in the American war, and of a Swedish frigate and her convoy in the one just concluded, are memorable examples.

But a recent instance has occurred, in which the rights of the United States, as a neutral nation, were grossly violated....and the dignity of their government outraged, in the most indecent manner,....by public ships of war belonging to Great-Britain. This was in the case of captain Phillips, commander of the Baltimore sloop of war, belonging to the United States. The Baltimore was convoying a fleet of American merchantmen, bound to the Havanna; when, on November 16, 1798....being then in sight of the Moro Castle, he fell in with a British squadron, under the orders of commodore Loring. This commander sent an officer on board the Baltimore, who carried away fifty-five of her men to the commodore's ship, the Carnatic of seventy-four guns. Captain Phillips had previously resisted the *demand* to give up any of his men....They were therefore *forcibly* taken from his ship, by captain Loring; who had under his command, at the time, three ships of the line and two frigates. The British commander, not content with the perpetration of this offence against the Law of Nations, proceeded to conduct still more aggravating: his squadron captured three merchant-vessels, belonging to captain Phillip's convoy, which were cut off from their entrance into port, and were all made prizes, within gun-shot of the Moro.

The American government manifested some sensation of the insult and injury, sustained on that occasion. Orders were issued from the Navy-Department, December 29, 1798, to the commanders of armed vessels in the service of the United States; by which they were commanded, that on no pretence whatever, they should permit the *public* vessels of war under their respective commands to be *detained or searched*,....nor any of the *officers* or *men* belonging to *them*, to be taken from them, by the ships or vessels of any foreign nation,....so long as they should be in a capacity to repel such outrage on the honor of the American flag*. On the second of January, following, a resolution passed the House of Representatives, in these words:.... "Resolved, That the President of the United States be requested to cause to be laid before this House, such information as may have been received, relative to the impressment of

* The remainder of this circular is in these words...."If force should be exerted to compel your submission, you are to resist that force to the utmost of your power; and, when overpowered by superior force, you are to strike your flag, and thus yield your vessel as well as your men; but never your men without your vessel. You will remember however, and it is strictly enjoined by the President, that your demeanor be respectful and friendly to the vessels and people of all nations in amity with the United States; and that you avoid, as carefully, the commission of, as the submission to, insults or injuries."

any seamen belonging to the United States' sloop of war, Baltimore, or any other *public* armed vessel of the United States, into any ship or vessel belonging to the king of Great-Britain."

It is, however, worthy of notice, that the *detaining* or *searching public* ships of war belonging to the United States....and the taking *officers* or *men* from *that* description of vessels, *only*,....seem to have constituted the offence on the part of the British; in the opinion of the then administration. There is not the most distant allusion, either in the resolution of the House of Representatives, or in the orders from the Navy-Department,....to the *capture* of the *merchant-vessels*, which were under the *protection* of the Baltimore: nor do the *orders* seem to contemplate any criminality, in the ships of war of a foreign power, detaining or searching, either *private* ships of *war* or *merchant-vessels*, belonging to American citizens, as neutrals....The *resolution* has relation to no other part of the transaction, than the *impressment of seamen* belonging to the Baltimore, or any other *public* armed vessel of the United States. Thus, by the most obvious implication, *trading* vessels belonging to citizens of the United States were abandoned to *search*, *detention*, and *capture*,....under *British* constructions of public law, founded in error and injustice; and some of which, the administration of this country had, themselves, admitted to be not only "contrary to our interests", but "*unwarranted by the Law of Nations**.

There is no case, we conceive, that more strongly evinces the necessity of the practice of *searching* being established on its just and proper foundation, and the exercise of the power restricted within it's legitimate bounds,....than the one just recited. Nor could any case occur, which would shew, in a more striking manner, the culpable neglect of *duty*, with which Mr. Jay is chargeable,....in not introducing into his treaty, some provision for effectually securing American seamen from British impressment, capture, or detention.

* See note, page 220.

A DISSERTATION

ON THE

FREEDOM OF NAVIGATION

AND

MARITIME COMMERCE.

SECTION V.

CONTAINING MISCELLANEOUS OBSERVATIONS AND REFLECTIONS, ARISING OUT OF THE MAIN SUBJECT; TOGETHER WITH THE GENERAL RESULT.

THE miseries inflicted on the human race, by war, have been too fatally experienced by all nations, at one period or another, to render any particular recital of them necessary; and yet, whilst man prides himself on being a rational creature, this scourge of the species continues to curse mankind; even in an age which may, in many respects, be justly styled an enlightened one.

That rude and barbarous nations should be actuated by the impulse of the animal passions, and those ferocious propensities which man possesses in common with the brute creation, to commit hostilities on their fellow-men, is much less a matter of astonishment than regret: for, the powers of the human mind, if destitute of cultivation, do not very greatly transcend the instinctive sagacity of many other animals. At the same time, man's natural reason, unimproved by the refinements of civilized society, and unaided by the precepts of a pure religion and its conforming morality, is placed so far above the instinctive faculty of the brute creation, as to render it, when under the dominion of the animal passions, infinitely more mischievous. It is the *right direction* of reason, which alone gives the intellectual faculties of man a just claim to superiority over the instinct of other animals. The latter can scarcely deviate from its true course, because it is directed by the more uniform laws of *mere* animal nature: But that rational freedom of the will, which is an essential and peculiar attribute of the human mind, does, by its very constitution, render the faculty of reason liable to error, in its operations; when either the animal impulses of our nature, are permitted to gain an ascendancy over that faculty,....or, when it is subjected to the controul of false conceptions.

The principles of moral right and wrong exist, absolutely and invariably, in the nature of things: They are founded in the constitution of the moral world. The practice and observance of the former, constitute virtue; and the latter, vice. Man's true happiness can, by no possibility, comport with vicious inclinations and pursuits; nor can misery, in his condition, be ever occasioned by the practice of virtue.

Whence then, it may be asked, proceeds that variegated mass of vice and wretchedness, that pervades the world?....If virtue leads to happiness, why are men vicious; and if vice be the parent of evil, even to the vicious man himself, why does not reason teach him to shun it?....And further, what good cause can be assigned, why an enlightened age is not also a virtuous one? The answers to these questions result in a simple proposition, founded on an evident truth;....that the generality of mankind form false estimates of the constituents of human happiness. *This* is the source to which we may justly trace a great portion of the evils, with which man finds himself surrounded, in the progress of human life.

The contemplation of this truth leads us, therefore, fairly to conclude, that, notwithstanding the boasted wisdom of the age in which we live, the great science of *Morality* is not only partially, but imperfectly, understood. This is undoubtedly the truth. If it were otherwise, we should perceive a declension of vice and a melioration of the condition of mankind; keeping pace with the rapid progression of every branch of natural science, and proportionate improvement of all the arts, that subserve as well to the ornamental as the useful purposes of life. But this, it is to be lamented, is not the fact. For although it is certain, that, in many respects, we are wiser than our ancestors....and, in some, even better; there are others, in which we have, most assuredly, retrograded.

The vast accession that has been made by the moderns, to the variety and utility of all the fabrics of art,....and the great extension of commerce among the nations of the earth, which the augmented objects of their intercourse serve to promote,....seem admirably suited to encrease the comforts of human life, and to cement by ties of mutual benefits the great brotherhood of mankind. If such were, in reality, the effects produced by the commercial operations of great and distinct communities of men, with each other, respectively; the philanthropist would then have cause to rejoice. In such case, foreign commerce would prove to be,....what by its nature it is capable of being made,....a blessing to the world. When, on the contrary, means so well adapted to promote the welfare of our species, are preverted, by folly and infatuation, to purposes tending to the oppression of nations and the annoyance of mankind; then, indeed, is there sufficient reason to deplore the true cause of so great an evil. This, however, is not to be traced to the nature of commerce itself; but to the inordinate thirst of gain, which states, whose principal pursuits are trade and manufactures, encourage in those who negociate them.

An extensive and (as it is called) flourishing foreign trade, yields wealth to individuals and power to states. The acquisition of both, if kept within reasonable limits, is equally useful and desirable. If the commerce of nations were left free to pursue its natural course, it would not, probably, exceed those limits. A liberal interchange of the various productions of nature and of art, among different climes and people, would be the fruits of such a traffic. It would be the means of disseminating throughout the various regions of the earth, those things that contribute to the substantial comforts of mankind. But the false and mischievous policy that has been adopted, in different degrees, by all commercial states,....subjecting commerce to an infinite variety of such artificial regulations, as are rendered subservient to the production of enormous wealth, by the sacrifice of private rights, public honor, and the legitimate interests of nations,....has destroyed the just equilibrium of trade. The few are aggrandized at the expense of the many. And, an augmentation of the financial resources of trading nations being a principal end proposed by their respective governments, in all their commercial regulations,....the power thus acquired by the more potent states, furnishes an apt engine for the oppression of the weaker. Unnatural restrictions on the mutual commerce of nations, necessarily produce an unnatural kind of competition among them. Thus arise misunderstandings, animosities and strife; and power, impelled by avarice, rarely wants specious pretexts for exercising acts of injustice. Hence, we trace a prolific source of those numerous naval wars, that have so long spread desolation through the world: and in this way, have misery and oppression become, too generally, substitutes to those blessings, which a just and liberal conduct in the commercial intercourse of nations, would naturally promote.

The evils arising from this state of things, are manifold. Independently of those flowing, directly, from foreign wars; others, more immediately of a domestic nature, are the inevitable consequences. Luxury among the people, and misrule in the government of the state, naturally follow the accumulation of vast wealth in the hands of the few:*....ambi-

* "In nátions enriched by commerce, and among families loaded with opulence by the avarice of their forefathers, the mere wantonness of unbounded plenty will occasion a corruption of manners, dangerous to all that renders society happy; but favorable to the despotic principle. Pleasure of the meanest kind will be the first and the last pursuit. Splendor, external show, the ostentation of riches, will be deemed objects

tion rears its head; oppression ensues; a general depravity of morals pervades the community; and the bonds of humanity are loosened. Hypocrisy is substituted for religion, which, thus modified, is made an engine of state. Even the manly and generous principles of true honor are utterly discarded; and, in their place, succeed the base and insidious circumventions of cunning and intrigue. The nation is, at length, divisible into two classes of men,....the oppressors and the oppressed.... And, when it has sunk to this condition of debasement, it is not difficult to foresee, that, eventually, either an entire depression of the people and an extinguishment of all their civil rights, or an utter subversion of despotic rule, must, by a convulsive struggle, terminate the scene. This catastrophe may be long prevented, by fraud and power: but it will not be the less certain, how long soever the ultimate

of prime consequence. *A Court* will be the place of exhibition; not of great merits, but of fine garments, graceful attitudes, and gaudy equipages,.....every frivolous distinction, which boldly claims the notice due to virtue, and assumes the dignity which public services ought solely to appropriate."....See a little work, entitled, *The Spirit of Despotism*....printed in London, in 1795, and re-printed in Philadelphia, the same year.

issue of national vice, rapine, and injustice, may be protracted.

Gloomy as this picture is, we may readily turn our eyes to portions of the old world, that exhibit a prospect, to which, even at present, it bears a striking resemblance. It was in the contemplation of such a scene as we have described; as one which might by possibility be realised in our own country; that the late Dr. Rittenhouse was led into the following reflections*...." That Being, (says the philanthropic astronomer) before whose piercing eye, all the intricate foldings and dark recesses of the human heart become expanded and illuminated, is my witness, with what sincerity, I wish for the happiness of the whole race of mankind: how much I admire that disposition of lands and seas, which affords a communication between distant regions, and a mutual exchange of benefits: how sincerely I approve of those social refinements, which *really* add to our happiness:....how I delight in a participation of the discoveries made from time to time, in nature's works, by our philosophic brethren in Europe. But when I consider that *luxury*

* See his oration delivered before the American Philosophical Society, at Philadelphia, on the 24th of February, 1775.

....and her constant follower, *tyranny*....who have long since laid in the dust, never to rise again, the glories of Asia,....are now advancing, like a torrent irresistible, whose weight no human force can stem, and have nearly completed their conquest of Europe; luxury and tyranny, who, by a vile affectation of virtues they know not, pretend at first to be the patrons of science and philosophy, but at length fail not effectually to destroy them,.... agitated, I say, by these reflexions, I am ready to wish....vain wish! that nature would raise her everlasting bars between the new and old world, and make a voyage to Europe as impracticable, as one to the moon. I confess, indeed, that by our connections with Europe, we have made most surprizing, I had almost said unnatural, advances towards the meridian of glory: but by those connections too, in all probability, our fall will be premature. May the God of knowledge inspire us with wisdom to prevent it: Let our harbours, our doors, our hearts, be shut against *luxury*."

We have cause, however, to be thankful, that the evils, which the benevolent Rittenhouse so feelingly deprecated, are not likely ever to assail our country, in so alarming a degree. Our vast extent of a fruitful territory, under various climes, abounds with all things necessary for the use of man; and furnishes many besides, which the refinements of social life and polished manners seem to render indispensible. We are more naturally independent of foreign nations, for the necessaries and comforts of our being, than the inhabitants of any other region of the globe: and the topical position, as well as physical strength, of our country, give us a pre-eminent degree of security, against any hostile attempts, that the injustice, jealousy, or mad ambition of other nations, might make, upon our territory and internal repose. The culture of the soil, and such pursuits of agriculture as are connected with its peculiar products, in the different climates of the United States, will for ages be the predominant occupation of our citizens. The population of our sea-ports, and other considerable towns, will ever bear a singularly small proportion to our numbers of a plain, frugal, and industrious people, spread over a territory of great extent. The habits and pursuits of the latter are alike favorable to virtue, and unpropitious to the introduction of luxury. And, in addition to these national advantages, resulting from the physical condition of this great Republic, it enjoys a constitution of civil polity, both in relation to its federate and state governments, eminently suited to promote the general welfare.

But, although the United States may be justly considered as an agricultural nation, foreign commerce must nevertheless constitute an important branch of their trade. The surplus of their native productions, together with some articles of wrought materials, will be exchanged with transmarine countries, for such of their respective manufactures, and other commodities, as the consumption of the United States may require; and a great proportion of this trade will be subservient to the agricultural and landed interests of the country. The general interests of the nation demand that its trade with foreign nations, be carried on in its own shipping; and this, it will be the policy of the government to encourage, by peculiar privileges. This marine trade will, however, require, that the protection of the government be extended to our maritime *rights*, under the Law of Nations.

In this way, then, we recur to that state of things, which inevitably subjects us to the injurious and unlawful controul of those states, who are in the practice of violating the maritime rights of others. It is therefore necessary that we *understand* those rights, in order that we may know how far it is our duty to *defend* them.

Believing, as we do, that the real and permanent welfare of all nations can only be promoted by a strict adherence to justice and good faith*, in their transactions with each other; and confident as we are in our opinion, that this position is supported by the principles of eternal truth; we are naturally led to examine into the cause of the enormous deviations from those principles, that are manifested in the conduct of enlightened nations.

Writers on the science of morals maintain those fundamental principles of natural equity,

* "Observe good faith and justice towards all nations; cultivate peace and harmony with all: religion and morality enjoin this conduct;....and can it be, that good policy does not equally enjoin it?....It will be worthy of a free, enlightened, and at no distant period, a great nation, to give mankind the magnanimous and too novel example of a people always guided by an exalted justice and benevolence."....President Washington's address to the people of the United States,....September 17, 1796.

which oppugn the conduct and practice in many instances, of statesmen who rule in those very countries, to which such writers belong. How then is this to be accounted for, on rational grounds? We conceive that the solution of the problem will result in this simple point....*the general decay of morality;* occasioned principally, as we have before observed, by the little attention that is paid to the just and proper cultivation of this highly important science*. It is not because the principles of this science are uncertain or obscure, that they are so little understood. They are so far from being uncertain, that they have their foundation in the unerring laws of nature; and so far from being obscure, that they are capable of demonstration. But M. Barbey-

* "'Tis substantially true, that virtue, or morality, is a necessary spring of popular government. The rule indeed extends, with more or less force, to every species of free government. Who, that is a sincere friend to it, can look with indifference upon attempts to shake the foundation of the fabric?"....President Washington's address, of the 17th, September 1796, to the people of the United States....The President appears to have been justly sensible of the connection, which necessarily subsists between true religion and morals,.... when, in the same address, he says;....."Of all the dispositions and habits which lead to political prosperity, religion and morality are indispensible supports."

rac* has assigned a good reason for those imputations that have been cast on the science of morality....“ There has even been (says he) an uninterrupted succession of men, who, seduced by a secret desire to shake off the troublesome yoke of duty, and to indulge themselves securely in the gratification, if not of their sensual and gross desires, yet, at least, of their more delicate and refined inclinations, have employed all the faculties of their souls, to destroy the evidence of the clearest and most acknowledged truths, in order to involve in their ruin all certainty of the rules of virtue.” And again, speaking of this perplexity, in which some pretend moral science is involved, he observes, “ that the frequent causes of this perplexity, is *interest;* which, joined with the *prejudices of education* or *custom,* obscure the clearest dictates of right reason: Of this (continues M. Barbeyrac) we every day see numberless instances. The greatest part of mankind are so much blinded with an excessive and mistaken self-love, that all their penetration, and integrity of mind, entirely forsake them, as soon as ever any one

* In his Historical and Critical account of the science of Morality, sect. 3.

matter comes in debate, the decision whereof is attended with *loss* or *gain.* And yet they shall easily determine, and that without any hesitation, many other things, a thousand times more difficult, when they examine them cooly, and with a mind wholly *disinterested.*"

In fact, the only perplexity that has ever attached itself to the science of morals, is that which has been introduced into it by the *false construction and application of its principles*, in books written on the subject; some palpable instances of which, we have exposed, in the preceding sections: and this, M. Barbeyrac has judiciously noticed, in these words.... "You will meet with several authors, who influenced either openly or secretly by party-principles, have made it their sole aim, while they were composing treatises on certain questions in morality or politics, to endeavour to find out, *not what was most conformable to the invariable rules of good sense and equity*, but whatever seemed most proper to justify their favourite opinion; or the pretensions and maxims of the sovereign under whose dominion they lived."

Had the science of morality been cultivated by ecclesiastics, (to whom it so properly belongs both to cultivate and enforce its precepts,*) with half the attention they have paid to the discussion of those controversial points, that have agitated the various sects of Christians, without their having any necessary connection with the essential doctrines of Christianity,....there would have been no pretext, at the present day, for ascribing to that science, doubts and perplexities. M. Barbeyrac† observes, that the light of the Reformation restored among protestants, in a great measure, purity both of doctrine and practice; but yet, that it cannot be truly said, that even the reformers themselves, and their successors, have always exactly pursued the true spirit of Christianity. He notices the horrible maxims of intolerance and persecution, on account of religion, maintained by some eminent ecclesiastics, who appear to have been, in other respects, pious and good men;....and also the disposition shewn by others, for reviving the

* M. *Barbeyrac* quotes the following just remark, on this subject, from the preface of M. and Madame *Dacier*, to the moral reflections of *Marcus Antoninus*....It is certain, that *morality* is the daughter of *religion;* that they go hand in hand, together; and that the perfection of the latter, is the standard of perfection in the former.

† Historical and Critical Account of Morality, sect. 11.

maxim of St. Austin, that such as believe not in the Christian revelation, cannot be looked upon as lawful possessors of the goods of this world. Many of the clergy have not only neglected a due cultivation of moral science, themselves; but among them are found opposers of some of the most celebrated lay-authors, who have treated on that subject. Grotius's work, on the *Right of War and Peace*, no sooner appeared in the world, as Mr. Barbeyrac observes, than " the ecclesiastics, instead of returning thanks to the author for it, every where declared against him: and his book was not only put into the expurgatory index of the Roman Catholic inquisitors; but many, even Protestant divines, laboured to cry it down. And thus it fared, too, with M. Pufendorf's book, of *The Law of Nature and Nations*. The Jesuits of Vienna caused it to be prohibited; and many Protestant divines, both of Sweden and Germany, did their best, to make this excellent work share, every where, the same fate."....But this strange and infatuated spirit of hostility to the inculcation of morality, which has appeared among some of the ministers of the Christian religion*,

* We have not the remotest design to apply these observations to the clergy, indiscriminately :....such an extensive cen-

seems also to have actuated the ancient Jewish priesthood. "Amongst the Jews (continues

sure would be alike unmerited and unjust. The *calling* with which that order of men is invested, is of the most honorable nature; and a very great portion of its members approve themselves worthy the character of Christian ministers, by the exemplary purity of their lives, and by inculcating the divine precepts of their Master. Those precepts are derived from the fountain of eternal truth; and having the same common origin with the genuine principles of Morality, it follows, that true Religion and Morals are inseparable. A serene and placid piety, manifesting itself in works of justice, charity, humility, and good will towards all men, are the genuine characteristics of the spirit of Christianity. These dispositions are amiable in men of any description:....And when the clergy....to many of whom the republic of letters are under great obligations,.... unite to these qualities of the heart, the embellishments of literature and useful science; they then become truly estimable, and reflect the highest honor on their order.

But when we discover among them, men cloathed with the dignified character of a Christian preacher, forsaking the meek and benevolent spirit of Christianity;....when we behold such men, with an intolerant zeal, pursuing theological controversies on unessential points of doctrine, and supporting their own interpretation of mysteries, which will remain forever inexplicable,....throwing out of view the practice of good works;.... when we find them sophisticating truth, to answer temporal purposes;....when we see them grasping, with avidity, at wealth and worldly influence; and, impelled by unworthy prejudices, propagating unhallowed principles of disunion and uncharitableness:.....we repeat it,.....when *such* men are discovered among the professors of Christianity, *they* justly merit censure. It is to such *prostitutions of the clerical character*....and not to the priesthood itself, nor to any particular sect of Christians,....

M. Barbeyrac*), it does not appear that the priests applied themselves to this science: And from the time that prophecy ceased among that chosen people of God; that is to say, after their return from the Babylonish captivity; the doctors and public interpreters of the Law began insensibly to corrupt morality;....so far were they from explaining the true principles thereof, and deducing from them, their natural consequences; as they might easily have done, with the help and assistance of that revelation of which they were the depositaries. But being entirely taken up with the civil and ceremonial law; and besides, filled with carnal prejudices, and scrupulously attached to the letter of the law, they either did not at all penetrate into, or else did entirely destroy, the sense of the Legislator. They, under pretence

that our observations are meant to be applied. Conduct of *that* description brings a reproach on Religion; and such of its unworthy ministers, who pursue it, can scarcely fail to infect with their own appropriate odium, those truly valuable members of their order, who are entitled to the respect and esteem of all good men. The usefulness and reputation of the meritorious part of the Clergy are deeply concerned, in having the vices and follies of their false brethren exposed:....the latter may be offended by any attempt to develope their real character and views; but,....*qui capit, ille facit.*

* Hist. and Crit. account of Morality, sect. 7.

that God, to suit himself to the weakness of the Jewish nation, had prescribed to them a great number of rites and ceremonies, insisted much more upon the performance of the exterior worship, and the practical punctilios of devotion, than the purity of the heart, with an *exact conformity to the rules of virtue:* and, what was still worse, by their false glosses, and by their human traditions, *they came at last to destroy, entirely, several of the most incontestible principles of the Law of Nature.*" We shall conclude our observations on this head, with one further remark of the same author*. "If (says he) we consider how few good books of morality we have,....in comparison of the infinite number of controversial writings which croud our libraries and booksellers' shops; we may from thence readily conclude, that *morality is a study greatly neglected.*" Having already remarked, that the deviation from the principles of truth and justice, which appears, in many respects, in the political conduct of statesmen, otherwise enlightened, manifests *an actual decay of morality*,....it is conceived that this observation is, in no respect, more strongly

* Hist. and Crit. account of Morality, sect. 11.

corroborated, than in the frequency of Wars among commercial nations;....wars, too generally produced by fraud and injustice,....by misconstructions and actual infractions of their independent rights. If nations were to act with liberality, good faith, and justice, in their mutual intercourse, there could not be any just cause for wars, among them: for, in matters which regard the internal polity of any particular state, other nations have no right to interfere*; though they may lawfully lend their

* It is a clear and indisputable point, that the government of one country has no right to interfere, unsolicited, in the internal affairs of any other independent nation. How unjustifiable, then, was the conduct of Lord Grenville; when, in a conference with Mr. T. Pinckney, the American minister to Great-Britain, (in 1794), he declared....that one reason for his government issuing the royal instructions of the 8th of January, 1794, was, "by this conduct, to take away every pretext from evil-disposed persons among us; who, according to the intelligence he had received, were endeavouring to irritate our (the American) people against Great-Britain, as well as to oppose the measures of our own government; and, in short, to reduce us to the present situation of France,....a misfortune which they deprecated, as well for our sakes, as for the common welfare and tranquillity of mankind!"....His Lordship appears to have been wonderfully anxious about *our* prosperity,...."for *our* sakes," too....(let it be remembered, this was on the 9th of January, 1794); and to have had a great solicitude for the "common *welfare* and *tranquillity of mankind!*" Yet it will be found, that, with President Washington's message of February 24, 1794,

aid to an oppressed state, on its special requisition, against a more powerful oppressor....M.

there was sent to Congress a letter from Mr. T. Pinckney, our minister to London, forwarding his conversation with this same Lord Grenville, "*concerning British agency, in fomenting the Indian War, and Algerine Hostility*."....What an admirable commentary on his Lordship's *professions*, and how striking a proof of their *sincerity!*

But what right had the British secretary....or those from whom he received his "intelligence"....to decide, that the political opinions of any part of "our people," designated them as "evil-disposed persons,"....in relation to "our own government?"....We are at a loss to divine, what sort of political logic it must be, by which he could justify his attempt to determine, whether the "measures" of our government respecting our own independent concerns,....were right or wrong! Indeed, his lordship seems to have been sensible, at the time, that he himself was wrong, in undertaking to judge of matters with which he had nothing to do; and in giving his decided judgment concerning them, to the representative of that nation, whose business alone it was to determine concerning them: for Mr. Pinckney says, in detailing the conversation, the British secretary prefaced his remarks, by observing, that one reason for issuing the instructions, was, "what he could not mention to me officially, but what he still thought it right I should be apprized of, that no misunderstanding of their motives might be entertained; that he was aware of the delicacy of speaking to a foreign minister concerning the internal state of his country,....neither could he expect an answer from me, on the subject; but that their second reason was," &c. (giving the reason before quoted.)...."I, of course, (continues Mr. Pinckney,) said nothing of our internal affairs, nor of those of France."

We in the United States have reason to wish for "our own sakes" at least, if not for "the common welfare and tranquillity of mankind,"....that the public functionaries of nations may

Pufendorf truly asserts, "that nothing is more consonant to the Law of Nature, than that no man should offer unjust violence or injury to another; and, on the other hand, than that all men should shew kindness and humanity to one another, and be particularly exact in the observation of agreements and compacts. And when men duly attend to, and obey these laws, they may be said to enjoy *Peace;* which is a state most agreeable to human nature,....which tends most to promote its happiness and security,....and indeed, which the *Law of Nature* was given to men, principally to establish and preserve. Nay further, *Peace* is a state proper to human nature, *as such;* since it ariseth from a principle peculiar to mankind, above the brutes: whereas *War* flows from principles common to both.

The *just* causes of war are very few. M. Pufendorf reduces them to three* heads;

acquire discretion enough to know, that it is indecorous and impolitic in them, as well as unlawful, to meddle with the internal affairs of other countries.

* In this he agrees with Grotius. But Heineccius asserts, that there are but *two* just causes of war. "One is (says he), when a foreign people injures another people, or attempts to rob them of their liberty, wealth or life: the other is, when one people denies to another their perfect right. The first is a just

though they might, perhaps, be reducible to the single point of a *defence* against actual aggressions of hostility: And this would appear the more proper, as, besides various lawful means of obtaining redress and satisfaction, which an injured nation may possess, without resorting to an *offensive* war, it is not precluded from an indubitable right to take such preparatory measures, as it may deem suitable, to repel hostile aggressions on the part of the offending power.

But the *unjust* causes of war are innumerable. Some of them are so obviously unlawful, as to be exempt from all imputation of doubtfulness: And among these, are to be ranked *Avarice* and *all extravagant desire of increasing Wealth;* as, also, *Ambition*, and *the hopes of enlarging Rule and Dominion, of growing great, and purchasing a false fame and glory, by the Oppression of others**. Yet, as M. Pufendorf observes†, "*Avarice* is a cause of

cause of *defensive* war,....the last, of *offensive;* and therefore the third, first mentioned by Grotius, viz. *the punishment of crimes*, is not to be admitted as a just cause of war; the rather, that it is certain an equal cannot be punished by an equal; and therefore one nation cannot be punished by another." book ii. chap. ix. sect. 193.

* Pufend. book viii. chap. vi. sect. 5.

† Ibid.

war, usually concealed, and dissembled with great care; because it supposes *a base and sordid spirit.* But *ambition* is generally favoured in the world, under the name of Gallantry and Fortitude: And it is commonly thought greatness and bravery of mind, *to grasp after, and fight for, what belongs to other men.*" Hence, M. de Vattel says*.... "I do not therefore place among the objects of offensive war, *Conquests*, or the desire of invading the *property of another*: such a latitude, destitute even of pretence, is not the object of a formal war, but that of a *robbery*."

War is, in itself, so enormous an evil, and, in its effects, productive of such misery to mankind; that it is incumbent on us, as rational beings, to do all in our power towards removing the causes which produce it. Let us hope, that the enlightened nations of the earth will, ere very long, discover, that it is not only a dictate of duty, but of true political wisdom, to observe such a spirit of equity, good faith and liberality, in all their intercourse and dealings with each other, as may tend to diminish the *causes* of misunderstandings among them.....Their utter extinguishment, we can,

* Book iii. chap. i. sect. 5.

perhaps, never expect: but it will be a great point gained, for the cause of humanity, if a considerable diminution of the evil can be effected; and especially, if this be accomplished by means of an improved morality, in the conduct both of national governments and private citizens.

A late ingenious and interesting writer*, remarks, that the construction of the Law of Nations for which England contends, with respect to maritime commerce....a construction founded on usurpation and supported by power,....has arisen out of the naval wars of the past century; all of which have been excited, maintained, directed and prolonged, by England. This writer, after noticing the maritime superiority of England, makes these remarks....“ This superiority has given to that power an opportunity of bringing forward *pretensions*, which the relative weakness of neutral states has almost enabled her to establish *as Rights*. The result of this has been

* The author of an anonymous work, lately published at Paris, entitled...*De l'Etat de la France, à la fin de l'an VIII.* This work appears to have been written about the period that our last envoys to France were negociating the convention between the United States and that Republic.

two distinct maritime codes....one of which is the code of *every other nation;* the other, that of *England only.*"

It is impossible that *two* distinct codes of Law, bearing relation to the same objects, can have a *rightful* obligatory force; where the objects of those distinct codes are *rights, derived from nature;* and where the same rights are differently defined in the two codes, according to *principles* essentially varying from each other, in their nature. As long, therefore, as Great-Britain will, in time of war, adhere to *her* construction of maritime Law, affecting the rights of all neutral nations; and persist in a determination to maintain *that* construction, in consequence of her naval superiority, ...*contrary to justice* and *against the sense of all other nations*,....merely for her own exclusive aggrandizement*;.....so long will one great

* "Let us suppose a nation entering most eagerly, and without listening one moment to terms of accommodation, into a most dangerous war, *professedly* to exterminate the bad *principles* and morals of a neighbouring people, and to defend *law, order* and *religion*. It is impossible to imagine but that a nation acting in this manner, and with this profession, *must* regulate all its *own* public conduct, especially in a war of this kind, according to the *strictest* law, order, and religion. Will that nation oppose an Armed *Neutrality*, instituted to prevent the interruption of *neutral* commerce? Will she maintain her re-

source of national strife continue to harrass the quiet of mankind. Those states which are influenced by their *Interests*, as well as by a solemn duty and a due sense of national honor, to maintain their *Rights*, cannot be expected tamely to surrender them, to the arrogant pretensions of any power under heaven.... Rights, involving such considerations as these, are of too sacred a nature to be yielded up, without an arduous struggle; much less ought they to be bartered away, for such pretended equivalents, or indemnifications, as a consciousness of superior power, in any state, actuated by a monopolizing avarice and rapacious ambition, might deign to grant, as a commutative boon.

Nothing more preposterous can be conceived, than a nation calling itself free and independent, and valuing itself on its rights;

putation for *justice*, if she should be the first and most violent in destroying this neutrality? Will she break the Law of Nations, by insulting ambassadors? Will she endeavour to *starve* a *whole* nation, with whom she is at war....not only the rulers and warriors, but infants, women, and aged people,....by preventing the importation of *corn?* Will she *forge* assignats? Will she continue the *slave-trade?* A conduct like this appears to be not only inconsistent with the pretended defence of *law*, *order*, and *religion;* but at once proceeding from the *spirit of Despotism*, and promotive of it." Spirit of Despotism, sect. 32.

and at the same time suffering its political independence to be violated, and the rights of its citizens to be invaded, by a foreign state. It is the duty of a state to protect in their rights, to the utmost of its power, all its citizens; and these rights, in the case of nations which carry on a maritime commerce with others, extend, in an appropriate modification, beyond the territory of the state. Its citizens, therefore, when navigating the ocean (which is the common dominion of all nations), in pursuit of their lawful commerce, are entitled to claim the protection of the Law of Nations, for their natural rights, on that element. And, this being a Law whose precepts are equally obligatory on all Nations, under those circumstances wherein its application becomes proper; every state is bound to take care, that the benefits, and the protection of their rights, resulting from that Law, be extended to its citizens. As long, however, as these rights remain liable to different constructions, that potent maritime nation which maintains the false construction, will pursue a correspondent conduct; unless it be controuled by the united efforts of other powers, in support of their natural rights. Until this be done, an ample stock of the efficient causes of wars, oppressions, rapine, injustice, and prostration of morals, will continue to operate. National independence will become a mere nullity....a *vox et præterea nihil.* While the maritime rights of neutral nations remain in their present controverted and unprotected condition; the consequences, pointed out by the French writer before quoted*, will inevitably continue. Among others, he observes that "the *commerce of neutrals*, in time of war, becomes subject to *a foreign jurisdiction*, arbitrary and of course illiberal. Their merchants are amenable to a variety of military tribunals; which, although they are declared to be founded for the simple purpose of deciding on the legality or illegality of certain acts of hostility, present, nevertheless, the idea of the *usurpation*, *by a single nation*, of a *right* which ought to be *common to all*, and a *forced acquiescence* of every power, at peace, *in the will of a power at war*."...." That the vessels of the belligerent powers seek not so much the glory of conquest, as *the profit of capture;* they cruise less *to protect their own commerce*, than

* In his work, *De l'Etat de la France, â la fin de l'an VIII.*

to harrass that of neutral powers; and the nations at war look forward to naval victories, not only as the means of establishing their relative superiority, *but with the view of enabling them to dictate upon the ocean, as a conquered province.*" The same writer remarks, that "the general maritime right of nations demands, in time of war, an unlimited freedom of navigation for neutral powers. This general rule (says he) being once established and well guaranted, there would result a broad system of moderation and reciprocity in *commerce*, which (finding a perfect security in the territories and under the flag of neutral states) would there unfold all its powers, f r the centre of exchange, concentrate all the springs of general reproduction; and would preserve inviolate all the elements of industry, until the moment when peace should restore that harmony of commercial intercourse, which unites all nations."

The great *desiderata*, in that system of general policy which regards *the common rights of every people, concerning their exterior relations*, are, *a definitive recognition and establishment of those rights*, and *the adoption of an efficient guarantee for their protection.* If these were once attained, wars between nations could scarcely find means to originate; and, in those few cases where they might happen to arise, they would be soon terminated. One of the main sources of what are denominated *justifiable* wars, would no longer furnish their *causes*. *These* would therefore be prevented: And the *operation* of the *unjust causes* of war, would at the same time be repressed. The most powerful maritime state would cease to find even its *supposed interest* promoted by war, when it should not be permitted to violate the rights of others with impunity. An efficient establishment of the just principles of the Law of Nations would not only restrict the *causes* of war, within very narrow limits; but would have a direct tendency to diminish its horrors and atrocities, in its prosecution. The barbarous and dishonest practice of *privateering* would be abolished; and this would, of itself, extinguish one powerful inducement to the commencement of naval wars.

There does not, perhaps, exist in the public conduct of any enlightened nation, pretending to political liberty, a measure more discordant with humanity and natural equity, than that of *privateering*. Public war is the proper concern of the state. It can never be justly undertaken for any other cause, than either for the purpose of national defence; or, of obtaining redress for public wrongs, on the failure of proper pacific means used for that end. Vattel defines war to be, " that state in which a *nation* prosecutes *its* right by force*." If the citizen of one independent country be grossly injured in his rights, by the citizen of another,....whilst beyond the jurisdiction of the former, and therefore out of reach of remedy from its municipal laws,.... the injured party is entitled to demand redress and protection, through the medium of the constituted authorities of his country. Civil government being instituted for the security of the individual, and the due protection of his natural rights; no member of the community can, in any case, lawfully take upon himself to avenge wrongs done to him, personally; further than to defend himself, against an actual aggression of forcible injury, at the moment of its commission. A nation injured in its rights by another nation, or by its private

* Book iii. chap. i. sect. 1.

citizens in certain circumstances, may be compelled, by the atrociousness of the injury and the incompetency of any other means to furnish redress, to seek reparation by war. But, in resorting to this, in such case, *reparation for the injury sustained* can, alone, be lawfully sought for: because, although Grotius considers the *punishment* of the offending party as one of the legitimate objects of war,....Heineccius*, and his annotator Dr. Turnbull, very properly affirm, that "the *punishment of crimes* is not to be admitted as a just cause of war; the rather, that it is certain an equal cannot be punished by an equal; and therefore one nation cannot be punished by another."

Upon what ground, then, is the business of *privateering* to be justified? The *making of war* is the prerogative of the *State; private warfare being confessedly unlawful*, and therefore proscribed. A war, strictly *defensive*, can with no propriety tolerate the fitting out *privateers*, for the *sole* purpose of *annoying* the enemy, by *offensive* operations. And *reparation* for injuries sustained, affecting the public rights of the state, is the object of *offensive*

* Book ii. chap. ix. sect. 192.

hostilities. When these injuries are done to a private citizen, while navigating the high seas, in pursuit of his lawful commerce; the state of which he is a member may grant to him *letters of reprisal**, by which he may be

* "If there be no controversy between nations and states themselves, when we lay hands upon persons or effects belonging to another republic in peace with us, on the account of justice refused to any of our society, this cannot be called *war*, but is making *reprisals*. But since this may very probably give rise to a war, it ought not to be done by any private person, but with the approbation of the Sovereign; and it ought to be carried no further than to make satisfaction to our member, to whom justice was refused."....Heineccius's system of Universal Law, book ii. chap. ix. sect. 203.

This law of *Reprisals* is founded on principles infinitely more just than those of *Privateering*. The former is a measure of *peace*; adopted for the special purpose of enabling the injured party, and him only, to procure satisfaction for the injury sustained, after other means of obtaining redress have failed; and the *quantum* of such satisfaction is not to exceed that of the actual injury. The *things* seized by the party making reprisals (for, according to the manners of modern Europe, says M. de Vattel, Ανδροληψια, or the seizure of *men*, is seldom put in practice, and is seldom if ever justifiable in time of peace), may be applied to his own advantage till he has obtained what is due for interest and damage; or they may be kept as a pledge, till a full satisfaction shall have been made. The effects seized are preserved, while there is any hopes of obtaining satisfaction or justice. As soon as this hope is lost, they are confiscated, and *then* the reprisals are accomplished. The way of reprisals, M. Vattel observes, is a more easy, safe, and mild means, than war, of bringing nations to reason, who suffer the violated

enabled to obtain *indemnification.* As for *reparation*, considered as one of the just objects of war, Grotius observes, that " it belongs to what is or was properly *our own.*" In no case, then, does either the necessity or the propriety of privateering exist.

He, therefore, who....having procured for a private armed ship of war, a commission

rights of other nations to remain unredressed: And " a Sovereign has no right to oppose force, or to make war against him, who, in such a case, by ordering the making of reprisals, only exercises his just right."

In another respect, reprisals are free from the injustice which belongs to privateering. An inoffensive merchant who is despoiled of his property and effects, at sea, by a private armed vessel of an enemy-nation, cannot have recourse to the Sovereignty of his own country, for indemnification: because, while the private citizens of one nation are permitted by the existing mode of warfare, to plunder the private citizens of another, under the authority of the state; so long must the individuals, belonging to warring nations that authorize such injustice, encounter all the hazards and oppressions, to which this sort of warfare is subjected. But, according to Vattel, " he who makes use of reprisals against a nation, on the goods of its members *indiscriminately*, cannot be taxed with seizing the wealth of an innocent person, for the debt of another: for, *in this case*, the Sovereign is to *recompense* those of his subjects, *on whom the reprisals fall....This is a debt of the state or nation*, of which each citizen ought only to support his quota."....See Vattel, book ii. chap. xviii. sect. 345....And, in the same chapter, the reader will find the doctrines supported, which are here laid down, concerning *reprisals.*

for that purpose,....deprives of their property and lives, defenceless mariners and trading men, engaged in their peaceable and honest occupations,....is not exempt from a *conscientious* imputation of robbery and murder. Being authorized by the *state* to rob, plunder, and destroy the goods and lives of those, from whom he may not have received even the slightest personal injury,....he has thus a kind of legal sanction for the act. But this species of warfare, carried on by the private citizens of one state, against the unoffending private citizens of another, while engaged in the lawful occupations of industry and peace, is unwarranted by any of the justifiable objects of war. It is opposed to every principle of morality, and to the precepts of natural law. Conforming to the dictates of a mistaken and barbarous policy, it is alike repugnant to reason and religion. It is, in fact, neither more nor less than a *licensed piracy*, of the most mischievous kind*; however

* In the course of debate in the British house of commons, on the 29th of April last, it was stated....in proof of the iniquitous conduct pursued by British privateers in the West-Indies, ...that, out of three hundred and eighteen cases of appeals from condemnations in those islands, under captures there made by

sanctioned it may be, by human laws, or countenanced by national depravity.

such privateers,....not above thirty-five were confirmed by the court of appeals in England. Thus, even according to the decisions of the English Court of Admiralty in their own causes, nearly *nine-tenths* out of a given number, of the captures of American vessels, recently made by British privateer cruizers in the West-Indies, were admitted to have been illegal!

But this is not the only kind of injustice and insult to which the neutral commerce of the United States has been subjected, during the recent war, by the piratical depredations of these cruisers. The personal rights of our citizens have been grossly violated, and our flag shamefully insulted, by these lawless sea-rovers; though, in one instance to which we allude, the *public* armed ships of war of Great-Britain have been much more criminal than even their *privateers*....They have, both, forcibly taken and detained American seamen, for the purpose of manning and fighting their own ships; contrary to good faith, the practice of civilized states, and the plainest principles of the Law of Nations. The author of a treatise on neutral rights ....entitled, *De l'Etat de la France, a la fin de l'an VIII*....and written about the beginning of September, 1800,....asserts, that there were then more than forty thousand *neutral* seamen under the British flag; "exposed without reason, without advantage, and without honor, to all the hazards of war."....If the British nation think proper, with all their boast of the security which their government affords, for the personal liberty of the subject, to permit the impressment of their own seamen; it is a matter to which we have nothing to say. But, when the constitution of our country does not permit its government, on any pretence whatever, to exercise so cruel a tyranny over the personal rights of its own citizens; the guardians of our liberties are under a sacred obligation, not to suf-

There can be little doubt that the United States may, in due season, obtain the concurrence of almost every maritime power in the civilized world, for the abolition of this iniquitous system of piracy and murder. The treaty, concluded in 1785, between the United States and Prussia, had, to the great honor of both states, already accomplished this desirable end, so far as regarded the two contracting parties. The stipulations of that treaty were predicated on those principles, that conform to the just purposes of war; which contemplate an ascendancy over, though not a permanent destruction of, the efficient and

fer a foreign nation to perpetrate so great an enormity, with impunity. It was the duty of Mr. Jay to have made by his treaty, effectual provision for guarding against this evil: For it will appear, by the message of the President to Congress, of the 5th of December, 1793,....that, amongst the various points which arose, as matters dependent for adjustment between the United States and Great-Britain,....one was, "the exposure of American Seamen to impressment" by the British. Mr. Jay was nominated as envoy extraordinary to his Britannic majesty, the 16th of April following....But Mr. Jay made no provision whatever, in his treaty, for securing American seamen from British impressment: and the omission to do so, corresponds perfectly with the general tenor of this gentleman's diplomatic services, in his mission to the Court of London. See the case of Captain Phillips, before mentioned.

operative power of the state, by the beligerents, respectively. For those pursuits, which are the ordinary occupation of a people in time of peace, and which do not serve by their direct operation or immediate use to annoy an enemy, can never be rightfully destroyed by a warring nation. And it is upon this principle, that *military* implements and stores are deemed contraband of war; and, as such, are prohibited to be carried to a nation engaged in hostilities: whilst the prohibition is not extended to the ordinary objects of commerce. The efficient warlike strength of a state at war, is sought to be diminished and controuled, by the military counteraction of its enemy: but the extermination of its peaceable inhabitants, and the plunder or destruction of the fruits of their honest industry, can only be dictated by a savage ferocity and the most depraved wickedness. The 23d article of our late Prussian treaty is in these words.... "If war should arise between the two contracting parties, the merchants of either country, then residing in the other, shall be allowed to remain nine months to collect their debts and settle their affairs, and may depart freely, carrying off all their effects, without molestation or hindrance: And all women and children, scholars of every faculty, cultivators of the earth, artizans, manufacturers, and fishermen, unarmed and inhabiting unfortified towns, villages or places; and in general, all others whose occupations are for the common subsistence and benefit of mankind, shall be allowed to continue their respective employments, and shall not be molested in their persons, nor shall their houses or goods be burnt, or otherwise destroyed, nor their fields wasted by the armed force of the enemy, into whose power, by the events of war, they may happen to fall; but if any thing is necessary to be taken from them, for the use of such armed force, the same shall be paid for at a reasonable price. *And all merchant and trading vessels employed in exchanging the products of different places, and thereby rendering the necessaries, conveniencies, and comforts of human life more easy to be obtained, and more general, shall be allowed to pass free and unmolested; and neither of the contracting powers shall grant or issue any commission to any private armed vessels, empowering them to take or destroy such trading vessels or interrupt such* *commerce**."....Here we perceive, that not only private armed vessels of the two nations were

* The latter clause of this article of the *old* treaty (distinguished by *italics*)....namely, that relating to navigation and maritime commerce,....is the only part of it, which, in the possible event therein contemplated, would be likely to have any *actual*....and, consequently, *beneficial* operation. Yet the *whole of this clause is omitted*, in Mr. John Q. Adams's new treaty with Prussia; while the preceding clause is copied verbatim into the new treaty, of which it constitutes the 23d article. Thus, by retaining the provisions *only*, contained in the corresponding article of the extinct treaty, which, it was barely possible, could ever *really* affect either of the contracting parties,....an *useless* display is made, of liberal policy and humanity: whilst those stipulations of the same treaty, equally liberal and humane, which were calculated to produce great and substantial good, were abandoned by Mr. Adams.

The *manner* in which the position....that *free ships make free goods*....is renounced by the existing Prussian treaty, has an appearance of disingenuousness. The old treaty was signed by Mr. Adams, the late President, as one of the three ministers appointed on the part of the United States, to conduct that negociation: and that treaty explicitly acknowledged the principle above mentioned. Therefore, as the new treaty was negociated under the administration of Mr. Adams....and his son having been commissioned by him, to conduct the negociation, ...it became necessary, in order to preserve some appearance of consistency, not to abandon so important a neutral right as that in question, definitely, and in express terms. To divert, as much as possible, an imputation of inconsistency, and of a *total* abandonment of that right,....a measure, which has the semblance of an *expedient*, is fallen upon:....the operation of the principle is virtually *suspended*....under the pretence that it has "not been sufficiently respected" by the belligerent powers,

prohibited from molesting the marine commerce of each other, in the event of war be-

during the two last wars, and especially in that which then continued. It is a very extraordinary reason to be assigned by the public functionaries of a free country, for relinquishing by the stipulations of a treaty a *national right*,....that such right had been, and continued to be, violated! A similar pretext might be readily found, for surrendering almost every political right we enjoy. England is, notoriously, the power that has almost incessantly, during late wars, committed the grossest infractions of the maritime rights of neutrals: Yet even this nation recognized the principle, of *free ships making free goods*, by her commercial treaty with France, so late as 1786. Mr. Adams's treaty with Prussia seems, indeed, to admit, that this principle... which "has not been sufficiently respected"....is founded in *right:* for, although the fabricator of this treaty stipulated a suspension....or rather, violation....of the principle, *during the existing war*,....he has introduced a clause by which "the two contracting parties propose, *after the return of a general peace*, to agree either separately between themselves, or jointly with other powers alike interested, to concert with the great maritime powers of Europe, such arrangements and such permanent principles, as may serve to consolidate the *liberty* and the *safety* of the neutral navigation and commerce, in future wars."

If Mr. Adams had found any difficulty in obtaining from the Prussian government, during the present war, a revival of the stipulation, that free ships should make free goods,....he was under no obligation to renew the treaty with that power. The original treaty had expired by its own limitation, nearly eighteen months before General Washington retired from the Presidency: and upwards of two years and four months, more, elapsed....after his successor attained to that dignity....before the new treaty was concluded. Thus, there was an interval of almost four years, in which no treaty existed between the United

tween them; but their public ships of war were subjected to the same restriction.

We have every reason to believe that France would readily concur with the United States, and other maritime powers, in freeing navigation and transmarine commerce from the bondage under which it has laboured. The late French author, before quoted,* asserts,....that France has been the first to propose, that neutral navigation should be forever liberated from every species of restraint...That all cruising against trading vessels should be abolished......That commerce, with all its agents and relative advantages, should be privileged and protected, under every possible circumstance, from the violence of war."....And the liberality which that nation has mani-

States and Prussia. It is therefore to be presumed, that no great inconvenience could have resulted, from the postponement of the negociation to a more favorable period; if the moment fixed upon for the purpose, had rendered unjustifiable stipulations unavoidable. But this was not the fact....No necessity for entering into such, did exist at the time.

It is somewhat remarkable, that the ratifications of this treaty were not exchanged, till nearly a twelvemonth after its signature. This bears date the 11th of July, 1799....It was finally ratified at Berlin, the 22d of June, 1800;....and officially announced here, the 4th of November following.

* See the work *De l'Etat de la France, a la fin de l'an VIII.*

fested, with respect to neutral rights, in its treaties with others, assure us that the same liberal spirit will influence her future conduct, on similar occasions*.

* Our first treaty with that nation, formed more than two years before the Armed Neutrality, contains the most just and liberal stipulations, concerning neutral rights; and the convention concluded between the United States and the French Republic, on the 30th of September, 1800, is equally favourable in that respect. The republican government of France has repeatedly manifested a desire of concerting such measures with other nations, as would serve to secure the freedom of navigation and maritime commerce, in time of war. Mr. Fauchet, in his letter of the 7th Germinal, 2d year, (29th of March, 1794), to the secretary of state, says...." I feel a pleasure in reflecting, and observing to you, that it is not the fault of the French, if commercial property, *even of enemy nations*, has not been respected amidst the horrors of war. This proposition of *natural right* was made by one of our legislative assemblies, to the *British*,....*who rejected it*."....It is true, that the rights of neutral nations have been actually violated by France, as well as by Great-Britain, during the present war; and the lawful commerce of the United States has suffered greatly, from the injuries perpetrated by both. The irritation produced thereby, was, in both cases, great; in the former, it was extreme,....having been heightened by causes, which it is unnecessary for us to notice. The differences that subsisted between this country and France, which operated so prejudicially upon our commerce and internal harmony, are now, happily, in a train of amicable adjustment:....We have, therefore, no inclination to recur to the subjects of controversy, that agitated the two nations,....either for the purpose of criminating or extenuating the late conduct of France towards the United

The northern powers, including the Batavian Republic, have fully evinced, by the

States. A very late *French* writer frankly acknowledges, that the rights of neutrals have been violated, by acts of his government, in the course of the present war. After observing, that France has been the first to propose to all other nations, interested in its success, an uniform and just code of maritime Law,....in order to reform the defects of the present European systems (if they deserve the name of systems), which owe their origin to the abuse of *power*, prostrating *right;* he adds these remarks....“ At the commencement of the present war, France proposed the only measure which could relieve commerce from its fetters, and neutral powers from their state of slavery. Since that period,....harrassed by the evils of her situation, exasperated by the animosity of her enemies, disgusted by the indifference of those who ought to assist her, and irritated by the partiality of those who ought at least to have remained neutral in the struggle, in which she was engaged, ...she did not feel herself warranted in supporting a system of moderation, which, in the critical state of her affairs, would have bordered upon folly. She, in her turn, began to impose severe laws; and thereby contributed to the losses of neutrals, and the general destruction of commerce. I do not mean at all to justify a fault (continues this writer), which she has had the magnanimity to acknowledge, and the merit of repairing: a fault, which resulted from a general error; and from the *ignorance* in which France, as well as the whole of Europe, remained for a long time,....as to the *true principles of public power*, and the *proper application* of the *rules of public Law*.”....This extract is made from a work, before quoted, entitled....*De l'Etat de la France, a la fin de l'an VIII*....said to have been written by a person in an official station, and to have been submitted, before its publication, to the council of state.

treaty of armed neutrality of 1780, their solicitude to maintain the just rights of neutrals, in time of war. And whatever may be the issue, under imperious circumstances at the present moment, of the convention lately entered into*, by the neutral powers of the north of Europe, we have too much confidence in their magnanimity, justice, and sense of their own interests, to entertain the least doubt of their concurring, ultimately, in support of the rights of neutral nations. Spain may be counted upon with equal certainty, from the disposition she discovered in the year 1780, relative to this object.

The inhuman principles, upon which the late war against France has been conducted, naturally produced that degree of irritation, which is thus offered as some apology for the infringement of neutral rights, that it occasioned. And hence Mr. Fauchet says, in the letter just before quoted,....“ I shall only indulge myself in this single reflection, that the horrible system of *violating the Law of Nations*, in order *to starve a nation* who cannot be conquered by force of arms, has *not been invented by France;* and, that it would be as unjust as barbarous, to require that she should allow *provisions* to pass to her enemies, while those destined for her, are taken by them.”

* This convention was entered into, at Petersburg, on the 16th of December, 1800. Its object was, “ to re-establish, *in their former shape*, the engagements, which, in the years 1780 and 1781, constituted the system of *the armed neutrality*.”

Thus, the co-operation of all the principal maritime powers of Europe (England excepted,) jointly with the United States of America, can unquestionably be obtained; for the great purpose of establishing, upon a secure basis, a maritime code of law, founded on reason and the principles of natural equity.

The leading principles on which this work, so interesting to humanity and the rights and dignity of all states, should be established, are, in our conception, very obvious; and we fully accord in opinion on this head, with the writer last mentioned*. He comprises the whole system of a new maritime code of law.... to be founded on natural justice and the rights of nations,....in these two regulations; which we give in his own words.

"1st, The abolition of all cruising against trading vessels. In time of war, the right of sovereignty, as exercised and acknowledged ashore, shall be extended, with all its attributes, to the flags of such states as take no part in the existing hostilities."

"2d, The navigation of every country, in time of peace, shall be secure from any kind of

* The author of *L'Etat de la France, a la fin de l'an VIII.*

prohibition; with the single exception of the coasting trade between different ports of the same nation, and of the intercourse between distant colonies and the mother country."

Here then is a foundation, upon which a well defined and perspicuous code of maritime law may be established; according to the principles of natural equity, and the just rights of nations. The violation of these rights, that has been experienced by all nations which carry on a maritime commerce, evinces the necessity of their adopting, in concert with each other, proper measures for guarding against a continuance of the evil. As long as statesmen of particular countries conceive themselves under a kind of political obligation to conform to those mistaken theories of jurists, respecting the natural rights of states, which concern their mutual relations; so long will an ample source of national litigation continue, to supply means of disturbing the peace and order of society....of impairing the independent rights of nations....and of undermining the morals and the liberties of the people. Yet such is the evil, that at present exists: and such it must remain; until those erroneous opinions concerning certain fundamental principles of universal Law, which have acquired some sort of sanction from the influence of celebrated authors, shall be forced to yield to the irresistible energy of truth and reason.

But the evil, enormous as it is, is not without a remedy. Necessity is often the parent of good, to mankind. The injustice that has been produced by the operation of those false constructions of the Law of Nations, maintained by many writers, manifests the fallacy of their doctrines; because wrong must necessarily result from principles founded in error. Injury is the natural fruit of injustice: And neutral nations have too sensibly experienced the injustice we mention, by its effects, not to discern the necessity of resorting to an effectual remedy for the evil.

Whether that state of irritation which is produced in the public mind, during an extensive and desolating war, does not render such a season an improper one, for any definitive negociation, concerning those important rights which concern the interest and independence of states, and the freedom and welfare of the great society of mankind,....those whose duty it is to decide, are the competent judges. We should rather conceive, however, that a period of profound peace....at least, among the great maritime nations of the world....would be the most suitable to the occasions*.

But whenever this great work shall be undertaken, it must be accomplished by means

* It is a circumstance which alleviates, in a considerable degree, the mischievous tendency of Mr. Jay's treaty, that some of its most odious stipulations may be annulled in two years after the expiration of the present war. For by the last clause of the twelfth article, it is agreed, that the parties to that treaty "will then renew their discussions, and endeavour to agree, whether in any and what cases, neutral vessels shall protect enemy's property;....and, in what cases provisions and other articles, not generally contraband, may become such." By the twelfth article of the existing treaty between the United States and Prussia, "the two contracting parties propose, after the return of a general peace, to agree either separately between themselves, or jointly with other powers alike interested, to concert with the great maritime powers of Europe, such arrangements and such permanent principles, as may serve to consolidate the liberty and the safety of the neutral navigation and commerce, in future wars."....And this measure,....so contemplated by the American and Prussian governments, in July, 1799,....has a particular aspect to the principle of free ships making free goods; it being expressly mentioned with reference thereto, in the article quoted. The "arrangements," proposed in the Prussian treaty, may be adopted speedily after the conclusion of the present war:....And, as our conventional obligations to Great-Britain, in that particular....as well as with respect to the stipulations concerning contraband,....will cease in two years after the war; the principles that may be adopted by the United States, for the purposes above mentioned, may commence, in regard to Great-Britain, from the end of that period.

of negociation. It is thus, that those controverted rights, which produce such disputes between states, as generally terminate in a resort to arms,....can be most equitably accommodated. Mr. Vattel observes, that "the differences that arise between nations, or their conductors, have their source either from rights in litigation, or from injuries. A nation ought (says he) to preserve the rights which belong to it; and the care of its safety and glory, does not permit it to suffer injuries. But, in fulfilling what it owes to itself, it is not permitted to forget its duties towards others. These two views, combined together, furnish the maxims of the Law of Nations on the manner of terminating disputes between different states." The same author, treating of the means which the Law of Nature recommends to put an end to national disputes.... after reciting the several methods proper for that purpose,....remarks....that, "in order to put into practice any of these methods, it is necessary to speak with each other and to confer together. Conference and congresses are then a way of reconciliation, which the Law of Nature recommends to nations, as proper to put an amicable period to their differences. Congresses (continues Vattel) are assemblies of plenipotentiaries, appointed to find out methods for a reconciliation, and to discuss and adjust their reciprocal pretensions. In order to expect a happy success from them, it is necessary that these assemblies should be formed and directed by a sincere desire of peace and concord."

Having previously discussed those controverted principles of the Law of Nations, which respect their relations to each other.... and, consequently, their mutual rights, duties and obligations,....we here see a legitimate and peaceable mode pointed out, for their adjustment. It would therefore be superfluous, in us, to pursue the subject of the present dissertation beyond its present limits. We have no inclination to encroach upon the duty or prerogative of others.

With regard to the object, to which our attention has been directed, on this occasion, we have no hesitation in pronouncing it to be one of primary importance. Conscious, nevertheless, of our inability to treat the subject in the manner that its magnitude demands; we have confined ourselves to that mode of discussion, and to those limits, which seemed best calculated to promote the cause of truth and justice, with such imperfect lights as we yet possess. And zealously attached, as we are, to the honor and true interests of our country; it will be to us a source of sincere and heartfelt gratification, if this essay shall, in any degree, serve to promote the national welfare, or the happiness of the American people.

SUPPLEMENTARY OBSERVATIONS.

THE last ten years have produced political events of so extraordinary a nature, as to have almost baffled all calculation. Things have, in many instances, run so counter to what prior experience had taught us to expect, from the ordinary progress of human affairs, that all reasoning on probable future events in the politics of Europe, deduced from their recent state, affords very doubtful conclusions. The political aspect of the European nations has been greatly changed, by the consequences of the French Revolution. Innovations upon those ancient systems of state-policy, that favoured the despotic principle of rule, have advanced with such rapidity, as has alarmed some of those governments, most tenacious of that principle. Hence we have witnessed such nations shamefully violating the most sacred obligations of justice and good faith; in hopes of preserving thereby, a little longer, the precarious remains of usurped power and unlawful dominion.

There is, however, another cause, to which the recent abandonments of the just principles of national policy, by some states, in particular instances, may be attributed;....*imperious necessity*. A nation may, by an extraordinary concurrence of circumstances, be placed in such a situation, as to compel them to renounce even *important rights*,....at least *for a time;* in order to secure, permanently, their *indispensible interests*.

We shall leave it to our readers to determine, to which of the two causes, above mentioned, is to be ascribed the wonderful occurrence, which is the subject of the following observations.

What we here allude to, is the convention concluded at Petersburg, between Russia and Great-Britain, the 5....17th June, 1801.

By the 3d article of this convention, it is agreed (*inter alia*) between the contracting parties, that, " having determined to put under a safeguard the liberty of the commerce and navigation of their subjects, in case either of them should be at war, whilst the other remains neutral,"...." the effects embarked on the neutral vessels shall be free; excepting the contraband of war, and the property of enemies."....The 7th article declares the principles and the measures adopted by the convention, to be permanent; and that its stipulations shall serve as a constant rule for the contracting powers, in matters of commerce and navigation. And, by the 8th article, it is provided, that the kings of Denmark and Sweden shall immediately be invited, in the name of the two contracting parties, by the emperor of Russia, to accede to the convention; and at the same time, to renew and confirm their respective treaties of commerce with his Britannic majesty.

What a spectacle does this exhibit to the world! We behold the youthful Alexander, just seated on the imperial throne of all the Russias, surrendering to Great-Britain an important maritime right, to which Russia was entitled, while she maintained the character of a neutral nation in time of war:....a right, which his illustrious mother, only one-and-twenty years before, had entered into a solemn treaty with the other maritime powers of the north, to defend by force;....a right, which was again confirmed, but a few months ago, by his father's ministry, in the convention negociated between Russia, Denmark and Sweden,.....the purpose of which was, "to re-establish, in their former shape, the engagements, which, in the years 1780 and 1781, constituted the system of the armed neutrality." But the most extraordinary circumstance of all, is, that the treaty of amity, commerce, and navigation, between Russia and Sweden, which contains an express recognition, of the same right, was finally ratified by the present emperor, Alexander,....only six days before he ceded that right to Great-Britain, in the late convention between the two powers.*

* The recent convention between Russia and Great-Britain was concluded the 5th (17th) of June last. And the treaty between Russia and Sweden, was concluded at St. Petersburg, on the 1st (13th) of March, preceding; ratified at Landscrona, the 11th of April; and ratified, definitively, at St. Petersburg, on the 30th of May (11th of June), all of the year 1801.

The late emperor, Paul, died in the night between the 11th and 12th of march, O. S:....that is to say, on the 23d or 24th of that month. Consequently, the treaty here mentioned,.... though it was probably the last negociated by Russia, during the reign of that ill-fated prince,....received the final ratification

The principle, that *free ships make free goods*, is one of the fundamental rights of neu-

of that power, within three months after the accession of Alexander I. to the Russian throne. The 24th article of this treaty declares *(inter alia,)* "that, with the exception of *warlike* contraband, the goods of subjects of the belligerent powers, in neutral bottoms, are free."....The same article contains this remarkable passage....“ Convinced of the principles laid down in the convention concluded at St. Petersburg, on the 16th of December, last year, *for the general good of trading nations,*.... the two crowns declare, that they make *it the invariable rule of their conduct.*"....The parties then enumerate the following important principles....besides the one just before quoted,....which “ they further declare that *they acknowledge*:" viz.

“ That neutral ships may freely sail for the ports and coasts of the belligerent powers."

“ That such ports, only, are to be considered as blockaded, where, from the proximity of ships of war, there shall actually be danger in entering."

“ That neutral vessels can be detained, only, on just grounds, and evident facts."

“ That no convoy shall be searched, when the commander of the ship of war, convoying them, declares that there is no contraband on board."

Such are the principles formally acknowledged by Russia and Sweden, and solemnly stipulated between them, for twelve years,....so late as the 11th of June last;....only six days before the former power declared, in favor of Great-Britain, that the effects embarked on neutral vessels should be free,....*excepting* the contraband of war, and the *property of enemies!* But the former treaty was the *voluntary* act of the Russian and Swedish governments: whereas no one can hesitate to believe, that the abandonment of the principle....that *free ships make free goods*....in the latter, was not the result of choice, on the part

trals; the security of which, was stipulated by the treaty of Armed Neutrality; and the principles, contained in that treaty, are stated by the late empress of Russia....in her declaration to the courts of London, Versailles and Madrid,....to be "coincident with the *primitive right of nations*, which every people may *reclaim*, and which the belligerent powers cannot invalidate, *without violating the Laws of Neutrality*, and without disavowing the maxims they have adopted in the different treaties and public engagements."....The 9th article of the treaty itself declares, that the *obligations* enforced thereby are to serve as *the groundwork of all treaties that should be set on foot thereafter:* that, meanwhile, *all* that is thereby agreed upon should be deemed as *binding* and *permanent*, in regard both to mercantile and naval affairs, and should have the force of *Law*, in determining the rights of neutral nations. And the 10th article, after declar-

of Russia; but of circumstances, to the controuling influence of which, that power deemed it expedient to submit, at the moment. What stability can be expected, in a treaty, concluded under such circumstances as this last?....With what sincerity can any power be expected to adhere to engagements, which cannot but be considered as derogatory from its interest, its honor, and its public faith?

ing the chief aim and principal object of the treaty to be, the securing the freedom of trade and navigation,....contains an invitation to all other neutral powers to become parties to the treaty, by acceding to it. Accordingly, Sweden and the States General did expressly accede to it; as did Prussia afterwards, in a more informal manner. France, Spain, and the United States of America, then three of the belligerent powers, at the same time expressed their entire approbation of the principles of this treaty: And even Great-Britain, another of the belligerents, not only manifested a willingness to accede to similar principles, in a proffered negociation with the States-General, before the end of the American revolutionary war; but did in fact, three years after its termination, renew, in her commercial treaty with France, a recognition which she had before repeatedly made, of the principle, that free ships make free goods.

Never were the principles that serve as the foundation of *Rights*, more fully or more generally recognized, in any public treaty, than those which the treaty of Armed Neutrality was intended to establish: Nor was any one ever concluded under circumstances which imposed on all the parties, but more particularly on Russia, more sacred obligations to adhere to their engagements with rigid fidelity.

Denmark was one of the original contracting parties to the treaty of Armed Neutrality; and Sweden, the first power that acceded to it: Yet we see Russia, the founder of that celebrated confederacy, stipulating with Great-Britain....against whom the confederation was principally aimed,....that the kings of Denmark and Sweden should be *invited*, by the emperor of *Russia*, to accede to the recent convention between himself and the king of Great-Britain! And what is the boon that is held forth, for inducing those powers to accept the invitation, and thereby violate their plighted faith?....“ His Britannic majesty engages, in such case, to deliver up and make restitution to each of the said powers, all the prizes which have been made on them; as also all the territories and countries of their dominion, which have been conquered by the arms of his Britannic majesty, since the rupture, in the same state in which these possessions were found at the time they were taken by the troops of his Britannic majesty.”...Thus,

Great-Britain obtains from Russia, a cession, on her part, of important neutral Rights,.... under the impending menace of committing immediate hostilities* against her, as she had

* We think ourselves fully warranted, by a recent occurrence in the imperial parliament of Britain, in having hazarded a suggestion, that the late convention between that country and Russia, was produced by the *compulsory* measures of the former; and was by no means the result of a free choice, on the part of any one of the northern powers....In the debate on the British king's speech, occasioned by the peace, lord *Lovaine* (who moved the customary address to the throne, in the House of Commons,)....after observing, that this convention was "a subject of congratulation,"...proceeded thus:..."An *expedition* justly conceived, and promptly executed, had *forced* them (Russia, Denmark and Sweden,) to consent to the *limitation* of the exercise of *Rights*, the extension of which was unjustly claimed, and that claim attempted to be enforced by arms; of Rights, the abuse of the exercise of which, could not for a moment be endured,....injurious, as it necessarily must be, to the commerce and prosperity, the rights and interest, of *Britain*. This event (continues his lordship) also formed another, and a striking proof, of the *superiority of our arms*, and the bravery and gallantry of those employed to fight the battles of the country."

Here, then, is an *explicit avowal*, by a distinguished member of the British Government....and made, in our opinion, on principles as indefensible, as the terms in which it was expressed are indecorous,....that the late convention, between Great-Britain and Russia, was *not a voluntary act* of the latter,....*nor one willingly acceded to*, by either Denmark or Sweden.

Mr. *Woodhouse*....who followed lord Lovaine, on this occasion,...."rejoiced at the convention with the northern powers,.... in which the *Rights of Britain* were maintained with undevia-

already done against Denmark and Sweden, ...by a powerful fleet in the Baltic: and the two latter powers are invited, at the same time, to barter *their* neutral rights, also; for the restitution of prizes made on them, and territories conquered from them, in consequence of lawful measures they had taken for the protection of those very rights!....Such is the morality which actuates Great-Britain, in the plenitude of her maritime power; and such the conduct of those, who were bound by the highest obligations of justice and honor, to have resisted her encroachments on their *Rights!*

ting firmness, and the abuse of those Rights, which were conceded to the enemy, guarded against with every possible strictness.".....Thus, Mr. Woodhouse was not content with supporting the assertion of his legislative colleague; but, referring to *Rights, common to all independent nations*, he speaks of them as if they appertained to *Britain, exclusively*,....and those exercised by Russia, Denmark and Sweden, as *Rights* "which were *conceded* to the enemy!"....And, besides the strange doctrines thus advanced by these gentlemen, they further declare the due "*exercise*" of those "*Rights*," claimed by neutrals, to be an "*unjust extension*" and an "*abuse*" of them; although the very term "*Rights*," which they use, implies....that their *exercise* must be *legal*:....It is absurd to talk of a people *possessing Rights*, which it is *unlawful for them to exercise*....But such policy and such measures need no further comment.

But what can Great-Britain promise herself, from stipulations entered into, under such circumstances?....Can she believe, that Russia, Denmark and Sweden, (if the two latter have actually accepted the invitation of the former,) will have more hesitation to infringe the convention of June 1801, when it shall suit their convenience,....obtained *as* it was; than in violating the stipulations of the Armed Neutrality, which were entered into voluntarily, and in the most solemn and deliberate manner?.... The interests of those powers....as well as a sense of wounded honor, which they must experience,....ought to forbid Great-Britain entertaining any such belief....The policy of courts forbids it. Russia has herself declared, in the face of the world, that one of the rights which her present monarch has ceded, by his late convention with Great-Britain, is founded on principles, "coincident with the primitive right of nations, *which every people may reclaim.*"....Is there any one who does not know, that many of the principles of Machiavelian policy are yet fashionable in the courts of princes? England knows it well. Let us then hear, what Machiavel would say, to states who had been constrained, by imperious necessity, to renounce their *rights*....“ It is not scandalous to break such promises, as are *extorted by force*: for, in promises relating to the public,....if they be obtained by force; when the force ceases, the promise ceases with it, and may be neglected without any disgrace. Of this, all history is full of examples, and there is not a day but presents us with new: for, as we see princes make no conscience of performing any thing, that they are obliged to, *by force*, especially if the force be removed; so they are as little tender of their *promises* in other things, when the *cause* which pressed them to promise, is taken away*.”...The same learned and sagacious author admits, that it is honorable for a prince to keep his word: but he contends, that “ a prince who is wise and prudent, cannot, nor *ought not* to, keep his parole, when the keeping of it is to his *prejudice*, and the *causes* for which he promised, *removed*.†”

We are far from advocating the politics of Machiavel; because many of his principles are clearly repugnant to morality and justice, and highly mischievous in their tendency. His unqualified assertion, that promises, *gene-*

* See the discourses of Nicholas Machiavel, chap. xlii.

† See Machiavel's Prince, chap. xviii.

rally, are not binding, if obtained *by force*,.... is wholly indefensible: it goes to the subversion of an important principle of morals, and is extremely dangerous to the tranquillity of nations; for, if this doctrine were to be admitted, every belligerent nation, that should be compelled, by the disasters of its arms, to conclude a treaty of peace with its enemy...imposing, as is usual in such cases, hard conditions on the vanquished,....would deem themselves justified in resorting, anew, to hostilities, against their former adversary; in order to "reclaim" (in the language of the Russian Declaration) what they had before lost.

It is conceived, nevertheless, to be a proposition founded in reason and natural justice, that no nation can *lawfully* make war upon another; for the *purpose* of compelling them to cede those *primitive rights*, to which they are entitled under the Law of Nature. Consequently, a cession of such rights, obtained by means of *force*, *unlawfully exercised for that end*, cannot justly preclude the injured nation from *reclaiming*, at a proper opportunity, the rights they had so lost. For, although "a pact is not invalid, if it be made with one who had a *right* to use violence,"....as in the case of a war undertaken upon a *just cause;* yet, "it is clear, that one is not bound by his promise to a robber, or to any one who *unjustly* uses violence against him*."....The analogy will hold between pacts and public treaties, in this case; the *reason* of the distinction being equally applicable to both.

If a contrary doctrine were to prevail, a powerful state might, at its pleasure, oppress one more weak or defenceless; and the latter could have no security for the enjoyment of those inherent and unalienable rights, which are derived from the Law of Nature. Even powerful states, themselves, if taken unexpectedly or by surprize, might be *forcibly* compelled to surrender such rights; in order to avert imminent dangers, more immediately affecting their national independence. In either case, most deplorable, indeed, would be the condition of a nation, if such compulsory cession of their privileges should debar them of a *right to regain them*, when in their power! No principle of natural justice would warrant a construction of the Law of Nations, which would deprive them of that right:....Nay, the

* See Heineccius, book i. chap. xiv. sect. 395.

maxim of Natural Law, that *no right can be founded on an injury*, directly opposes the admission of any such construction.

These observations are offered in order to demonstrate, how little probability there is, that those powers, who have been constrained by imperious circumstances to cede such of their national rights, as they have heretofore evinced a zealous determination to maintain, will submit to a *permanent* surrender of them. It may be readily perceived, that they will consider themselves justifiable upon the principles which they have, themselves, avowed, ...in "*reclaiming*" them. Although the cession that has been made, in the case under consideration, does indirectly affect all neutral states; it is, nevertheless, more immediately the concern of the parties in the transaction: to them, therefore, it belongs, to view it in such light....so far as it regards themselves,.... as they may deem it proper.

We had completed our dissertation on the maritime rights of neutrals, before the public prints announced the purport of the recent treaty between Russia and Sweden, and the convention between Russia and Great-Britain: ....Those events occasioned these additional observations. We were apprehensive, however, that the hostile measures lately pursued by Great-Britain, in the Baltic, would compel Russia, Denmark and Sweden, to abandon.... at least temporarily,....the stipulations of their convention of the 16th December, 1800. Under this impression we observed, towards the close of our treatise, that, whatever might be the issue of that convention, under the imperious circumstances of the moment,.....we placed too much confidence in their magnanimity, justice, and sense of their own interests, to entertain the least doubt of their concurring, ultimately, in support of the maritime rights of neutrals. How far the nature of their present engagements leave them at liberty to do this, it is their province to decide:....They are not ignorant of their rights; and, it is presumed, they know how to appreciate them.

But, let the ultimate conduct of Russia, Denmark and Sweden, with respect to their maritime rights as neutrals, be what it may; we are persuaded that our own country..... together with France, Spain, Prussia, and the Batavian Republic, as well as most of the other European states, which enjoy a considerable marine commerce,....will not consent on their part, to abandon those rights, on which the freedom of navigation and commerce, appertaining to them all, so much depend.

In the foregoing treatise we have endeavoured to shew, *what those rights are;* and we trust this is done in such manner, as amounts to a clear demonstration, that they are founded on the immutable principles of Reason and Natural Justice.

It is true, that notwithstanding Russia, in her character of a *neutral* power, has, by her recent convention with Great-Britain, excepted the property of nations at war from protection, in her ships; she has, nevertheless, obtained from Great-Britain a recognition of *other* neutral rights, which are of great importance. The stipulations respecting articles Contraband of war, and the right of Search, are here referred to.

Neither hemp, pitch, tar, wood, iron, nor any of the raw materials, employed in the manufacture of fire-arms, or other implements of war, are included in the list of contraband. Therefore, all naval stores, and every thing necessary to the construction of ships, are admitted to be (what they rightfully are) articles of free commerce:.....And so, also, are provisions.

Thus, although Russia has ceded to Great-Britain one of her important rights, as a neutral nation,.....the latter has, on her part, greatly relaxed her unjust pretensions, with respect to others. Russia, while neutral (and Denmark and Sweden likewise, if they have become parties to the convention of June 5.... 17th between Russia and Great-Britain), may carry to a nation engaged in war, "timber for ship-building, tar, rozin, hemp, and cordage, ...and, generally, whatever may serve directly to the equipment of vessels,"....together with "provisions:" But, by Mr. Jay's treaty, *we* have procured nothing that has even the appearance of an equivalent, for our cession of the principle...that free ships make free goods; ....for he has admitted all the articles thus described, to be contraband, with the exception of "unwrought iron and fir planks." And it ought not to be forgotten, that Messrs. C. C. Pinckney, Marshall, and Gerry, laboured to prove to the French government, in 1798, that the character of contraband of war ought to be attached, among other articles, to "naval stores, timber (for ship-building), *horses*,

....and even *provisions* in certain junctures, where there are hopes of reducing the enemy by *famine*." Consequently, the United States ....although they abound with those articles, which Mr. Jay, and our envoys to France in 1798, thought proper to denominate contraband,....are prohibited from carrying them to any nation with which Great-Britain may be at war; while the latter nation declares it not to be unlawful for the northern powers to carry the same articles to an enemy-nation!

The right of Search is also put on a footing, by the Russian and English convention, much more consonant to the Law of Nations, than that on which it stood by the late doctrines of the British court of Admiralty. Privateers are very properly interdicted from making any search, whatever, of vessels belonging to the respective parties, sailing under convoy of a ship of war of either power: And an ingenious writer, in a very respectable London print, makes the following remarks on the right of search, as defined in the convention....“ It gives up the right of search, to a degree far beyond what we calculated. If a Swedish* frigate, for instance, shall now be convoying a fleet of Swedish merchant-ships to France, and an English ship of the line falls in with them, the English ship is to send an officer on board the Swedish frigate, who is to inspect the papers of the Swede, and if there appear no cause of suspicion, then none of the Swedish merchantmen are to be at all examined, but the fleet is to pass on. He must trust to the Swedish frigate's taking cognizance of the cargoes and conduct of the mer-

* The writer of the observations quoted in the text (which appeared in the Morning Post) seems to have written them in full confidence that Sweden would accede, if she had not already done so, to the convention between Russia and Great-Britain. It does not appear, however, from the purport of the latest advices from Europe, that either Sweden or Denmark have become parties to that treaty:....On the contrary, they early indicated a strong disinclination, on the part of those powers, to participate therein; and Prussia has manifested a marked disapprobation of that negociation. Let the policy of Denmark and Sweden, on this occasion, be finally what it may, we find, by the Berlin prints of the 6th of June past, that, on the last day of the preceding month, M. de Rosencranz, the Danish ambassador at the Court of Berlin, exchanged with the Prussian cabinet-minister, Count Haugwitz, the act of ratification, respecting the *accession of Prussia* to the convention for *preserving the Rights of neutral maritime powers*, signed at Petersburg, on the 16th of December, 1800.

chantmen. She is responsible for them: they are, as it were, stowed in her hold....part of her cargo; and if her papers appear fair, then we are not at liberty to investigate those of the merchantmen. Our right of search, therefore, extends no further than seeing that the Swedish frigate, convoying the merchantmen, has regular papers and documents, to shew of what their cargoes consist. We are not allowed the privilege of questioning the crews of the merchant-men, or, by personal inquiries and examination on board their ships, discovering facts which cannot be learned in the frigate. We have the disadvantages which a court of law would labour under, of taking written evidence instead of personal testimony. We cannot cross-examine the parties concerned. Lord Robert Fitzgerald, in his writings, has accused the Danish Government of conniving at the exportation of warlike stores to France, and of a general spirit to favor the succouring of the French. The speeches of the late and present ministers, in parliament, were to the same effect. If Denmark and Sweden be so inclined, now,....it is only necessary to practise a little fraud on board the convoying frigate, and their wishes will be attained;

they cannot be detected. But such a fraud is unnecessary, since tar, hemp, iron, &c. are no longer contraband of war*. We have secured the faith of the neutral powers, by granting them full liberty to do all which might tempt them to be perfidious."

Such are the comments of an Englishman, on the result of the late negociation between his government and that of Russia. The former appear to have acquiesced in a great relaxation of their pretensions, respecting the contraband of war and right of search,

* In the year 1798, Mr. Lawford, a British commodore, sent an officer on board a Swedish frigate, convoying a fleet of merchantmen, to ask of what their cargoes consisted, and to what ports they were bound. The answer was, they were laden with hemp, pitch, tar, deals, iron, &c. and that they were mostly bound to ports in the Mediterranean. Upon this reply, the commodore neither desired to see any papers, nor made any search ; but, having called a council of war, he sent to the admiralty for instructions,....in the meanwhile, keeping company with the convoy. On the arrival of these instructions, he carried the whole fleet into Margate Roads. Such of the vessels as had cargoes of pitch, tar, hemp, and iron, were detained; and the others were released.

Hence we find the admiralty, in England, laying it down as law, that these articles were contraband of war; and, in the case of one of the detained ships, Sir William Scott expressly stated them, from the bench, to be of that description, and, as such, authorizing the detention of the whole convoy.

....in order that they might the more readily obtain from the latter a concession in favor of the British position....that neutral ships do not afford a lawful protection to enemy's goods. If, however, the abandonment of the legitimate principle, that free ships make free goods, was made by Russia, in this instance, on the grounds of such a compromise,....we should conceive a concession of that nature, induced by such considerations, to be highly derogatory from her national honor. The preceding conduct of the northern powers, and especially of Russia....together with the extraordinary predicament in which they were placed, at the time of the negociation,....warrant us, we think, in attributing the cession of an important neutral right, to motives much more compatible with the dignity of a nation.

But the writer we have just quoted, in the continuation of his remarks, considers the right of search, as modified in the convention with Russia, to be "a mockery:" For, presuming on the practice of those frauds and deceptions, by the northern powers, which he has hinted at....though such as, we are inclined to believe, no respectable government would, knowingly, tolerate,....he thinks the stipulation, which prohibits their carrying enemy's goods, a nullity. Under this impression, he says...."France can now import and export every article, in neutral bottoms, as well as if the whole British navy were locked up in port."....If, however, we could admit a belief, that the Russians, in consequence of the mode of search prescribed in the Russian convention with England, would avail themselves of the facility which that mode affords, of covering enemy's goods, ...thus defeating the end of an adverse stipulation, by unworthy means;....we should not deem the clandestine enjoyment of the mere benefits of a right extorted from them, desireable, under such circumstances.

The remaining stipulations of the convention accord with the principles of the Armed Neutrality of 1780. The third article provides....

"That the vessels of the neutral power shall be freely navigated to the ports, and on the coasts, of the nations at war."

"That, to prevent any equivocation or misunderstanding upon what is to be considered contraband of war, his imperial majesty of all the Russias and his Britannic majesty declare, conformably to the 11th article of the treaty of commerce concluded between the two crowns, the 10....21st, February, 1797, that they acknowledge the following articles to be such; viz. *cannons, mortars, fire-arms, pistols, bombs, grenades, bullets, balls, fusils, flints, matches, powder, salt-petre, sulphur, cuirasses, pikes, swords, belts, cartridge-boxes, saddles and bridles; excepting, however, such quantity of said articles, as may be necessary for the defence of the vessel and of the ship's company.*"

"That, to determine what characterizes a blockaded port, this denomination shall be given to such only as, when, by the disposition of the power who attacks it, with vessels at anchor or sufficiently near, there is a manifest danger in entering."

Thus, in fact, this convention....excepting its unjustifiable abandonment on the part of Russia, of the position, that free ships make free goods,....adheres to the principles of the Law of Nations, respecting the maritime Rights of Neutrals, stipulated in the treaty of Armed Neutrality. The writer above quoted thinks, the manner in which the right of search is restricted, makes it "a mockery,"....and, consequently, that the exception of enemy-goods from protection, in the neutral ship, is nugatory. He expresses his opinion, that the convention " gives to the confederacy all they asked, and relinquishes every claim, in the defence of which Mr. Pitt involved this country (Great-Britain) in a war with the powers of the Baltic. It falls as much short of those privileges, which we think necessary to the protection of our naval greatness, as Mr. Pitt's demands went beyond them."

Although we cannot coincide in the opinion, that this convention " gives to the confederacy all they asked ;" because it renounces a Right, which that confederacy have, in other instances, maintained: we consider it, nevertheless, as being favorable to the just claim of neutrals, in other respects. Great-Britain, in this very recent case, has greatly fallen from the loftiness of her pretensions, in regard to the contraband of war....the right of search.... blockaded ports....and the right of neutrals to sail freely along the coasts, and into the ports (not effectively blockaded), of belligerent nations. The rigid and injurious doctrines she has held in modern times, on those points, have been as strenuously supported by her statesmen and crown-lawyers, on the pretended ground of legitimacy; as that, on which they advocate the right of seizing enemies' goods in neutral ships. But we trust it has been satisfactorily shewn, that the principle, of free ships making free goods, is the *legitimate* one. Great-Britain is, therefore, equally bound, in *justice*, to concede this point; as she was, to recede from her pretensions concerning other neutral rights, in her convention with Russia: and, on the other hand, all neutral states are under an obligation to maintain every *right*, which belongs to them, respectively, in that character.

THE END.

APPENDIX.

ALTHOUGH extracts have been given, in the body of this treatise, from the following State-papers,....in order to illustrate the subject of the work; it was conceived, that partial quotations might be unsatisfactory to many readers. The writer has therefore thought it adviseable to subjoin those papers, entire, by way of an APPENDIX. Every person desirous of bestowing on the subject that attention which it merits, will, by this means, have a more full opportunity of gratifying his inclination: and the importance of the documents, thus brought into one view....especially those relating to the celebrated league of the Armed Neutrality,....renders any apology for the insertion of them, here, unnecessary.

The writer had not an opportunity of seeing Professor *Schlegel's* recent treatise on Neutral Rights, until he had very nearly completed the foregoing Dissertation: he could not, therefore, avail himself of the advantage, which he might have derived from a perusal of that work. He was fortunate enough, however,....after the printing of this book had very considerably advanced,....to have access to the library of his learned friend, PETER S. DU PONCEAU, Esq. of Philadelphia, (containing a valuable collection of works on Universal Law);....in sufficient time to furnish some interesting matter, which has been comprised in three or four of the notes....The writer takes this opportunity of making his acknowledgments to *Mr. Du Ponceau*, for some useful hints then suggested by him, on this occasion.

If the writer could, also, have had earlier recourse to *Chalmers's Treaties*, than he actually obtained,.... that collection would have enabled him to give, in his Dissertation, a more perfect catalogue of those treaties, which contain the stipulation, that *free ships make free goods*. The list exhibited, although it may not be in all respects accurate, is, notwithstanding, fully adequate to the purposes for which it was introduced:....Perfect accuracy was, in those respects, by no means essentially necessary.

APPENDIX.

No. I.

THE MARITIME TREATY (KNOWN BY THE NAME OF THE TREATY OF ARMED NEUTRALITY) BETWEEN THE EMPRESS OF RUSSIA AND THE KING OF DENMARK; ACCEDED TO BY THE KING OF SWEDEN, AND THE STATES-GENERAL OF THE UNITED PROVINCES.

ART. I. THEIR respective majesties are fully and sincerely determined to keep upon the most friendly terms with the present belligerent powers, and preserve the most exact neutrality: they solemnly declare their firm intention to be, that their respective subjects shall strictly observe the Laws forbidding all contraband trade with the powers now being, or that may hereafter be, concerned in the present disputes.

II. To prevent all equivocation or misunderstanding of the word Contraband, their imperial and royal majesties declare, that the meaning of the said word is solely restrained to such goods and commodities, as are mentioned under that denomination, in the treaties subsisting between their said majesties and either of the belligerent powers. Her imperial majesty abiding principally by the X and XI articles of the treaty of commerce with Great-Britain; the conditions therein mentioned, which are founded on the Rights of Nations, being understood to extend to the kings of France and Spain; as there is at present no specific treaty of commerce between the two latter and the former. His Danish majesty, on his part, regulates his conduct in this particular, by the first article of his treaty with England, and the 26th and 27th of that subsisting between his said majesty and the king of France, extending the provisions made in the latter to the Catholic king; there being no treaty *ad hoc*, between Denmark and Spain.

III. And whereas, by this means, the word *contraband*, conformable to the treaties now extant, and the stipulations made between the contracting powers, and those that are now at war, is fully explained; especially by the treaty between Russia and England, of the 20th of June, 1766; between the latter and Denmark, of the 11th of July, 1670; and between their Danish and most Christian majesties, of August 23d 1642; the will and opinion of the high contracting powers are, that all other trade whatsoever shall be deemed, and remain free and unrestrained.

By the declaration delivered to the belligerent powers, their contracting mejesties have already challenged the privileges founded on Natural Right, whence spring the Freedom of Trade and Navigation, as well as the Right of Neutral Powers: and being fully determined not to depend in future merely on an arbitrary interpretation, devised to answer some private advantages or concerns, they mutually covenanted as followeth:

1st. That it will be lawful for any ship, whatever, to sail freely from one port to another, or along the coasts of the powers now at war.

2nd. That all merchandize and effects belonging to the subjects of the said belligerent powers, and shipped on neutral bottoms, shall be entirely free; except contraband goods.

3d. In order to ascertain what constitutes the blockade of any place or port, it is to be understood to be in such predicament, when the assailing power has taken such a station, as to expose to imminent danger, any ship or ships that would attempt to sail in or out of the said ports.

4th. No Neutral ship shall be stopped, without a material and well-grounded cause: and in such cases, justice shall be done to them, without loss of time; and besides indemnifying, each and every time, the party aggrieved are thus stopped without sufficient cause, full satisfaction shall be given to the high contracting powers, for the insult offered to their flag.

IV. In order to protect officially the general trade of their respective subjects, on the fundamental principles aforesaid, her imperial and his royal majesty have thought proper, for effecting such purpose, each respectively to fit out a proportionate rate of ships of war and frigates. The squadron of each of the contracting powers shall be employed in escorting convoys, according to the particular circumstances of the navigators and traders of each nation,

V. Should any of the merchantmen belonging to the subjects of the contracting powers, sail in a latitude where there shall be no ships of war of their own nation, and thus be deprived of the protection; in such case, the commander of the squadron belonging to the other friendly power shall, at the request of said merchantmen, grant them sincerely, and *bona fide*, all necessary assistance. The ships of war and frigates, of either of the contracting powers, shall thus protect and assist the merchantmen of the other: provided nevertheless, that, under the sanction of such required assistance and protection, no contraband be carried on, nor any prohibited trade, contrary to the Laws of Neutrality.

VI. The present convention cannot be supposed to have any relative effect; that is, to extend to the differences they may have arisen since its being concluded: unless the controversy should spring from continual vexations, which might tend to aggrieve and oppress all the European nations.

VII If, notwithstanding the cautious and friendly care of the contracting powers, and their steady adherence to an exact Neutrality, the Russian and Danish merchantmen should happen to be insulted, plundered, or captured by any of the armed ships or privateers, belonging to any of the belligerent powers: in such case, the ambassador or envoy of the aggrieved party, to the offending court, shall claim such ship or ships, insisting on a proper satisfaction,....and never neglect to obtain a reparation for the insult offered to the flag of his court. The minister of the other contracting power shall at the same time, in the most efficacious and vigorous manner, defend such requisitions, which shall be supported by both parties with unanimity. But in case of any refusal, or even delay in redressing the grievances complained of; then their majesties will retaliate against the power that shall thus refuse to do them justice, and immediately agree together on the most proper means of making well-founded reprisals.

VIII. In case either of the contracting powers, or both at the same time, should be in any manner aggrieved or attacked, in consequence of the present convention, or for any reason relating thereto; it is agreed, that both powers will join, act in concert for their mutual defence, and unite their forces, in order to procure to themselves an adequate and perfect satisfaction, both in regard to the insult put upon their respective flags, and the losses suffered by their subjects.

IX. This convention shall remain in force for and during the continuance of the present war; and *the obligation enforced thereby, will serve as the ground-work of all treaties that may be set on foot hereafter:* according to future occurrences, and on the breaking out of any fresh maritime wars which might unluckily disturb the tranquillity of Europe. Meanwhile, *all that is hereby agreed upon, shall be deemed as binding and permanent*, in regard both to mercantile and naval affairs; and shall have the force of *Law, in determining the Rights of Neutral Nations.*

X. *The chief aim and principal object of the present convention being to secure the Freedom of Trade and Navigation*, the high contracting powers have antecedently agreed, and do engage to give to all other neutral powers free leave to accede to the present treaty, and, after a thorough knowledge of the principles on which it rests, share equally in the obligations and advantages thereof.

XI. In order that the powers, now at war, may not be ignorant of the strength and nature of the engagements entered into by the two courts aforesaid, the high contracting parties shall give notice, in the most friendly manner, to the belligerent powers, of the measures by them taken; by which, far from meaning any manner of hostility, or causing any loss or injury to other powers, their only intention is to protect the trade and navigation of their respective subjects.

XII. This convention shall be ratified by the contracting powers, and the ratifications interchanged between the parties in due form, within the space of six weeks, from the day of its being signed, or even sooner, if possible. In witness whereof, and by virtue of the full powers granted us for the purpose, we have put our hands and seals to the present treaty.

Given at Copenhagen, July the 19th, 1780.

CHARLES D'OSTEN, called SOKEN.
J. SCHACK RATLAU.
A. P. COMPTE BERNSTORFF.
O. THOFT.
H. EIKSTEDT.

Acceded to, and signed by the Plenipotentiaries of the court of Sweden, at St. Petersburg, 21st of July,

1780: and by the States-General accepted, November 20th, 1780; and signed at St. Petersburg, January 5th, 1781, with the addition only of article....

XIII. If the respective squadrons, or ships of war, should meet or unite, to act in conjunction, the command in chief will be regulated according to what is commonly practised between the crowned heads and the republic.

No. II.

DECLARATION OF THE EMPRESS OF RUSSIA, TO THE COURTS OF LONDON, VERSAILLES AND MADRID.... DATED, FEBRUARY 26, 1780.

THE empress of all the Russias has so fully manifested her sentiments of equity and moderation, and has given such evident proofs, during the course of the war that she supported against the Ottoman Porte, of the regard she has for the rights of neutrality and the liberty of universal commerce, as all Europe can witness. This conduct, as well as the principles of impartiality that she has displayed during the present war, justly inspired her with the fullest confidence, that her subjects would peaceably enjoy the fruits of their industry and the advantages belonging to a neutral nation. Experience has, nevertheless, proved the contrary. Neither the abovementioned considerations, nor a regard to the rights of nations, have prevented the subjects of her imperial majesty from being often molested in their navigation, and stopped in their operations, by those of the belligerent powers.

These hindrances to the liberty of trade in general, and to that of Russia in particular, are of a nature to excite the attention of all neutral nations. The empress finds herself obliged, therefore, to free it, by all the means compatible with her dignity and the well-being of her subjects: but, before she puts this in execution, and with a sincere intention to prevent any future infringements, she thought it but just to publish to all Europe the principles she means to follow, which are the properest to prevent any misunderstanding, or any occurrences that may occasion it. Her imperial majesty does it with the more confidence, as she finds these principles coincident with the primitive right of nations, which every people may reclaim, and which the belligerent powers cannot invalidate without violating the Laws of Neutrality, and without disowning the maxims they have adopted in their different treaties and public engagemets.

They are reducible to the following points:

1st, That all neutral ships may freely navigate from port to port, and on the coasts of nations at war.

2dly, That the effects belonging to the subjects of the said warring powers shall be free in all neutral vessels, except contraband merchandize.

3dly, That the empress, as to the specification of the above-mentioned merchandize, holds to what is mentioned in the tenth and eleventh articles of her treaty of commerce with Great-Britain, extending her obligations to all the powers at war.

4thly, That, to determine what is meant by a blocked-up port, this is only to be understood of one which is so well kept in, by the ships of the power that attacks it, and which keep their places, that it is dangerous to enter into it.

5thly, That these principles serve as a rule for proceedings and judgments upon the legality of prizes.

Her imperial majesty, in making these points public, does not hesitate to declare, that to maintain them, and to protect the honour of her flag, the security of the trade and navigation of her subjects, she has prepared the greatest part of her maritime forces. This measure will not, however, influence the strict neutrality she does observe, and will observe, so long as she is not provoked and forced to break the bounds of moderation and perfect impartiality. It will be only in this extremity, that her fleet have orders to go wherever honour, interest, and need may require.

In giving this solemn assurance with the usual openness of her character, the empress cannot do other than promise herself that the belligerent powers, convinced of the sentiments of justice and equity which animate her, will contribute towards the accomplishment of these salutary purposes, which manifestly tend to the good of all nations, and to the advantage even of those at war. In consequence of which, her imperial majesty will furnish her commanding officers with instructions, conformable to the above mentioned principles, founded upon the *primitive laws of people, and so often adopted in their conventions.*

No. III.

THE MEMORIAL PRESENTED TO THEIR HIGH MIGHTINESSES BY PRINCE GALLITZIN, THE RUSSIAN MINISTER, ON THE PART OF THE EMPRESS HIS SOVEREIGN.

High and Mighty Lords,

THE underwritten envoy extraordinary from the empress of all the Russias has the honour to communicate to you a copy of the declaration which the empress, his sovereign, has made to the belligerent powers. Your High Mightinesses may look upon this communication as a particular mark of the attention of the empress for the republic, which is equally interested in the reasons which occasioned the declaration. He has further orders to declare to your High Mightinesses, in the name of her imperial majesty, that how desirous soever she may be on the one hand to maintain the strictest neutrality during the present war, yet her majesty is as determined to take the most efficacious means to support the honour of the Russian flag, the security of the trade, and the navigation of her subjects, and not suffer either to be hurt by any of the belligerent powers: that, in order to prevent, on this occasion, any misunderstanding or false interpretation, she thought it necessary to specify in the declaration the limits of a free trade, and what is called contraband. That, if the definition of the former is founded upon the clearest notions of Natural Right, the latter is literally taken from the treaty of commerce between Russia and Great-Britain, by which her imperial majesty means incontestibly to prove her good faith and impartiality towards each party; that she consequently apprehends that the other trading powers will immediately come into her way of thinking relative to neutrality.

From these considerations, her imperial majesty has ordered the underwritten to invite your High Mightinesses to make a common cause with her, as such an union may serve to protect the trade and navigation, and at the same time observe a strict neutrality, and to communicate to your High Mightinesses the regulation she has in consequence taken.

The same invitation has been made to the courts of Copenhagen, Stockholm, and Lisbon, in order that by the united endeavours of all the neutral maritime powers, a natural system, founded on justice, might be established and legalised in favour of the trade of neutral nations, which, by its real advantages, might serve for a rule for future ages.

The underwritten does not doubt but your High Mightinesses will, without delay, take the invitation of her imperial majesty into consideration, and concur in immediately making a declaration to the belligerent powers, founded on the same principles as that of the empress, explaining, at the same time, the nature of a free and contraband trade, conformable to their respective treaties with the other nations.

For the rest, the underwritten has the honour to assure your High Mightinesses, that if, to establish such a glorious and advantageous system upon the most solid basis, they wished to open a negociation with the above-mentioned neutral powers on this subject, the empress, his sovereign, is ready to join you.

Your Mightinesses will easily see the necessity of accelerating your resolutions upon objects of such importance and advantage for humanity in general. The underwritten begs of you to give him a speedy answer.

DEMETRI PRINCE GALLITZIN.

Hague, April 3d. 1780.

No. IV.

ANSWER FROM THE KING OF SPAIN, TO THE DECLARATION OF THE EMPRESS OF RUSSIA.

THE king, being informed of the empress's sentiments with respect to the belligerent and neutral powers, by a memorial remitted to Comte de Florida Blanca, on the 15th inst. by Mr. Etienne de Zinowief, minister of her imperial majesty: the king considers this as the effect of a just confidence which his majesty has on his part merited; and it is yet more agreeable that the principles adopted by this sovereign should be the same as have always guided the king, and which his majesty has for a long time, but without success, endeavoured to cause England to observe, while Spain remained neuter. These principles are founded in justice, equity and moderation; and these same principles Russia and all the other powers have experienced in the resolutions formed by his majesty; and it has been entirely owing to the conduct of the English navy, both in the last and the present war (a conduct wholly subversive of the received rules among neutral powers) that his majesty has been obliged to follow their example; since the English paying no respect to a neutral flag, if the same be laden with effects belonging to the enemy, even if the articles should not be contraband, and that flag not using any means of defending itself, there could not be any just cause why Spain should not make reprisals, to indemnify herself for the great disadvantages she must otherwise labour under. The neutral powers have also laid themselves open to the inconveniences they have suffered, by furnishing themselves with double papers, and other artifices, to prevent the capture of their vessels; from which have followed captures and detentions innumerable, and other disagreeable consequences, though in reality not so prejudicial as pretended; on the contrary, some of these detentions have turned to the advantage of the proprietors, as the goods, being sold in the port where they were condemned, have frequently gone off at a higher price than they would have done at the place of their destination.

The king nevertheless, not contented with these proofs of his justification, which have been manifested to all Europe, will this day have the glory of being the first to give the example of respecting the neutral flag of all the courts that have consented, or shall consent, to defend it, till his majesty finds what part the English navy takes, and whether they will, together with their privateers, keep within proper bounds. And to shew to all the neutral powers how much Spain is desirous of observing the same rules in time of war as she was directed by whilst neuter, his majesty conforms to the other points contained in the declaration of Russia. To be understood, nevertheless, that, with regard to the blockade of Gibraltar, the danger of entering subsists, as determined by the fourth article of the said declaration. These dangers may, however, be avoided by the neutral powers, if they conform to those rules of precaution established by his majesty's declaration of the 13th of last March, which has been communicated to the court of Petersburg by his minister.

FLORIDA BLANCA.

At Aranjuez, April 18, 1780.

No. V.

ANSWER FROM THE COURT OF GREAT-BRITAIN TO THE DECLARATION OF THE EMPRESS OF RUSSIA: SENT TO THE BRITISH ENVOY AT ST. PETERSBURG, APRIL 23d, 1780.

DURING the course of the war, wherein his Britannic majesty finds himself engaged through the unprovoked aggression of France and Spain, he hath constantly manifested his sentiments of justice, equity, and moderation, in every part of his conduct. His majesty hath acted towards friendly and neutral powers according to their own procedure respecting Great-Britain, and conformable to the clearest principles generally acknowledged as the Law of Nations, being the only law between powers where no treaties subsist, and agreeable to the tenor of his different engagements with other powers; those *engagements* have *altered* this *primitive law**, by mutual stipulations, proportioned to the will and convenience of the contracting parties.

* This, we contend, they could not *rightfully* do....See the *Note* subjoined to the Declaration of Denmark to the courts of London, Versailles and Madrid.

W. B.

Strongly attached to her majesty of all the Russias, by the ties of reciprocal friendship and common interest, the king, from the commencement of those troubles, gave the most precise orders respecting the flag of her imperial majesty, and the commerce of her subjects, agreeable to the law of nations, and the tenor of the engagements stipulated by his treaty of commerce with her, and to which he shall adhere with the most scrupulous exactness.

The orders to this intent have been renewed, and the utmost care will be taken for their strictest execution.

It may be presumed, not the least irregularity will happen; but in case any infringements, contrary to these repeated orders, take place, the courts of admiralty, which in this, like all other countries, are established to take cognizance of such matters, and *in all cases do judge solely by the law of nations, and by the specific stipulations of different treaties*, will redress every hardship in so equitable a manner, that her imperial majesty shall be perfectly satisfied, and acknowledge a like spirit of justice, which she herself possesses.

No. VI.

ANSWER FROM THE KING OF FRANCE TO THE DECLARATION OF THE EMPRESS OF RUSSIA.

THE war in which the king is engaged, having no other object than the attachment of his majesty to the freedom of the seas, he could not but with the truest satisfaction see the empress of Russia adopt the same principle, and resolve to maintain it. That which her imperial majesty claims from the belligerent powers is no other than the rules already prescribed to the French marine, the execution of which is maintained with an exactitude known and applauded by all Europe.

The liberty of neutral vessels, restrained only in a few cases, is the direct consequence of neutral right, the safeguard of all nations, and the relief even of those at war. The king has been desirous, not only to procure a freedom of navigation to the subjects of the empress of Russia, but to those of all the states who hold their neutrality, and that upon the same conditions as are announced in the treaty to which his majesty this day answers.

His majesty thought he had taken a great step for the general good, and prepared a glorious epocha for his reign, by fixing, by his example, the rights which every belligerent power may, and ought to acknowledge, to be due to neutral vessels. His hopes have not been deceived, as the empress, in avowing the strictest neutrality, has declared in favour of a system which the king is supporting at the price of his people's blood, and that her majesty adopts the same rights as he would wish to make the basis of the maritime code.

If fresh orders were necessary to prevent the vessels of her imperial majesty from being disturbed in their navigation by the subjects of the king, his majesty would immediately give them; but the empress will no doubt be satisfied with the dispositions made by his majesty in the regulations he has published. They do not hold by circumstances only, but they are founded on the right of nations, and quite suitable to a prince who finds the happiness of his own kingdom in that of general prosperity. The king wishes her imperial majesty would add, to the means she has fixed to determine what merchandizes are reckoned *contraband* in time of war, precise rules in the form of the sea-papers, with which the Russian ships will be furnished.

With this precaution, his majesty is assured nothing will happen to make him regret the having put the Russian navigators on as advantageous a footing as can be in time of war. Happy circumstances have more than once occurred to prove to the courts how important it is for them to explain themselves freely relative to their respective interests.

His majesty is very happy to have explained his way of thinking to her imperial majesty, upon so interesting a point for Russia, and the trading powers of Europe. He the more sincerely applauds the principles and views of the empress, as his majesty partakes of the same sentiments which have brought her maiesty to adopt those measures which must be to the advantage of her own subjects, and all other nations.

Versailles, April 25th, 1780.

No. VII.

DECLARATION OF THE KING OF DENMARK AND NORWAY, TO THE COURTS OF LONDON, VERSAILLES, AND MADRID.

IF the most exact and perfect neutrality, with the most regular navigation, and the most inviolable respect to treaties, could have kept free the commerce of the subjects of the king of Denmark and Norway, from the inroads of the powers with whom he is at peace, free and independent, it would not be necessary to take measures to insure to his subjects that liberty to which they have the most incontrovertible right. The king of Denmark has always founded his glory, and his grandeur, upon the esteem and confidence of other people. It has been his rule, from the beginning of his reign, to testify to all the powers, his friends, a conduct the most capable of convincing them of his pacific intentions, and of his desire to contribute to the general happiness of Europe. His proceedings have always been conformable to these principles, against which nothing can be alleged; he has not, till now, addressed himself, but to the powers at war, to obtain a redress of his grievances; and he has never wanted moderation in his demands, nor acknowledgments when they have received the success they deserved: but the neutral navigation has been too often molested, and the most innocent commerce of his subjects too frequently troubled; so that the king finds himself obliged to take proper measures to assure to himself and his allies, the safety of commerce and navigation, and the maintenance of the inseparable rights of liberty and independence. If the duties of neutrality are sacred, the law of nations has also its rights avowed by all impartial powers, established by custom, and founded upon equity and reason. A nation independent and neuter, does not lose by the wars of others the rights which she had before the war, because peace exists between her and all the belligerent powers. Without receiving or being obliged to follow the laws of either of them, she is allowed to follow, in all places (contraband excepted), the traffic which she would have a right to do, if peace existed with all Europe, as it exists with her. The king pretends to nothing beyond what the neutrality allows him. This is his rule, and that of his people; and the king cannot accord to the principle, that a power at war has a right to interrupt the commerce of his subjects. He thinks it due to himself and his subjects, faithful observers of these rules, and to the powers at war themselves, to declare to them the following principles, which he *has always held*, and which he *will always avow* and maintain, in concert with the empress of all the Russias, whose sentiments he finds entirely conformable with his own.

1st. That neutral vessels have a right to navigate freely from port to port, even on the coasts of the powers at war.

2nd. That the effects of the subjects of the powers at war shall be free in neutral vessels, except such as are deemed contraband.

3d. That nothing is to be understood under the denomination of contraband, that is not expressly mentioned as such in the third article of his treaty of commerce with Great-Britain, in the year 1670*, and the

* The twentieth article of this treaty is in these words; viz. "But lest such freedom of navigation, or passage of the one ally, and his subjects and people, during the war that the other may have by sea or land with any other country, may be to the prejudice of the other ally, *and that goods and merchandize belonging to the enemy may be fraudulently concealed, under colour of being in amity;* for the preventing of fraud and clearing all suspicion, it is thought fit, that the ships, goods, and men belonging to the other confederate, in their passage and voyages, be accompanied with letters of passport and certificate; the forms whereof to be as follows:" &c.

And, in like manner, the twelfth article of the treaty between England and Sweden, concluded in the year 1661, had declared, that, "For the evading of all suspicion and collusion, lest the free navigation or intercourse of one of the confederates, his subjects, inhabitants by land or sea, with other nations, while the other confederate is at war, should be carried on to the prejudice of the other confederate; and *lest the enemies' goods and merchandize should be concealed under the disguise of the goods of friends,* it is stipulated that all ships, carriages, wares, and men, belonging to the other of the confederation, shall be furnished in their journies and voyages with safe conducts, commonly called passports and certificates, such as are underwritten;" &c.

Two treaties between these powers and Great-Britain, as we have stated in page 42, (and one of which is the Swedish treaty above-mentioned), were cited by the British government, in their controversy with Prussia in 1753, to support their doctrine....that free ships do not afford a rightful protection to enemy's goods. But we have shewn, that no *legitimate* obligatory force can attach to any stipulation by treaty, which purports to be a cession of an important *Right,* derived from *Nature*....and, consequently, founded on *Natural Justice;*...although, conventional stipulations, that respect matters which are *in themselves indifferent,* and *which do not tend to infringe any Natural Right, common to all independent nations, and conducive to their well-being,* impose on the contracting powers an obligation, to observe them with the most scrupulous exactitude and good faith. It is evident, that both Denmark and Sweden, as well as Russia, conceived

26th and 27th articles of his treaty of commerce with France, in the year 1742; and the king will equally maintain these rules with those powers with whom he has no treaty.

4th. That he will look upon that as a port blocked up, into which no vessel can enter without evident danger, on account of vessels of war stationed there, which form an effectual blockade.

5th. That these principles serve for rules in procedure, and that justice shall be expeditiously rendered, after the rules of the sea, conformably to treaty and usage received.

6th. His majesty does not hesitate to declare, that he will maintain these principles with the honour of his flag, and the liberty and independence of the commerce and navigation of his subjects; and that it is for this purpose he has armed a part of his navy, although he is desirous to preserve, with all the powers at war, not only a good understanding, but all the friendship which the neutrality can admit of. *The king will never recede from these principles*, unless he is *forced* to it: he knows the duties and the obligations, he respects them as he does his treaties, and desires no other than to maintain them. His majesty is persuaded, that the belligerent powers will acknowledge the justice of his motives; that they will be as averse as himself to doing any thing that may *oppress the liberties of mankind*, and that they will give their orders to their admiralty

this distinction to be founded in truth and reason. The language of the two former, in their respective *Declarations* to the courts of London, Versailles, and Madrid, fully evinces their adherence to the doctrine on which that distinction is predicated: and the empress of Russia, in her declaration to the same courts (wherein she asserts, among other Neutral Rights, the *legitimacy* of the principle, *that free ships make free goods;* expressly says, "she finds these principles coincident with the *primitive Right of Nations, which every people may reclaim*, and which the belligerent powers cannot invalidate, *without violating the Laws of Neutrality*." &c.

W. B.

and to their officers, conformably to the principles above recited, which tend to the general happiness and interest of all Europe.

Copenhagen, July 8th, 1780.

No. VIII.

DECLARATION OF THE KING OF SWEDEN TO THE SAME COURTS.

EVER since the beginning of the present war, the king has taken particular care to manifest his intentions to all Europe. He imposed unto himself the law of a perfect neutrality; he fulfilled all the duties thereof with the most scrupulous exactitude; and in consequence thereof, he thought himself entitled to all the prerogatives naturally appertaining to the qualification of a sovereign perfectly neuter. But notwithstanding this, his commercial subjects have been obliged to claim his protection, and his majesty has found himself under the necessity to grant it to them.

To effect this, the king ordered last year a certain number of men of war to be fitted out. He employed a part thereof on the coasts of his kingdom, and the rest served as convoys for the Swedish merchant ships in the different seas which the commerce of his subjects required them to navigate. He acquainted the several belligerent powers with these measures, and was preparing to continue the same during the course of this year, when other courts, who had likewise adopted a perfect neutrality, communicated their sentiments unto him, which the king found entirely conformable to his own, and tending to the same object.

The empress of Russia caused a declaration to be delivered to the courts of London, Versailles, and Madrid, in which she acquainted them of her resolution to protect the commerce of her subjects, and to defend the *universal rights and prerogatives of neutral nations.* This declaration was founded upon such *just principles of the law of nations* and the subsisting treaties, that it was impossible to call them into question. The king found them entirely concordant with his own cause, and with the treaty concluded in the year 1666, between Sweden and France; and his majesty could not forbear to acknowledge and to adopt the same principles, not only with regard to those powers, with whom the said treaties are in force, but also with regard to such others as are already engaged in the present war, or may be involved therein hereafter, and with whom the king has no treaties to reclaim. It is the *universal law*, and when there are no particular engagements existing, it becomes *obligatory upon all nations.*

In consequence thereof, the king declares hereby again, " That he will observe the same neutrality, and with the same exactitude as he has hitherto done. He will enjoin all his subjects, under rigorous pains, not to act in any manner whatever contrary to the duties which a strict neutrality imposes unto them; but he will effectually protect their lawful commerce, by all possible means, whenever they carry on the same, conformably to the principles here above mentioned.

APPENDIX, No. IX.

ORDINANCE AND DECLARATION OF THE KING OF PRUSSIA, CONCERNING THE NAVIGATION AND MARITIME COMMERCE OF HIS SUBJECTS; MADE IN CONSEQUENCE OF THE ARMED NEUTRALITY.

FREDERIC R.

EVER since the beginning of the present maritime war, which has since spread over almost all the southern parts of Europe, the king has been particularly attentive to procure to all his subjects, who traffic by sea or practise navigation, all the security they were entitled to. To this end, his majesty has, by means of his ministers, requested of the belligerent powers, that they would give strict and precise orders to all commanders of their ships of war and privateers, to respect the Prussian flag, and to let all Prussian ships, laden with goods and merchandizes, which according to the law of nations are lawful, and not contraband, free and peaceably pass and repass, without causing them the least damage or retard; and much less to conduct them without any right or necessity into any foreign ports. To this request, the said powers have not only returned the most satisfactory answers, but have also given the most friendly assurances that it should be complied with in every respect.

To obtain this end, with still more certainty, his majesty has commanded all his ministers, residing at the courts of the belligerent powers, to interest themselves in the most efficacious manner, and by the most energetic representations, in favour of the Prussian subjects trading by sea, whose ships may have been taken, conducted in any foreign port, or, as it has often happened, pillaged and robbed in the open sea; and to insist that they be speedily released, and that all law-suits, which their capture may occasion, be decided with impartiality and without loss of time.

In order, therefore, to second these beneficial views of his majesty, and to enable the king's ministers to acquit themselves of these his royal orders in that respect, it is necessary that the subjects of his majesty, who may find themselves in that case, should either apply personally, or by means of a commissioner, to the king's minister at the court where complaint is to be exhibited, and that they should give him a true and circumstantial account of the subject of their complaint, in order that he may exhibit and support the same, where and when he shall see cause. They are, however, not to rely entirely and only on the intercession of the said minister, but they are likewise to exhibit their complaints, either by themselves or by their commissioners, before the admiralties or maritime colleges of the country where their ships may have been conducted, or wherein they may have sustained any damage; to support these complaints with the necessary proofs; to conform to the judiciary forms established in each country; and to plead and pursue their causes with all possible diligence, by means of their attornies, or other persons properly qualified. By these means, his majesty flatters himself, that they will obtain a prompt and impartial decision; but if the contrary should be the case, they shall then apply to the king's envoys, for them to lay before each court such complaints as the case may require, and to obtain due satisfaction.

But in order to secure the more, for the future, the navigation of his subjects from all insults, the king has, by his minister, requested her majesty the empress of Russia, and the two other northern maritime powers, who, as it is well known, have joined in a convention for maintaining the maritime neutrality, that they would be pleased, as powers with whom the king has the satisfaction to live in perfect harmony and friendship, to give orders to all commanders of their ships of war, to take the Prussian merchant ships, which they may meet with at sea, within sight, and within reach of their cannons, under their protection and convoy, and to assist and defend them, in all cases where they shall be attacked, or any ways molested by the ships of war or privateers of the belligerent powers.

Her majesty, the empress of Russia, has assured the king, by a written declaration from her ministry, that she has not only caused the most precise orders to be given to all commanders of her ships of war, that they shall protect, against all attacks and molestations whatever, the ships of the Prussian merchants and navigators, which they may meet with either at sea, or in any port, as belonging to a power allied with Russia, and which shall scrupulously observe the rules of maritime neutrality, as founded on the law of nations; but that she would likewise enjoin all her ministers at the courts of the belligerent powers, that whenever the Prussian envoys may have any complaint to exhibit at the court where they reside, concerning any hindrance or vexation caused to the maritime commerce of Prussian subjects, that they shall support the same, in the name of her imperial majesty, with all the good offices, influence, and assistance in their power; and that in return to this, her imperial majesty expects, that his majesty, the king of Prussia, would also furnish his ministers, residing at the courts of the belligerent powers, with instructions conformable to the convention of the northern maritime powers, with orders to support, likewise, by the most energetic representations, all the complaints of the ministers of the allied powers for the defence of maritime neutrality, in all cases where they may have any satisfaction to demand for the subjects of their sovereigns.

The king has accepted this amicable declaration of her imperial majesty with great pleasure and gratitude; and by a counter declaration, every ways conformable to the above, has signified his willingness to comply with the views of her imperial majesty, and in consequence thereof, has caused the necessary instructions to be given to his ministers residing at the different courts.

Already before this, his majesty had, on the occasion of another negociation with the court of Denmark, requesting his Danish majesty to grant the protection of his naval forces to the Prussian merchant ships, from whom his majesty had likewise received the friendly assurance, that the Danish ships of war should take under their protection and convoy all such Prussian ships as should conform to the treaties subsisting between the court of Denmark and the belligerent powers, with regard to contraband commodities. The king has caused the same request to be made to the court of Sweden, and he flatters himself with an answer from his Swedish majesty, equally favourable as those from their majesties the empress of Russia and the king of Denmark.

His majesty, therefore, thinks proper to acquaint all his subjects, who traffic by sea, or practise navigation, and all others whom it may concern, with the above arrangements, in order that they, or the captains and commanders of their ships may conform thereto; and that in case they should be attacked, molested, or taken by the ships of war or privateers of the belligerent nations, that they may apply to the Russian, Danish, or Swedish ships of war, that may be within their reach, to demand their protection and assistance, and that they may join, as much as possible, the fleets and convoys of these three northern maritime powers.

But the king's intention is merely to secure, by the above arrangements, the lawful commerce of his subjects, and not to cause any prejudice to the different powers at war, with whom he lives in perfect harmony, nor to favour any contraband dealings whatever; all the subjects of his majesty, who traffic by sea, or practise navigation, are hereby enjoined to observe the most exact neutrality, conformable to the laws of nature, and the rights and privileges of nations, almost universally acknowledged. But as the different treaties, respecting the maritime commerce, which several powers have concluded among themselves, might create some difference in these rights and privileges, it is principally to the known *declaration*, which her majesty, the empress of Russia has caused to be presented, last year, to the belligerent powers, and to the ordinance which his majesty afterwards issued, on the 8th of March, 1780, for the regulation of her colleges of commerce, to which the subjects of the king are to conform, with regard to their maritime commerce; the principles set forth therein being such as his majesty finds the most coinciding with the rights and privileges of nations in general, and with his own in particular.

In consequence thereof, it is ordered by this present edict, to all the Prussian subjects, who are in any ways concerned in the maritime commerce and navigation, as follows:

ART. I. That they shall not take any part, under what pretence soever, in the present war; and shall not carry to any of the belligerent powers, under the Prussian flag, any goods or merchandize generally acknowledged as contraband, and which constitute implements or ammunitions of war; such as cannons, mortars, flints, matches, gunpowder, salt-petre, pikes, sulphur, swords, and saddles. The subjects of the king shall also be cautious not to carry on board of their trading ships, any more of these articles than is absolutely necessary for their own use.

ART. II. All Prussian subjects are, on the contrary, allowed and permitted to carry, under the Prussian flag, as well to the belligerent as to neutral nations, all kinds of goods and merchandizes which are not comprehended in the foregoing article, and which cannot properly be construed as implements or ammunitions of war; nor are hereby prohibited, but particularly allowed, all the productions of all the different provinces of his majesty's dominions. His majesty expects, from the equity and friendship of the belligerent powers, that they will not henceforth permit their ships of war, or privateers, to molest or seize any Prussian ships laden with *masts*, *hemp*, *pitch*, *corn*, and other materials, *which, without being warlike stores*, may however be *converted* into such, and which constitute the principal and almost only object of the Prussian commerce....These powers, it is hoped are too *just, to expect that the commerce of a neutral nation should be suspended or entirely annihilated, on account of their broils and wars.* After these principles, it is likewise hoped, that the different powers at war will henceforth let freely pass and repass, without seizing or confiscating, all lawful cargoes, goods and merchandize, belonging to Prussian subjects, and which may be laden on board of ships belonging to the subjects of any belligerent nations; and in the same manner all lawful cargoes, goods and merchandize, belonging to the subjects of any *belligerent* powers, and that may be laden on board of Prussian ships; "for, in all these cases, his majesty will most efficaciously interfere in favor of his subjects trading by sea."

But as it is prudent to avoid contestations as much as possible, his majesty most earnestly recommends to all his subjects, to endeavour, as much as can be, to load their goods and effects on board of Prussian ships, and always to carry the same under the Prussian flag; as also not to employ themselves, more than need be, in any coasting trade; but to adhere principally to the Prussian commerce only, in order to avoid the better all accidents, misunderstandings, and difficulties.

Art. III. All Prussian ships, before they put to sea, shall provide themselves with proper passports and attestations from the admiralties, maritime colleges, or magistrates of the city or port from which they sail; as also with proper clearances, bills of lading, and other customary certificates, in which shall be expressed the quality and quantity of the cargo, the name of the proprietor, and of the person to whom the goods are sent, as well as the name of the place for which the ship is destined. All these papers shall in every respect be clear and not equivocal. They shall always be kept on board, and shall not be thrown into the sea, under any pretext whatever. All captains or commanders of ships are above all hereby forbidden to have on board of their ships any double, equivocal, or entirely false papers of passports; in which case, upon due conviction thereof, they shall not only be deprived of his majesty's protection, but also incur severe punishment.

Art. IV. All Prussian ships, taking in any cargo in a foreign port, shall likewise provide themselves with the necessary passports and clearances, which are customarily granted to trading ships in that port, in order that they may prove every where of what nation they are, what their cargo consists of, from whence they come, and for what port they are bound; and if any pirate or other should take the said papers from them by force, the king will consider it as an offence of the first magnitude.

Art. V. No officers, or other persons employed in the navy of any of the belligerent nations, shall be taken as passengers, or otherwise be found on board of any Prussian ship: nor shall any more than one-third of the crew, consist of natives of any of these nations.

Art. VI. All Prussian navigators are hereby strictly commanded, not to take any cargoes, goods, or merchandize, whatever, to any fortified place or port, that may be besieged, blockaded, or surrounded by the ships of war of any of the belligerent powers.

Art. VII. All Prussian navigators are likewise expressly forbidden to lend their names, papers, &c. to any other nation; for they are to carry on their trade in general in a manner conformable to the rights and customs of all nations, so that they may not occasion any prejudice to the rights of the belligerent powers, nor subject themselves to any reason of complaint.

All those of his majesty's subjects, who shall strictly conform to the tenor of this present edict, may rely on the king's most efficacious protection; but all those who shall neglect to conform thereto, shall not only be deprived of his protection, but may attribute to themselves all the dangers and damages which they may draw upon them, by a conduct contrary to the tenor of this present ordinance.

Given at Berlin, April 30, 1781.

By order of his majesty,

FINKENSTEIN.

E. F. DE HERTZBERG.

No. X.

LETTER FROM MR. FOX TO MONS. SIMOLIN....DATED MARCH 29, 1782.

SIR,

HAVING laid before his majesty an extract of the letter, which you did me the honor, Sir, of communicating from prince Gallitzin and Mons. de Marcoff, I have his majesty's commands to inform you, that the king, desirous of testifying his intentions towards their H. M. and of renewing that friendship which has been so unfortunately interrupted between old allies, who ought to be united in the bonds of mutual interest, is ready to enter into a negociation, for the purpose of setting on foot a treaty of peace, on the terms and conditions of that which was agreed to, in 1674, between his majesty and the republic: and that the better to facilitate the execution of a plan which his majesty has so much at heart, the king is willing to give immediate orders for a suspension of hostilities, if, on their part, the lords the States-General should think such a measure suitable to the object in view.

I am commanded by his majesty to explain to you, Sir, his sentiments on so important a subject, and desire you will impart the same to the ministers of her imperial majesty to their H. M. that they may be conveyed, without the least delay, to the ministers of the Republic; being of opinion that it is the most convenient step, with the mediation and good offices of her imperial majesty, to put an end to the scourge of that war, which unfortunately subsists between the two nations.

I have the honor to be, &c.

C. J. Fox.

No. XI.

MEMORIAL FROM PRINCE GALLITZIN AND MONS. DE MARCOFF, TO THE STATES GENERAL.

THE underwritten, joint ministers of the empress of all the Russias, in consequence of the orders given them, to accelerate, as much as in them lies, the salutary work of the mediation entrusted to her imperial majesty, think it their duty to lose no time to communicate to your high mightinesses a copy of a letter written to Mons. *Simolin*, their sovereign's minister at London, by Mr. *Fox*, secretary of state to his Britannic majesty. It will convince your H. M. of the intentions of his B. M. to be sincerely reconciled to the Republic, on the conditions, by yourselves established, in your resolution of the 14th ult. by which you again accept of the empress's mediation: the preliminary concession, made on the part of

Great-Britain, concerning the principal article of the treaty of 1674, seems to level all the obstacles which had hitherto prevented your entering upon a negociation for a final peace. If, in the interim, the proposal made in the said letter, of a suspension of hostilities, should be thought conformable to the interest of the nation, nothing could be more so to the principles of humanity in general, which actuate the empress, and to her private sentiments of benevolence and affection for this state; especially, as such a measure has the double advantage of preventing the useless effusion of blood; and from this instant *restoring* to the Republic, *the enjoyments of the rights of freedom in trade and navigation, which fall to the share of neutral nations*, and especially those that have acceded *to the principles of the Armed Neutrality.*

Full of confidence in the disposition equally peaceful, and conformable to the real welfare of the state, which your H. M. have always manifested in the most solemn and positive manner; the underwritten flatter themselves, that you will not hesitate to make a proper use of the letter they have the honor to communicate, in order to take a quick and decisive resolution, that may tend to restore peace and harmony with your old friend and ally, upon terms as honorable as they are advantageous.

P. GALLITZIN.
MARCOFF.

APPENDIX, No. XII.

A SECOND LETTER FROM MR. FOX, TO M. SIMOLIN.... DATED ST. JAMES'S, FOURTH MAY, 1782.

SIR,

I HAVE not at all delayed to lay before his majesty the communication, which you did me the honor of making to me the first of this month. His majesty has received it as a new mark of the friendship of her imperial majesty, and as a proof of the lively and sincere interest which she takes in the restoration of the peace of Great-Britain and her ancient ally. I believe it will be needless to remark to you, sir, that his majesty has understood, with the greatest satisfaction, that he has adjusted his councils in all points conformable to the measures which his majesty had already taken to second the good offices of the court of Petersburg. The king moreover promises himself, that her imperial majesty understands, with pleasure, that he has anticipated her counsels, *in having offered to the Hollanders the entire liberty of navigation, according to the treaty of* 1674, *between Great-Britain and the Republic;....a treaty, by which the principles of the Armed Neutrality are established, in their widest extent, to all the contracting parties.* His majesty, then, does not make any difficulty to say, that he will accept, as the *basis* of a separate peace between him and the States General, *a free navigation, according to the principles demanded by her imperial majesty, in her declaration of the* 26*th of February,* 1780.

You will permit me to remark, that, in communicating to you the sentiments of his majesty, I believe I need not repeat what I had the honor to write to you by his majesty's orders, on the 29th of March last. If that letter has not produced the effects, which her imperial majesty seems to have promised would be the effect of such a step towards a reconciliation, and on which alone, according to the report of the ministers of her imperial majesty at the Hague, the Republic made the negociation for a peace with Great-Britain to depend; and if, notwithstanding the moderation which his majesty has taken pains to prove on this occasion, in terms the least equivocal,....the Republic shall persist to oppose every idea of a separate peace; the king will always have the satisfaction of having acted in such a manner, as to manifest the price he sets on the friendship of her imperial majesty, and the respect he has for her councils.

I have the honor to be, &c.

C. J. Fox.

No. XIII.

ADDITIONAL INSTRUCTIONS TO THE COMMANDERS OF HIS MAJESTY'S SHIPS OF WAR, AND PRIVATEERS THAT HAVE OR MAY HAVE LETTERS OF MARQUE AGAINST FRANCE. GIVEN AT OUR COURT AT ST. JAMES'S, THE EIGHTH DAY OF JUNE, 1793, AND IN THE TWENTY-THIRD YEAR OF OUR REIGN.

(L. S.) GEORGE R.

1st. THAT it shall be lawful to stop and detain all vessels loaded wholly or in part with *corn*, *flour* or *meal*, bound to any port in France, or any port occupied by the armies of France, and to send them to such ports as shall be most convenient; in order that such corn, meal or flour, may be purchased on behalf of his majesty's government, and the ships be released after such purchase, and after a due allowance for freight, or that the masters of such ships on giving due security, to be approved of by the Court of Admiralty, be permitted to proceed to dispose of their cargoes of corn, meal or flour, in the ports of any country in amity with his majesty.

2d. That it shall be lawful for the commanders of his majesty's ships of war and privateers, that have, or may have, letters of marque against France, to seize all ships, whatever be their cargoes, that shall be found attempting to enter any blockaded port, and to send the same for condemnation, together with their cargoes, except the ships of Denmark and Sweden, which shall only be prevented from entering on the first attempt, but on the second shall be sent in for condemnation likewise.

3d. That in case his majesty shall *declare* any port to be blockaded, the commanders of his majesty's ships of war, and privateers that have or may have letters of marque against France, are hereby enjoined, if they meet with ships at sea, which appear from their papers to be destined to such blockaded port, but to have sailed from the ports of their respective countries, before the *declaration* of the blockade shall have arrived there, to advertise them thereof, and to admonish them to go to other ports; but they are not to molest them afterwards, unless it shall appear, that they have continued their course with intent to enter the blockaded port, in which case they shall be subject to capture and condemnation, as shall likewise all ships wheresoever found, that shall appear to have sailed from their ports, bound to any port which his majesty shall have *declared* to be blockaded, after such *declaration* shall have been known in the country from which they sailed, and all ships which in the course of the voyage shall have received notice of the blockade in any manner, and yet shall have pursued their course with intent to enter the same.

G. R.

APPENDIX, No. XIV.

LETTER FROM MR. JEFFERSON, SECRETARY OF STATE, TO MR. T. PINCKNEY, MINISTER PLENIPOTENTIARY FROM THE UNITED STATES WITH GREAT-BRITAIN.

Philadelphia, September 7th, 1793.

SIR,

WE have received, through a channel which cannot be considered as authentic, the copy of a paper, styled, "Additional Instructions to the Commanders of his majesty's ships of war, and privateers," &c. dated at St. James's, June 8th, 1793. If this paper be authentic, I have little doubt but that you will have taken measures to forward it to me. But as your communication of it may miscarry, and time, in the meanwhile, be lost, it has been thought better that it should be supposed authentic; that, on that supposition, I should notice to you its very exceptionable nature, and the necessity of obtaining explanations on the subject, from the British government; desiring, at the same time, that you will consider this letter as provisionally written, only; and as if never written, in the event that the paper, which is the occasion of it, be not genuine.

The first article of it permits all vessels, laden wholly, or in part, with *corn*, *flour*, or *meal*, bound to any port in France, to be stopped, and sent into any British port, to be purchased by that government, or to be released only on the condition of security given by the master, that he will proceed to dispose of his cargo in the ports of some country *in amity with his majesty*.

This article is so manifestly *contrary to the Law of Nations*, that nothing more would seem necessary, than to observe that it is so. Reason and usage have established, that when two nations go to war, those who chuse to live in peace, retain their natural right to pursue their agriculture, manufactures, and other ordinary vocations; to carry the produce of their industry, for exchange, to all nations, belligerent or neutral, as usual; to go and come freely, without injury or molestation; and, in short, *that the war among others, shall be, for them, as if it did not exist.* One restriction on their natural rights, has been submitted to, by nations at peace; that is to say, that of not furnishing to either party *implements merely of war*, for the *annoyance* of the other; nor any thing, whatever, to a place *blockaded* by its enemy. What these implements of war are, has been so often agreed, and is so well understood, as to leave little question about them, at this day. There does not exist, perhaps, a nation in our common hemisphere, which has not made a particular enumeration of them, in some or all of their treaties, under the name of *Contraband.* It suffices, for the present occasion, to say, that *corn*, *flour*, and *meal*, are not of the class of Contraband; and, consequently, remain *articles of free commerce.* A culture, which, like that of the soil, gives employment to such a proportion of mankind, could never be suspended by the whole earth, or interrupted for them, whenever any two nations should think proper to go to war.

The state of war, then, existing between Great-Britain and France, furnishes no legitimate right either to interrupt the agriculture of the United States, or the peaceable exchange of its produce with all nations; and consequently, the assumption of it will be as lawful hereafter as now, in peace as in war. No ground, acknowledged by the common reason of mankind, authorizes this act now; and unacknowledged ground may be taken at any time or all times. We see then, a practice begun, to which no time, no circumstances, prescribe any limits, and which strikes at the root of our agriculture; that branch of industry, which gives food, clothing, and comfort, to the great mass of the inhabitants of these States.

If any nation, whatever, has a right to shut up, to our produce, all the ports of the earth, except her own, and those of her friends, she may shut up these also, and so confine us within our own limits. No nation can subscribe to such pretensions; no nation can agree, at the mere will or interest of another, to have its peaceable industry suspended, and its citizens reduced to idleness and want. The loss of our produce, if destined for foreign markets, is a tax too serious for us to acquiesce in. It is not enough for a nation to say, we and our friends will buy your produce. We have a right to answer, that it suits us better to sell to their enemies as well as their friends. Our ships do not go to France to return empty; they go to exchange the surplus of one produce, which we can spare, for surplusses of other kinds, which they can spare and we want; which they can furnish on better terms, and more to our mind, than Great-Britain or her friends. We have a right to judge for ourselves, what market best suits us; and they have none to forbid us the enjoyment of the necessaries and comforts, which we may obtain from any other independent country.

This act, too, tends directly to draw us from that state of peace, in which we are wishing to remain. It is an essential character of *Neutrality*, to furnish no aids (not stipulated by treaty) to one party, which we are not equally ready to furnish to the other. If we permit corn to be sent to Great-Britain and her friends, we are equally bound to permit it to France. To *restrain* it, would be a *partiality* which might lead to war with France; and, between restraining it *ourselves*, and *permitting her enemies* to restrain it unrightfully, is no difference. She would consider this as a mere pretext, of which she would not be the dupe; and, on what honourable ground could we otherwise explain it? Thus, we should see ourselves plunged, by this unauthorized act of Great-Britain, into a war, with which we meddle not, and which we wish to avoid, if justice to all parties, and from all parties, will enable us to avoid it. In the case, where we found ourselves obliged, by treaty, to withhold from the enemies of France, the right of arming in our ports, we thought ourselves, in justice, bound to withhold the same right from France also; and we did it. Were we to withhold from her, supplies of provisions, we should, in like manner be bound to withhold them from her enemies also; and thus shut to ourselves all the ports of Europe, where corn is in demand, or make ourselves parties in the war. This is a dilemma, which Great-Britain has no right to force upon us, and for which no pretext can be found in any part of our conduct. *She* may, indeed, feel the desire of *starving* an enemy-nation; but she can have no right of doing it *at our loss*, nor of making *us the instrument* of it.

The president therefore desires, that you will immediately enter into explanations on this subject, with the British government. Lay before them, in friendly and temperate terms, all the demonstrations of the injury done us by this act; and endeavour to obtain a revocation of it, and full indemnification to any citizens of these states, who may have suffered by it in the meantime. Accompany your representations with every assurance of our earnest desire to live on terms of the best friendship and harmony with them, and to found our expectations of justice on their part, on a strict observance of it on ours.

It is with concern, however, I am obliged to observe, that so marked has been the inattention of the British court, to every application which has been made to them, on any subject, by this government, (not a single answer, I believe, having ever been given to one of them, except in the act of exchanging a minister), that it may become unavoidable in certain cases, where an answer of some sort is necessary, to consider their silence as an answer....perhaps this is their intention. Still, however, desirous of furnishing no colour of offence, we do not wish you to name to them any term for giving an answer. Urge one as much as you can without commitment; and on the first day of December, be so good as to give us information of the state in which the matter is, that it may be received during the session of congress.

The second article of the same instruction allows the armed vessels of Great-Britain to *seize*, for condemnation, all vessels on their first attempt to enter a *blockaded* port, *except those of Denmark and Sweden*, which are to be *prevented only*, *but not seized*, on their first attempt. Of the nations inhabiting the shores of the Atlantic ocean, and practising its navigation, Denmark, Sweden, and the United States, alone, are neutral. To declare, then, all *neutral* vessels (for, as to the vessels of *belligerent* powers, no order was necessary) to be legal prize, which shall attempt to enter a blockaded port, except those of *Denmark and Sweden*, is exactly to declare, that the *vessels of the United States* shall be lawful prize, and those of Denmark and Sweden shall not. It is of little consequence, that the article has avoided naming the United States, since it has used a description applicable to them, and to them alone: while it exempts the others from its operation, by name. You will be pleased to ask an explanation of this distinction, and you will be able to say, in discussing its justice, that in every circumstance, we treat Great-Britain on the footing of the most favoured nation, where our treaties do not preclude us; and that even these are just as favourable to her, as hers are to us. Possibly she may be bound by treaty, to admit this exception, in favour of Denmark and Sweden; but she cannot be bound by treaty to withhold it from us; and if it be withheld merely because not established with us by treaty, what might not we, on the same ground, have withheld from Great-Britain, during the short course of the present war, as well as the peace which has preceded it?

Whether these explanations with the British government, shall be verbal, or in writing, is left to yourself. Verbal communications are very insecure; for it is only to deny them or to change their terms, in order to do away their effect at any time; those in writing have many and obvious advantages, and ought to be preferred, unless there be obstacles of which we are not apprized.

I have the honour to be,
With great and sincere esteem,
Dear Sir,
Your most obedient servant,
THOMAS JEFFERSON.

No. XV.

ADDITIONAL INSTRUCTION TO THE COMMANDERS OF ALL OUR SHIPS OF WAR, AND PRIVATEERS, THAT HAVE, OR MAY HAVE, LETTERS OF MARQUE AGAINST FRANCE.

Given at our court of St. James's, the 6*th day of November,* 1793, *and in the* 34*th year of our reign.*

(L. S.) G. R.

THAT they shall stop and detain all ships laden with goods, the produce of any colony belonging to France, or carrying provisions, or other supplies, for the use of such colony, and shall bring the same, with their cargoes, to legal adjudication, in our courts of admiralty.

By his majesty's command,
HENRY DUNDAS.

APPENDIX, No. XVI.

INSTRUCTIONS TO THE COMMANDERS OF OUR SHIPS OF WAR, AND PRIVATEERS, THAT HAVE, OR MAY HAVE, LETTERS OF MARQUE AGAINST FRANCE.

Given at our court of St. James's, the 8th day of January, 1794.

G. R.

WHEREAS by our former instruction to the commanders of our ships of war and of privateers, dated the 6th day of November, 1793, we signified, that they should stop and detain all ships laden with goods, the produce of any colony belonging to France, or carrying provisions or other supplies for the use of any such colony, and should bring the same, with their cargoes, to legal adjudication. We are pleased to revoke the said instruction; and in lieu thereof, we have thought fit to issue these our instructions, to be duly observed by the commanders of all our ships of war, and privateers that have, or may have letters of marque against France.

I. That they shall bring in for lawful adjudication all vessels with their cargoes, that are laden with goods, the produce of the French West-India islands, and coming directly from any port of the said islands to any port in Europe.

II. That they shall bring in, for lawful adjudication, all ships, with their cargoes, that are laden with goods, the produce of the said islands, the property of which goods shall belong to subjects of France, to whatsoever ports the same may be bound.

III. That they shall seize all ships that shall be found attempting to enter any port of the said islands, that is or shall be blockaded by the arms of his majesty or his allies, and shall send them in, with their cargoes, for adjudication, according to the terms of the second article of the former instructions, bearing date the 8th of June, 1793.

IV. That they shall seize all vessels laden wholly or in part with *naval* or *military stores*, bound to any port of the said islands, and shall send them into some convenient port belonging to his majesty; in order that they, together with their cargoes, may be proceeded against, according to the *Rules** of Nations.

* It has been already noticed, that, under the *Denomination* of "Naval and Military Stores," various articles have been comprehended by the *British*, which are not admitted by *other* States to be *rightfully* included in that description of goods; and consequently, not considered as belonging to the list of *Contraband of war*.

The introduction, therefore, of the word "*Rules*," instead of *Law*, in this place appears not to have been accidental, or, as synonimous with Laws; but as a term better calculated to suit the purpose intended. One nation may establish *arbitrary* "*Rules*," directly repugnant to the principles of natural justice, and possessing no legitimate controul whatever, over the actions of any other: Whereas, the term *Law*, means such a Rule, as a *rightful obligation* is attached to; and, of course, the *Law of Nations*, as being founded in Reason and universal Justice, is obligatory on every people. Such regulations as these *Instructions* (as they are called) of the British crown, may be thus termed the "*Rules of Nations*; but they could not accord with the *Law* of Nations; the principles of which they contravene. W. B.

END OF APPENDIX.

INDEX

TO THE DOCUMENTS CONTAINED IN THE

APPENDIX.

INDEX.

ERRATA.

The following ERRATA escaped correction, in consequence of the inconvenience that attended the revision of the proof-sheets, occasioned by the Author's distance from Philadelphia. The reader is requested to correct these errors, with his pen.

Page 40, line 1,	for *known,*	read *know.*
46, line 4 of the note,	for *post hæc,*	read *posthæc.*
50, line 7 of the note,	for *eaa,*	read *ea.*
62, line 8,	for *Thomafius,*	read *Thomasius.*
70, line 19 of the note,	for *the,*	read *they.*
81, line 3 of the note,	for *of maintaining,*	read *so maintained.*
112, line 12,	for *neutral,*	read *natural.*
113, line 2 and 5 of the note,	for *present,*	read *recent.*
125, line 12,	for *continues,*	read *continue.*
143, line 10,	for *incapacited,*	read *incapacitated.*
180, line 2 of the note,	for *iniqui,*	read *inique.*
245, line 9,	for *one,*	read *our.*
261, line 14,	for *preverted,*	read *perverted.*
271, line 14,	for *this,*	read *the.*